FEMINIST INTERPRETATIONS OF JACQUES DERRIDA

17⁹⁵

RE-READING THE CANON

NANCY TUANA, GENERAL EDITOR

This series consists of edited collections of essays, some original and some previously published, offering feminist reinterpretations of the writings of major figures in the Western philosophical tradition. Devoted to the work of a single philosopher, each volume contains essays covering the full range of the philosopher's thought and representing the diversity of approaches now being used by feminist critics.

Already published:

Nancy Tuana, ed., *Feminist Interpretations of Plato* (1994)

Margaret Simons, ed., *Feminist Interpretations of Simone de Beauvoir* (1995)

Bonnie Honig, ed., *Feminist Interpretations of Hannah Arendt* (1995)

Patricia Jagentowicz Mills, ed., *Feminist Interpretations of G.W.F. Hegel* (1996)

Maria J. Falco, ed., *Feminist Interpretations of Mary Wollstonecraft* (1996)

Susan J. Hekman, ed., *Feminist Interpretations of Michel Foucault* (1996)

FEMINIST INTERPRETATIONS OF JACQUES DERRIDA

EDITED BY NANCY J. HOLLAND

THE PENNSYLVANIA STATE UNIVERSITY PRESS
UNIVERSITY PARK, PENNSYLVANIA

Library of Congress Cataloging-in-Publication Data

Feminist interpretations of Jacques Derrida / edited by Nancy J.
Holland.
     p.   cm. — (Re-reading the canon)
   Includes bibliographical references and index.
   ISBN 0-271-01634-5 (cloth : alk. paper)
   ISBN 0-271-01635-3 (pbk. : alk. paper)
   1. Derrida, Jacques. 2. Feminist theory. I. Holland, Nancy J.
II. Series.
B2430.D484F46   1997
194—dc20   96-28716
                                            CIP

It is the policy of The Pennsylvania State University Press to use acid-free paper for the first printing of all clothbound books. Publications on uncoated stock satisfy the minimum requirements of American National Standard for Information Sciences—Permanence of Paper for Printed Library Materials, ANSI Z39.48-1992.

Contents

Foreword   vii
Nancy Tuana

Acknowledgments   xi

Introduction   1
Nancy J. Holland

1   Choreographies: Interview   23
Jacques Derrida and Christie V. McDonald

2   Displacement and the Discourse of Woman   43
Gayatri Chakravorty Spivak

3   Ontology and Equivocation: Derrida's Politics of
    Sexual Difference   73
Elizabeth Grosz

4   Deconstruction and Feminism: A Repetition   103
Peggy Kamuf

5   Toward an Ethic of Desire: Derrida, Fiction,
    and the Law of the Feminine   127
Peg Birmingham

Editor's Note   147

6   Civil Disobedience and Deconstruction   149
Drucilla Cornell

7   The Force of Law: Metaphysical or Political?   157
Nancy Fraser

8   Sentiment Recuperated: The Performative in Women's
        AIDS-Related Testimonies   165
    Kate Mehuron

9   Crossing the Boundaries Between Deconstruction,
        Feminism, and Religion   193
    Ellen T. Armour

10 *Kolossos:* The Measure of a Man's Cize   215
    Dorothea Olkowski

    Suggested Further Readings   231

    Notes on Contributors   239

    Index   243

Foreword

Take into your hands any history of philosophy text. You will find compiled therein the "classics" of modern philosophy. Since these texts are often designed for use in undergraduate classes, the editor is likely to offer an introduction in which the reader is informed that these selections represent the perennial questions of philosophy. The student is to assume that she or he is about to explore the timeless wisdom of the greatest minds of Western philosophy. No one calls attention to the fact that the philosophers are all men.

Though women are omitted from the canons of philosophy, these texts inscribe the nature of woman. Sometimes the philosopher speaks directly about woman, delineating her proper role, her abilities and inabilities, her desires. Other times the message is indirect—a passing remark hinting at woman's emotionality, irrationality, unreliability.

This process of definition occurs in far more subtle ways when the central concepts of philosophy—reason and justice, those characteristics that are taken to define us as human—are associated with traits historically identified with masculinity. If the "man" of reason must learn to control or overcome traits identified as feminine—the body, the emotions, the passions—then the realm of rationality will be one reserved primarily for men,[1] with grudging entrance to those few women who are capable of transcending their femininity.

Feminist philosophers have begun to look critically at the canonized texts of philosophy and have concluded that the discourses of philosophy are not gender-neutral. Philosophical narratives do not offer a universal perspective, but rather privilege some experiences and beliefs over others. These experiences and beliefs permeate all philosophical theories whether they be aesthetic or epistemological, moral or metaphysical. Yet this fact has often been neglected by those studying the traditions of philosophy. Given the history of canon formation in Western philosophy, the perspective most likely to be privileged is that of upper-class, white males. Thus, to be fully aware of the impact of gender biases, it is imperative that we re-read the canon with attention to the ways in which philosophers' assumptions concerning gender are embedded within their theories.

This new series, *Re-Reading the Canon,* is designed to foster this process of reevaluation. Each volume will offer feminist analyses of the theories of a selected philosopher. Since feminist philosophy is not monolithic in method or content, the essays are also selected to illustrate the variety of perspectives within feminist criticism and highlight some of the controversies within feminist scholarship.

In this series, feminist lenses will be focused on the canonical texts of Western philosophy, both those authors who have been part of the traditional canon, as well as those philosophers whose writings have more recently gained attention within the philosophical community. A glance at the list of volumes in the series will reveal an immediate gender bias of the canon: Arendt, Aristotle, de Beauvoir, Derrida, Descartes, Foucault, Hegel, Hume, Kant, Locke, Marx, Mill, Nietzsche, Plato, Rousseau, Wittgenstein, Wollstonecraft. There are all too few women included, and those few who do appear have been added only recently. In creating this series, it is not my intention to reify the current canon of philosophical thought. What is and is not included within the canon during a particular historical period is a result of many factors. Although no canonization of texts will include all philosophers, no canonization of texts that exclude all but a few women can offer an accurate representation of the history of the discipline as women have been philosophers since the ancient period.[2]

I share with many feminist philosophers and other philosophers writing from the margins of philosophy the concern that the current canonization of philosophy be transformed. Although I do not accept the position that the current canon has been formed exclusively by power relations, I do believe that this canon represents only a selective history of the tradition. I share the view of Michael Bérubé that "canons are at once the location, the index, and the record of the struggle for cultural representation; like any other hegemonic formation, they must be continually reproduced anew and are continually contested."[3]

The process of canon transformation will require the recovery of "lost" texts and a careful examination of the reasons such voices have been silenced. Along with the process of uncovering women's philosophical history, we must also begin to analyze the impact of gender ideologies upon the process of canonization. This process of recovery and examination must occur in conjunction with careful attention to the concept of a canon of authorized texts. Are we to dispense with the notion of a tradition of excellence embodied in a canon of authorized texts? Or, rather than abandon the whole idea of a canon, do we instead encourage a reconstruction of a canon of those texts that inform a common culture?

This series is designed to contribute to this process of canon transformation by offering a re-reading of the current philosophical canon. Such a re-reading shifts our attention to the ways in which woman and the role of the feminine is constructed within the texts of philosophy. A question we must keep in front of us during this process of re-reading is whether a philosopher's socially inherited prejudices concerning woman's nature and role are independent of her or his larger philosophical framework. In asking this question attention must be paid to the ways in which the definitions of central philosophical concepts implicitly include or exclude gendered traits.

This type of reading strategy is not limited to the canon, but can be applied to all texts. It is my desire that this series reveal the importance of this type of critical reading. Paying attention to the workings of gender within the texts of philosophy will make visible the complexities of the inscription of gender ideologies.

Nancy Tuana

Notes

1. More properly, it is a realm reserved for a group of privileged males, since the texts also inscribe race and class biases that thereby omit certain males from participation.

2. Mary Ellen Waithe's multivolume series, A History of Women Philosophers (Boston: M. Nijhoff, 1987), attests to this presence of women.

3. Michael Bérubé, Marginal Forces/Cultural Centers: Tolson, Pynchon, and the Politics of the Canon (Ithaca: Cornell University Press, 1992), 4–5.

Acknowledgments

On the contrary it is a matter—desire beyond desire—of responding faithfully but also as rigorously as possible both to the injunction or the order of the *gift* ("give" ["*donne*"]) as well as to the injunction or the order of meaning.
　　　　　　　　　　　　　　　　　　　　—Jacques Derrida, *Given Time*, 30

There is an inherent difficulty with any expression of gratitude in relation to a text such as this one, in which the gift is the meeting place of the metaphysical and the feminine. Still, it is important to acknowledge that the contributors to this volume have given me not only their work, but also, in many cases and in many ways, their help and their friendship. The same must be said for referee Tina Chanter of the University of Memphis, and the general editor of this series, Nancy Tuana of the University of Oregon, without whom this volume would never have come about at all.

Primarily due to gifts from the late Paul and Jean Shulman Hanna, the Office of the Dean of the College of Liberal Arts at Hamline University has provided substantial financial support for the preparation of this volume. I also thank my department chair and friend Duane Cady for his support, both material and moral, and the Humanities Division secretaries. Finally, and as always, I must thank my husband and children—Jeffrey Koon, Gwendolyn and Justis—gifts and obligations that I treasure above all else.

Jacques Derrida and Christie V. McDonald, "Choreographies: Interview," is reprinted by permission of The Johns Hopkins University Press from *Diacritics* 12 (Summer 1982): 66–76. Copyright © 1982 by The Johns Hopkins University Press.

Gayatri Chakravorty Spivak, "Displacement and the Discourse of Woman," is reprinted by permission of Indiana University Press from Mark Krupnick, ed., *Displacement: Derrida and After*. Copyright © 1983 by Indiana University Press.

Drucilla Cornell, "Civil Disobedience and Deconstruction," is reprinted by permission of the author and the *Cardozo Law Review*. This article originally appeared in 13/4 *Cardozo Law Review* 1309.

Nancy Fraser, "The Force of Law: Metaphysical or Political?" is reprinted by permission of the author and the *Cardozo Law Review*. This article originally appeared in 13/4 *Cardozo Law Review* 1325.

Introduction

[Taking women students seriously] means that most difficult thing of all: listening and watching in art and literature, in the social sciences, in all the descriptions we are given of the world, for the silences, the absences, the nameless, the unspoken, the encoded—for there we will find the true knowledge of women.

—Adrienne Rich

[A]s Derrida has acutely noted, the logocentric tradition is bound up in subtle ways with the drive for purity—the drive to escape contamination by feminine messes—symbolized by what he calls 'the essential and essentially sublime figure of virile homosexuality.' "

—Richard Rorty

While one might not expect to find Adrienne Rich quoted in a book on the work of Jacques Derrida, nor necessarily to find Richard Rorty quoted in a book on contemporary feminist thought, both of the above passages would suggest at least some affinity between Derrida's deconstructive project, with its primary focus on "the silences, the absences, the nameless, the unspoken, the encoded" in traditional philosophical and literary texts ("the logocentric tradition"), and a feminist project that would insist on the absence of women and their lives from that tradition. At the same time, however, the same quotations underscore a deep tension between the two projects: Rich's search for "the true knowledge of women" can easily seem to be thwarted by deconstruction's continued focus, albeit a highly critical one, on male texts and male thinkers, the unending series of fathers begetting themselves upon their sons in an incestuous and fertile, as well as virile, hom(me)osexuality.[1] Worse yet, the very concept of "the true knowledge" of anything, but perhaps especially of women, would violate the deepest of deconstructive canons. How can these two projects be reconciled? Is this confusion a feminist mess, or an irreducibly postmodern one?

In this volume are brought together the work of eleven contemporary thinkers who concern themselves with both feminism and deconstruction, in an attempt to do what Elizabeth Grosz notes is no longer required of feminist Lacanians and Foucauldians, to give a justification for the possibility of a feminist deconstruction (see Chapter 3). While several of the articles are critical of Derrida's work, some quite strongly so, all recognize, at a minimum, that "deconstructive techniques" *can* have properly feminist uses.[2] At the other extreme, Derrida himself, in the relatively early (1982) interview reprinted here, speaks about "feminism" only with circumspection. Perhaps more aware than Rorty of the dangers of male discourse on the subject, Derrida dances around it, so to speak, as if just introduced to it. This collection is intended as a further introduction to the relationship between Derrida's work and feminism, making this text an introduction to a reintroduction, a pre-text to bring the two together.

As a preliminary step, this introduction will offer three guides for readers from different backgrounds to use in approaching these very interdisciplinary texts: brief explanations of three of the basic terms that are in play here ("postmodern," "deconstruction," and "feminism"), an even briefer exegesis of key concepts from the work of four "precursors" whose work has had a strong impact on the development of Derrida's thought (Edmund Husserl, Martin Heidegger, Emmanuel Levinas, and Jacques Lacan), and introductory explications of the basic arguments of the texts that follow. While the reader will quickly see that no hard line can be drawn here, as elsewhere, between text and pre-text, this is only (I write with some trepidation) an introduction.[3] The main event follows, and is not to be missed.

Concepts

Logos remains as indispensable as the fold folded into the gift, just like the tongue (*langue*) of my mouth when I tear bread from it to give it to the other. It is also my body.

— Jacques Derrida[4]

Postmodern.   The term "postmodern" is subject to substantial and valid criticism in footnotes to the contributions made to this collection by both Drucilla Cornell and Elizabeth Grosz (Chapters 6 and 3). At the same time, some definition of the term would seem to be essential. Therefore, I shall offer a brief explanation that should be adequate for understanding its use in the texts that follow.

I have chosen "postmodern" over Cornell's preferred "postmodernity" because the use of the former term in aesthetics and the arts, especially architecture, seems less troublesome to me than the relatively esoteric reference of the latter to the concept of "modernity," found in the work of critical theorists such as Theodor Adorno. Perhaps this reflects my philosophical background: in that field "modern" has, if not a clear definition, at least a clear set of texts to which it refers; that is, those running roughly from Hobbes and Descartes to Kant. (The problem for philosophy has always been what to call the philosophical thought that comes after that.) On this basis, certain features of the "modern," understood in terms of these texts, can then be cited in attempting to define what would be the "post/modern." Since, as already suggested, one crucial point in the essays below will be the impact of Derrida's work on the possibility of a feminist politics (an issue that seems in turn to hinge on how the political agent is understood), in defining both the modern and the postmodern I shall focus on the status of the Subject and its undoing in postmodern thought. It is important, however, to remember that this is a strategic choice, not merely a repetition of the modern privileging of the Subject—although it is unavoidably that as well.

The primacy of the modern Subject retains certain key features over almost two hundred years, starting in the middle of the seventeenth century with "Of Man" (part 1 of Thomas Hobbes's *Leviathan*) and René Descartes's "I think, therefore I am." (Actually, as many others have pointed out, this is a far less metaphysical claim in the original Latin, "*Cogito, ergo sum*," where the pronoun "I" is tacit). For Kant, at the turn of the nineteenth century, the "Psychological Idea" is still the basis for our understanding of the mysteries of substantial relations, which must be presupposed for either the causal completeness of the Cosmological Idea or the revelations of the Theological Idea to have any meaning. The modern Subject defined by the "I think" is also pivotal in the realm of political thought, as the object of monarchical power but also the locus of the growing list of "Rights of Man" that remains basic to the contemporary dialogue about the law. Such a Subject, defined in terms of its rationality, or its potential for rationality, is vital to all phases of modern philosophical thought in a way that no single paradigm of the modern can be said to be definitive in other fields, such as literature or the visual arts.

In fact, what is sometimes termed "modern" in literature or art can look very much like the dispersal of this philosophical Subject, its disintegration under the dehumanizing pressures of "modernity," in the sense of twentieth-century technological society. The writings of James Joyce or the psychoanalytic work of Sigmund Freud, for instance, would be "modern" in this sense, revealing the complexity and conflict repression leaves lurking beneath the seemingly unified Cartesian ego. From a postmodern perspective, however, this disintegrating modern self is still measured against the memory of integration and the promise of reintegration, of a psychoanalytic cure or utopian "natural man" or a sexual liberation.[5] In some other time, some other place we were, or will be, whole, rehumanized, and free. This narrative has an obvious power in much of modern feminist political thought—it is what makes it "modern"—and, for that reason, its postmodern critics can easily seem to be critics of such feminist thought as well.

The postmodern world is one in which even the memory, the hope, or the dream of an integrated Subject ceases to exist. It is a world of interminable psychoanalysis, of constant "*bricolage*" or making do with spare parts,[6] of a sexuality that can never restore the lost intimacy and immediacy at which it aims. The Subject, like the rights we attribute to it, is a myth. The myth of the atomic, powerful Subject has been thrown together from elements of Christian doctrine and Hellenic philosophy, with a large dose of Indo-European linguistics. What if English had kept the agentless but active Greek middle voice, the Latin suppression of the first person singular pronoun in the present tense, the Hebrew refusal to name God? Things happen; thinking is going on, so something exists; we cannot explain that existence—that is the message of the postmodern deconstruction of the modern Subject.[7] And what would be a postmodern feminist politics without its proper Subject?

> I will even venture to say that ethics, politics, and responsibility, *if there are any*, will only ever have begun with the experience and experiment of aporia. When the path is clear and given, when a certain knowledge opens up the way in advance, the decision is already made, it might as well be said that there is none to make: irresponsibly, and in good conscience, one simply applies or implements a program.[8]

With the loss of the Subject, the Psychological Idea, we lose everything on which ethics and politics would seem to depend, as Kant will not have been the first to tell us.

Deconstruction.   Although many of them challenge "postmodern," most of the authors included here have no argument with "deconstruction." Indeed, both Elizabeth Grosz and Peggy Kamuf offer their own quasi-definitions of it (Chapters 3 and 4). An easy way to begin to explain its meaning at this point is to show how postmodern discourse came to deconstruct even the alienated, fragmented Subject of late modernism. To do this, we have to return to Freud. In psychoanalytic discourse, the infant must learn two basic tasks if it is to enter the realm of the fully human. First, it must learn to separate and distinguish itself from the objects around it, most especially that object that is its mother. Second, it must learn to delay gratification, to wait for food and, eventually, for the release of other bodily tensions. This dual process of difference and deferral, which permanently denies us any possible return to the infantile pleasures that precede it, is captured in the French verb *différer*, which means both to defer and to differ. Since its noun form, "*différence*," has only the single meaning it shares with English, early on Derrida coined the term "*différance*" to retain the double meaning of the verb.

Drawing on the work of linguist Ferdinand de Saussure, Derrida uses differance as a polymorphous tool for deconstructing "metaphysical" discourse, which is defined here by the fact that all of its foundational concepts are structured in a series of isomorphic hierarchical oppositions: form/matter, subject/object, rational/irrational, but also right/left, light/dark, male/female, and, of course, true/false, good/bad. What differance tells us is that these oppositions have meaning only because of the posited difference between the two terms and, therefore, that neither of the terms has any meaning in and of itself, but always defers its final referent along the trajectory of the series. Since the terms and the oppositions are mutually interdependent, no term can be classified as unmarked (primary) or marked (deviant), but all are equally marked, equally secondary to the opposition itself. For Saussure, words exist only in such a system of differance. They always carry an internal reference to the other words in the language of which they are a part and so permanently delay any final arrival at the prelinguistic things themselves that words are supposed to name. Similarly, the modern Subject can be seen as a system of differance, as always other than it is, not as a tragic accident, but necessarily. This would be because it can only be the Subject it is by opposition to the material object that it is not (in Descartes), to the thing-in-itself that it is not (in Kant), to the sovereign that it is not (in Hobbes), to the God that it is not, to the madman that it is not, to the irrational laborer or woman that it is not, to the id/superego that it is not, and so forth.

Some explicit examples of deconstruction can be found in the essays collected here, but its use is implicit throughout this volume. Several of the authors emphasize that deconstruction is a *double* movement.[9] Along with its critical reading of traditional texts, it offers an affirmation of all that those texts would use hierarchical oppositions to subordinate or exclude—indeterminacy in all its forms, mystery, randomness, chaos, Nature, the body, emotion, absolute difference, infinite deferral and constant substitution—in two words, differance and Woman. By revealing the structure of differance at the base of any claim to truth or essence, deconstruction also says two things about women: they do not exist *as such* in traditional phallogocentric discourse (which is defined, as Rorty suggests, by their necessary exclusion), but they also do not exist outside that discourse as "women" in any essential or determinate meaning of the term because essence and determinate meanings have gone the way of Man and God. As I said at the outset, deconstruction would claim that there is no "true knowledge of women" in either of its (interestingly, systematically ambiguous) meanings. This loosening of the connection between the category "women" and a certain biologically identifiable group of humans provides the basis for another feminist concern that the interests of really existing women are being excluded from the realm of deconstructive thought just as they are excluded from traditional philosophy.[10]

Feminism. Although there is considerable debate among feminists about whether there is any "essence" that defines women as such,[11] it is also the case that much feminist thought continues to see itself as freeing women from the confines of patriarchal oppression so that we may realize our true inner natures. Given this perspective, to be told that both essence and truth must be "deconstructed" seems to present a serious challenge to the feminist project. Just as the status of a profession may decline when large numbers of women go into that field, it is easy to suspect it is no accident that, now that women can be Subjects, being a Subject no longer seems to be either desirable or possible. Couching that undesirability in a language that only the most dedicated and astute of graduate students can easily master only increases the feeling that perhaps we are only being disempowered, excluded, left to our own "feminine messes" once again.[12] From a postmodern perspective, on the other hand, much feminist discourse, particularly in the United States, remains deeply steeped in the modern concept of the atomic Subject that dominates Anglo-American philosophy. Feminist debates from all points on the spectrum seem to be about the rights of that Subject when she is female, how she might attain the privileges of male Subjects, how she can best protect herself from the predations of male Subjects, how she can cease to damage those Subjects even less powerful than she is, how her essence is to be realized, her true nature freed. As suggested earlier, this conflict provides one "plot" of the dialogue in this book.

Needless to say, there exists in this volume no single, coherent, monolithic sense of what feminism is. By agreeing to contribute, the authors have accepted that title for at least one piece of their work and, although most are commonly recognized as feminist thinkers, no more than that should be assumed. Some would deny any positive relationship between Derrida and feminism, most would have reservations about asserting baldly that one exists. One cannot necessarily tell from reading their contributions, nor do I necessarily know myself, which of these authors might be socialist or Marxist feminists, liberals, or radicals. In a sense, of course, we are all postmodern feminists, if only because we are fluent in that mode of discourse.[13] As I hope will be the case with the other volumes in this series, feminism will primarily be given here what can be called a "definition in use"; that is, what it means for these authors will become clear only through reading their work.

That being said, I must admit that it begs the question more than it should. At some point, invitations were issued, conversations were had (or not had), discriminations were made that could not wait until these texts were in hand to be made. If not a definition of "feminism," my initial tasks as an editor necessarily relied at least upon certain criteria of inclusion that I have some duty to make explicit. Not having done so at the time, I am in the position of the *bricoleuse* forced to give an account of why my pieced-together structure should stand, based only on the hope that it will. My own "definition in use" seems to have had two major components. First, I sought out thinkers who took gender issues seriously in their work, especially their previous work on Derrida or other postmodern writers. Second, their work had to reflect a deep conviction that "women are people"; that, whatever the limitations of the modern Subject, there was nothing that kept women either individually or collectively from qualifying to be one as much, or as little, as men did. Thus, a provisional definition of "feminism" for this volume might be the belief that sexual difference is a valid theoretical variable, at least within European discourse, and is so, in part, because of the traditional unjust exclusion of women from that discourse. What more exactly it might mean can be determined only from reading the contributions that follow.

Contexts

[I]t is torn from the mouth of a woman, so as to be given to the other. Why doesn't he clarify that in this work?
                                                                —Jacques Derrida

The work of many thinkers other than Derrida are discussed in these pages. In general, they can be classified into four very broad and overlapping groups: (1) literary figures (Shakespeare, the authors of AIDS-related testimonies); (2) historical figures (Plato, Descartes, Kant, Hegel, Marx, Neitzsche, Freud); (3) contemporary figures in the usual sense (Husserl, Heidegger, Levinas, Lacan); and (4) writers who are Derrida's literal contemporaries (Foucault, Irigaray, feminists of all sorts). These names, and many others, provide the con/texts of Derrida's work. Of these groups, however, I have chosen to focus specific attention on only the third, the contemporary figures whose work I believe the average reader of these pages will be least familiar with and whose specialized vocabulary I believe she will find the most difficult to understand. They represent a sort of middle background to all of these texts, not far enough away to be part of the broad background one can expect any reader to be familiar with, yet not close enough to come under the direct and detailed scrutiny of any of the authors (although Christie V. McDonald's amazing footnote to "Choreographies" [Chapter 1] goes a good part of the way). These are not offered even as good beginning accounts of the work of Husserl, Heidegger, Levinas, and Lacan, but merely as preliminary sketches, "outworks" that grew from the papers that follow and from which such an account might be built.

Derrida's first book was on Edmund Husserl's "The Origin of Geometry" in 1962.[14] In this early work many themes that have shaped Derrida's subsequent thought are already apparent, including themes with definite political connotations. This may be due to the political subtext of Husserl's own sense of the "crisis" in European science and culture in the 1930s, to which Derrida ties "The Origin" (OG 25), or to a tacit comparison with Hegel's philosophy of history, and therefore with Marx. In any case, for Husserl, the origin of geometry as a science can be understood only through a series of "reductions": a phenomenological reduction that separates geometrical shapes from our actual experience of space; an eidetic reduction that reveals the underlying structure of Ideas inherent in those shapes; and a historical reduction that takes this process in isolation from any empirical event. Derrida argues that in this attempt to create a geometry without "differance," Husserl's reductions exclude any relationship not only to spatially different Others with whom the geometer might/must communicate his ideas, but also to a temporally different Self who would require some sign (in memory) of what had been thought. Thus despite his elaborate metaphysics of time, Husserl's geometry exists only in a present moment of full self-presence; it can have no Other either in time or in space (OG 136–37). As Peg Birmingham notes (Chapter 5), this attempted absolute exclusion of the Other, rather than being "ideal," is a fiction, so the foundational truth of geometry lies in a history that is not truth but "a novel" (OG 144).

This fictitious "metaphysics of presence" is also the central focus of Derrida's seminal work on Husserl's "philosophy of language," *Speech and Phenomena*.[15] There he begins with Husserl's claim that the true linguistic sign must be "pure" expression, without any hint of "indication." Again Derrida notes that this can happen only in the self-presence of the present moment, for a Self without any possible

Other. If language actually communicates something to myself or another, then it must fall prey to the indeterminacy of differing and deferral, of "differance" (which first appears in this text). From this develop Derrida's arguments against the possibility of a "private language" and for the necessity of "writing" or the trace; that is, of differance and an implicit Other, even within the spoken word. The power of the spoken word, he claims, flows from the fiction of identity between thought and word generated by hearing oneself speak when the bodily nature of this process is ignored through idealization or "reduction." Thus the Other excluded by Husserl would be not only the spatially Other person or the temporally Other self, but also the metaphysical Other of my own body (*SP* 80–81). In this text, moreover, Derrida adds another dimension to these determinations of the Other, one that he will later link to Woman—the dimension of death: "*A voice without differance, a voice without writing, is at once absolutely alive and absolutely dead*" (*SP* 102; emphasis in original). This provides one link between Derrida's work on Husserl and his work on both Hegel and Husserl's apostate student, Martin Heidegger.[16]

It has been rumored in certain circles that Derrida has written at least a thousand unpublished pages on Heidegger. (Of course, some of these phantasmic pages may include *Of Spirit*[17] or other books that have been published since I first heard the rumor.) I note the rumor only to suggest the difficulty of summarizing in any finite space the content of Heidegger's thought, much less its relationship to Derrida's work. There is not even, in the case of Heidegger, any one central text on which this discussion could legitimately focus; even *Of Spirit* gives every sign of still being, in some important sense, a work in progress. In the face of such an impossible task, therefore, I have chosen purposefully to err on the side of explaining (far) too little by focusing rather narrowly on two key Heideggerian concepts: Dasein and the relationship to the ground of Being expressed by the German phrase "*es gibt.*"[18]

Dasein is a simple German term that takes on monumental proportions in Hegel and later in Heidegger. It means literally to be (*sein*) there (*da*). As the above discussion of Husserl suggests, the spatio-temporal reference is vital. The concept of Dasein relies on the fact that its existence is an issue for it. That is, Dasein is able to take a stand on its own existence, to have some perspective on it, to see itself as in some specific time and place, at a "there" where it need not necessarily be, where it someday will not be (hence the focus on death in Heidegger's early "existentialism"). Beings that have a being other than Dasein's (for example, primates) may engage in behavior similar to Dasein's, but will not have this sense of themselves as contingently existent, spatio-temporally located beings. Two important points about Dasein must be noted. First, although the term comes from Heidegger's early work, *Being and Time*,[19] the spatial reference can be found in the "later Heidegger" as well: for example, in the evocation of Rainer Maria Rilke's "Open" in "What are Poets For?"[20] Second, as Derrida points out in "Choreographies" (Chapter 1), the reason for the term "Dasein" was exactly to avoid the hierarchical oppositions, such as mind/body and human/nonhuman, that Heidegger was among the first to take as definitive of the "metaphysical." Thus, like his nemesis Friedrich Nietzsche, Heidegger can be seen as a pioneer of postmodern, even of deconstructive, thought. Derrida is quite open, in *Of Spirit* and elsewhere, about the dependence of his work on Heidegger's, as well as about the conflicts such a heritage generates.

Dasein, then, find ourselves in an Open, a space that allows our own existence to become a question for us. How does/did this happen? Unfortunately, that question has much more obvious answers in both French and German than in English. The best we can do in English, "there is," has an all but erased spatial reference that finds a stronger echo in the French "*il y a*" (literally, "it has here"), but the German "*es gibt*" (literally, "it gives"), while nonspatial, agrees with the French in properly identifying the impersonal, unknown, middle-voiced source of the existence of Dasein (which is, importantly, *not* a form of the verb "to be" in either language). Heidegger, in *Being and Time* for instance, tends to trace this impersonal source back to that which sends us (*uns schicken*) our history (*Geschichte*), so that Dasein is always already "there," but Derrida often prefers to focus on what is given, the gift. Part of the reason for that focus in "Choreographies" is that in the work of anthropologist Claude Lévi-Strauss, what is given in both trade and ritual, the essential gift, is always a woman.[21] Thus, what can be, and often is, interpreted as theological discourse in Heidegger can be also re-read as sexist, not to say phallogocentric, discourse.[22] This would be only one example of a perpetual ambiguity in Heidegger's work that would perhaps explain the credence given to the rumor about the thousand unpublished pages.

The complex relationship between Derrida's work and that of Emmanuel Levinas can be sketched somewhat more fully, based on three key texts by Derrida, "Violence and Metaphysics" from *Writing and Differ-ence*, "At This Very Moment in This Work Here I Am," and *The Gift of Death*.[23] Still, just as Derrida always makes it clear that his work remains within the Heideggerian problematic, so he says of Levinas that the questions raised about his work are "questions put to *us* by Levinas" (*WD* 84). Derrida presents *Totality and Infinity*[24] as a challenge to the "Greek" philosophies of Husserl and Heidegger, a challenge that seeks to reintroduce both the metaphysical and the ethical into a philosophical discourse that these two thinkers had sought to "cleanse" of them. Most important, the ethical is defined here as "a nonviolent relationship to the infinite as infinitely other, to the Other" (*WD* 83). Thus, a major element of Levinas's criticism of both Husserl and Heidegger is that each of them in his own way engages in a theorizing that ignores the concrete existence of human Others. The metaphysics that Levinas would restore, however, is not a metaphysics that would reestablish the traditional hierarchical oppositions of self/other, and so forth. The Other here is not the not-me, the other Subject, or anything that could be encom-passed within a system of the same in that way. It is the face-to-face encounter with the actually existing Other, and his/(her?) absolute demand for justice that Levinas would bring back into the philosophical realm.[25]

Two aspects of this restoration echo the work of Søren Kierkegaard. "Metaphysics and Violence" notes that metaphysical transcendence would be, on Levinas's account, desire for the Other, but always a renounced, Kierkegaardian desire. This is because it is precisely *as* Other that the Other is desired and so can never be possessed: "a metaphysics of infinite separation" (*WD* 93). *The Gift of Death* reminds us of another point found in Kierkegaard: that the demand of the concrete Other for justice is always a demand that lies outside the Kantian/Hegelian law, which speaks only of the universal, a law for which attention to the particular is sin (63). The similar argument against Heidegger would be that his rejection of metaphysics, by neutralizing humanity into Dasein, also erases the voice of the particular Other. Levinas characterizes both as a violence against the Other, as he does the attempt to speak *of* the Other through a general term or concept ("there is no concept of the Other" [*WD* 104]), rather than *to* him/(her?). Derrida, however, is as critical of Levinas's work as he is of Heidegger's, and for the same reason: "Once sexual difference is subordinated, it is always the case that the wholly other, who is *not yet marked* is *already* found to be marked by masculinity" ("ATVM" 40). He ends "Violence and Metaphysics" with a claim about *Totality and Infinity* to which several of the contributors to this volume refer: "it seems to us impossible, essentially impossible, that it could have been written by a woman" (*WD* 321).[26]

The relationship between Lacan and Derrida is less complex than that between Derrida and Heidegger, but more contentious than that between Derrida and Levinas. The key text here is *"Le facteur de la vérité"*[27] (which appears in *The Post Card*). Before turning to that text, however, it may be necessary to give a quick sketch of the Lacanian concepts of the Real, the Imaginary, and the Symbolic. Drawing on Freud, one can briefly summarize the Real as the infant's experience of the world as an impossible remainder of a lost past; the Imaginary as the preliminary, pre-Oedipal sense he attempts to make of the Real; and the Symbolic as the linguistic realm into which the Imaginary is retranslated as a result of castration anxiety. Thus, hunger would be Real, the loss of the breast an Imaginary abandonment by the all-powerful pre-Oedipal Mother, and weaning a Symbolic necessity imposed by the all-powerful Oedipal Father's desire for exclusive access to the mother's body. Due to differance, the (psychoanalytic) subject functions only within the Symbolic, has very limited access to the Imaginary, and has no access at all to the Real, although it is structurally implied in his behavior and, especially, symptoms. Thus, we cannot experience hunger as pure absence or, under normal circumstances, as abandonment, but only as a deprivation. Furthermore, the Symbolic is, for Lacan, the Law of the Father in which the mother plays a role only in her absence, in the threat of absolute lack or castration she represents. In the public, sane world of the Symbolic, all the positions are held by men—the woman, as such, famously does not exist at all.

"Le facteur de la vérité" notes the effect of this structure on the modern Subject: "If there is a subject *of the* signifier, it is in being Subject to the law of the signifier" (*PC* 422). In his "Seminar on 'The Purloined Letter,' "[28] Lacan equates femininity, castration, and Truth: the subject is castrated by the fear of castration, which is necessary for it to come to its own subjecthood/Phallus within a Symbolic it cannot control, a Truth that is always revealed by the castrated Woman. As one might imagine, indeed applaud, Derrida makes short shrift of this. "What follows is obvious: phallogocentrism as androcentrism" (*PC* 481). Echoing his comments on Heidegger and Levinas in "Choreographies," he notes that Lacan, like Freud, believes "there is only *one* libido, and

therefore no difference, and even less an opposition within libido between the masculine and the feminine, and moreover it is masculine by nature" (PC 482). The "neutral" human category—Dasein, the Other, libido—is always already male. While Derrida would not deny the structure of signification that Lacan delineates, he does, as Drucilla Cornell notes (Chapter 6), question its ultimate hegemony, concluding that "a letter does *not always* arrive at its destination, and from the moment that this possibility belongs to its structure one can say that it never truly arrives, that when it does arrive its capacity not to arrive torments it with an internal drifting" (PC 489). Even Lacan's transfer of sovereignty from the Subject to the Symbolic gives too much to the modern, the androcentric, the metaphysical.

Contents

Beyond any possible restitution, there would be need for my gesture to operate without debt, in absolute ingratitude.
—Jacques Derrida, "At This Very Moment"

Starting from Christie V. McDonald's citation of Emma Goldman's famous line, "If I can't dance I don't want to be part of your revolution," "Choreographies" quickly comes to the key question in this introduction: how to reconcile feminism as a liberatory political project with the deconstruction denial that there can be any "truth" or "essence" of the feminine, of "woman," or of the "human" that could provide the *telos* or endpoint for such a process of liberation. Undoubtedly calculating the possibilities for misquotation and misinterpretation, Derrida presents the problem in the form of a question—"Why must there be a place for woman? And why only one, a single, completely essential place?"—while also allowing for the provisional acceptance of such a place in specific political contexts. In the process, he and McDonald discuss many of the philosophers with whom he has concerned himself over the years. Again multiplying the (inevitable) possibilities of misreading, Derrida "credits" Nietzsche's "misogynistic" texts with exposing the two dogmas, "Woman as truth" and "the Truth about women," that provide the foundation for "phallogocentrism"; that is, for the philosophical virile hom(me)osexuality referred to above. Thus, they discuss the fact that Levinas and Heidegger posit a sexual but pre-gendered being as the foundational Dasein, or the absolute Other, even though such a "neutral" or unmarked being will always already be male, since to be "female" is to be marked as different. In the end, it seems that a new "concept" of woman will require a deconstruction of the concept of "concept" itself.

Gayatri Spivak (in Chapter 2) asks what seems to be the next logical question: Can Derrida's critique provide us a network of concept-metaphors that does not appropriate or displace the figure of woman? Starting with the reading of Nietzsche in *Spurs*,[29] she suggests "that the woman who is the 'model' for deconstructive discourse remains a woman generalized and defined in terms of the faked orgasm and other varieties of denial." This fetishized feminine would, of course, be also phallicized and thus neuterized, no longer feminine. To the extent that such a feminine governs Derrida's metaphors, they would only replicate, rather than repudiate, the Nietzschean gesture of displacement that he would criticize. Going beyond Nietzsche to Hegel, Freud, Genet, and Blanchot, Spivak argues that, because deconstruction, on this model, remains a male enterprise, that is, because sexual difference is irreducible, women can ask even deconstructive questions only from the position of men, can only speak in drag, as it were. This gesture, moreover, would reverse the strategy Derrida himself uses in his fictive "dialogues" with unnamed, but identifiably female, interlocutors.[30] Spivak's solution to the aporias created by the possibility of feminist deconstruction would be for feminists to "correct" Derrida in the same way that Marx "corrected" Hegel.

Elizabeth Grosz begins her "Ontology and Equivocation: Derrida's Politics of Sexual Difference" with a declaration that feminism has matured enough to withstand, if not always to welcome, internal criticisms of its own presuppositions. She argues that deconstruction can provide tools for such self-criticism that will result in "better" feminism, while acknowledging that there can be no "pure" feminism entirely outside the patriarchal system. She emphasizes the ways in which Derrida's work illuminates the gaps and lapses in that system through which feminist thought can develop. After rejecting several feminist criticisms of Derrida, she turns to the issue of the ontology of sexual difference; that is, the question of whether sexual difference is metaphysical "bedrock" or a variation on some underlying uniformity. This leads to Derrida's readings of the supposed gender neutrality of Dasein in Heidegger and the Other in Levinas. Grosz then considers what she sees as two problems with Derrida's work from a feminist perspective. First, she questions his tendency to confuse sexuality in the sense of pleasurable drives with sexuality in the sense of a (binary) sexed subjectivity, arguing that one can resolve one's sexuality in the first sense in a variety of ways that would be defined as different sexualities in the second sense. On the other hand, the problem presented by the complications that Derrida finds in any concrete (feminist) politics is seen as a positive aspect of his work. This necessary interdeterminacy in all that we do, Grosz believes, can serve as a creative force in feminist thought.

Peggy Kamuf also addresses the issue of sexual difference, but draws on radically different aspects of Derrida's work. She traces a trajectory from Shakespeare's *Othello* to Freud's theory of penis envy to argue that there is a vital connection between the construction of the modern Subject (that is, the Subject of modern politics) and jealousy. She points out that her own argument fails to distinguish between jealousy and envy because they become one and the same in light of the postmodern loss of the possibility of final possession (even of oneself as Subject), which is the crux of the usual distinction between the two. The collapse of the jealous modern Subject is then tied to the notion of repetition in *Speech and Phenomena*. Like Grosz, Kamuf points out the positive side of the "double bind" created by deconstruction, its affirmation of singularity and "autobiography" (Chapter 4). In contrast to a feminist politics based on the making of the modern Subject female, as a subject-without-jealousy, and the corresponding threat of the personal being swallowed into the (totalitarian) political, Kamuf finds a source of feminist strength in the present impossibility of knowing what sort of future such thinking may create for us.

Peg Birmingham's focus in "Toward an Ethic of Desire: Derrida, Fiction, and the Law of the Feminine" is on law seen in relationship to fiction, rather than to sociopolitical fact. Her starting point is the argument, found in Linda Alcoff and others, that because "woman" is only a "fiction" for Derrida, deconstruction can provide no basis for a positive feminist political agenda, but only a nominalist, if not nihilist, "negative feminism." By turning to the term "fiction" itself, in Derrida's very early introduction to Husserl's "The Origin of Geometry" and then in the very recent *Acts of Literature*,[31] Birmingham explores the rich possibilities presented by the "mere" fiction of woman, especially with regard to origins, embodiment, pro-creation, the erotic, and the law, which Derrida characterizes as the "silhouette" of the feminine. Although she questions this tendency to rely on negation, on the category of "the other," as a placeholder for woman/women in some of his work, she is able to recast Derrida's "nominalism" as performative and generative, rather than nihilistic, and ultimately to demonstrate the fertility of his thought for rethinking both ethics and desire from a feminist perspective.

Drucilla Cornell and Nancy Fraser both take the common starting point of Derrida's "The Force of Law: The 'Mystical Foundation of Authority,' "[32] but then move in quite different directions—one would almost say, on quite different levels. In "Civil Disobedience and Deconstruction," Cornell evokes the nonexistence of women, as such, within male-dominated discourse, as it is described by Lacan. She points out Derrida's insistence on the many ways in which male-dominated discourse *fails* to control its own rigid gender logic and how it might suggest a more optimistic view of the oppression of women than Lacan would allow. Conversely, she finds Derrida less optimistic than Levinas, who insists on a radical asymmetry of the ethical demand for justice in which I am precisely not the one to whom justice is owed but the one who owes it. Derrida, she argues, would insist on the necessity of basing any such asymmetry on a preexisting "phenomenological symmetry" in which both parties would have equal standing. It is the lack of such symmetry in contemporary gender relations, Cornell concludes, that would allow women to consider themselves not obliged to obey the law: they are subject to it without being genuinely recognized as its Subjects; that is, full members of the polity in which it has legitimacy. Women do not exist as such in the discourse of the law, so, she argues, they have no "natural duty" to obey the law.

Nancy Fraser draws her title, "The Force of Law: Metaphysical or Political?" from John Rawls's "Justice as Fairness: Political, not Metaphysical." In this article, she explores the opposition between transcendental and political arguments she finds in Derrida's discussion, and problematizes the priority he accords to the metaphysical. Her claim is that, since Derrida's argument in "The Force of Law" is concerned with the metaphysical basis of law, it is itself transcendental and so cannot ground any sort of normative judgment or generate meaningful political discussion. In other words, she would insist that to think about the conditions of possibility of the political is not yet to think politically, that is, is not yet to engage in a normative political critique. Such a claim challenges *both* feminist arguments that deconstruction cannot be feminist because it entails a nihilistic or amoral political position, and arguments, such as the one offered in "The Force of Law," that deconstruction is ethical at its core because it requires moral judgment and action based on responsibility alone, without any ultimate justification.[33] On the more practical level, Fraser argues (1) for making a distinction between the "metaphysical" violence or force necessary for the existence of any legal system at all and the very concrete ways in which any particular legal system uses *unnecessary* violence against its members; and (2) for the priority of normative political critique over the sort of negative transcendental argument offered in "The Force of Law."

Kate Mehuron's "Sentiment Recuperated: The Performative in Women's AIDS-Related Testimonies" (Chapter 8) addresses the relationship between deconstruction and activist discourse. She is concerned with the use of deconstruction both to read counterhegemonical "texts" that exceed or defy our usual understandings of what texts are *and* to use such texts in "reading" social institutions that would not ordinarily be considered texts at all. Thus, this is not a close reading of Derrida, but rather an "elegiac" reading of the testimonies of women living in the center of the AIDS pandemic: HIV-positive women and women who find themselves the friends/lovers/wives/ex-wives/care partners/survivors of people with AIDS (PWAs). Drawing on Derrida's critical reading of J. L. Austin's distinction between the constative, or representational, use of language and its performative use (its ability to change states of affairs in the world),[34] Mehuron offers the testimonies of these women as counterhegemonic texts in opposition to the powers that would seek to recuperate their sentiments to the conservative discourse of passive victimization. She wants to see them as potentially transformative performances, not descriptive, autobiographical narratives. With reference to Foucault and Spivak as well as Derrida, Mehuron explores both the possibilities and the limits of deconstruction for this kind of reading: she sees these testimonies as challenging the reader "to participate in politicized moments which seize, cut, or overturn the present in deliberative activities that are exterior to academic reflection."

Ellen T. Armour's "Crossing the Boundaries Between Deconstruction, Feminism and Religion" (Chapter 9) adds two new variables to the discussion of Derrida and feminism by comparing his work with that of Luce Irigaray and by focusing on religion as a realm of both feminist and deconstructive engagement. Her argument, against feminists who would reject Derrida but embrace Irigaray, is that Derrida's work provides a necessary *supplément*[35] to Irigaray's, particularly to her discussions of religion and the divine. Armour's reason for this claim is the same as her reason for considering religion a vital part of any feminist or deconstructive critique: Western religion is of a piece with the Western metaphysical tradition that develops out of Plato, and so is necessarily implicated in any serious rereading of that tradition. Thus, she turns to Derrida's deconstruction of the trope of "God-the-Father" found in "Plato's Pharmacy."[36] Armour regards this aspect of Derrida's work as important for feminism in itself, but also as a *supplément* to Irigaray's own questioning of "God-the-Father" and to her suggestion that women envision deity in female terms.

Dorothea Olkowski's "*Kolossos:* The Measure of Man's Cize" (Chapter 10) is a close reading of "Parergon," a text from *The Truth in Painting* in which gender is not discussed as such.[37] She questions the meaning that may, or may not, be drawn from this silence. Both Olkowski and Derrida focus on the concept of the sublime, and its relationship to the colossal, as developed in Immanuel Kant's *Critique of Judgment.*[38] As with the *pharmakon* in "Plato's Pharmacy," the phallic significance of the colossal plays a major role. From there the discussion shifts to the column and toward the Medusa, but, Olkowski points out, not quite all the way: "Derrida does not himself wish to be entangled in it here." She also incorporates Derrida's comments on pleasure and the beautiful from "Economimesis,"[39] contrasting the emphasis on the disinterested, abstract aesthetic judgment in both Kant and Hegel with the "negative pleasure" inspired by the unrepresentable excess of the colossal/sublime. Thus, the colossal would be both inside and outside the Kantian system of aesthetic value. In "Parergon," however, Derrida makes this point without reference to the other famous inside/outside (both metaphorical and literal) that Woman has always been in the phallogocentric tradition. In so doing, Olkowski suggests, he recapitulates the traditional philosophical silence about women, an insistence on judging everything by the "cize" of Man that goes back through Kant to Plato and Oedipus, and beyond.

Diversity of perspectives, diversity of persons; diversity of con/texts, diversity of conclusions—not a full range of possible feminist interpretations of Derrida, but a wide swath of the available middle ground. A wide-enough sampling, perhaps, for the reader to find some piece of it relevant, even critical, to her own developing thought about the important nexus of issues addressed by Derrida's work. Coming myself from a background that bridges in some ways the gap between Continental and Anglo-American philosophy, and working in a situation that requires me to teach texts from both traditions, it sometimes seems that the deepest contribution Derrida makes to feminist thought is simply that he takes it as a serious realm of philosophical investigation, something that is extremely rare in the history of European philosophy or in contemporary pragmatism, analytical philosophy, or phenomenology. Thus autobiographically it was Derrida who brought together most clearly and as if for the first time my work as a philosopher and as a feminist. To think of his work as somehow inimical to the feminist philosophical project is impossible for me. This volume, therefore, takes on both the form of a tribute—a gift, if you must—to a thinker who, if nothing more, does take feminism as a serious part of the philosophical enterprise, and the form of an argument that would justify such a tribute. Whether all, or any, of the contributors would agree in seeing their work in that way is doubtful but, as editor, the final introductory word is mine.

Notes

1. See Jacques Derrida, *The Post Card: From Socrates to Freud and Beyond*, trans. Alan Bass (Chicago: University of Chicago Press, 1987), especially the section entitled "Envois." The locution "hom(me)osexuality" was recommended by Ellen Armour, who borrowed it from Luce Irigaray.

2. See Nancy Fraser's "The Force of Law: Metaphysical or Political?" (Chapter 7).

3. On the general impossibility of my current task, see Jacques Derrida, "Outwork, prefacing" in *Dissemination*, trans. Barbara Johnson (Chicago: University of Chicago Press, 1981), 1–59.

4. Jacques Derrida, "At This Very Moment in This Work Here I Am," in *Re-Reading Levinas*, ed. Robert Bernasconi and Simon Critchley, (Bloomington: Indiana University Press, 1991), 20, hereafter in this section cited as "ATVM" with a page reference.

5. For one postmodern version of the argument about sexuality, see Michel Foucault, *The History of Sexuality*, vol. 1: *An Introduction*, trans. Robert Hurley (New York: Pantheon, 1978). For a more general account of the emergence of the modern Subject, see also his *The Order of Things*, trans. unattributed (New York: Vintage, 1973), especially "Las Meninas," 3–16.

6. Although flawed in many ways, the work of Claude Lévi-Strauss remains a key step in understanding postmodernism (which is also always necessarily poststructuralism). The reference here is to Lévi-Strauss's *The Savage Mind*, trans. unattributed (Chicago: University of Chicago Press, 1966), 16–36. For Derrida's commentary on this topic, see especially "Structure, Sign, and Play in the Discourse of the Human Sciences" in *Writing and Difference*, trans. Alan Bass (Chicago: University of Chicago Press, 1978), 278–93.

7. On the feminist implications of this loss of the modern Subject, see also Peggy Kamuf's contribution to this volume (Chapter 4).

8. Jacques Derrida, *The Other Heading*, trans. Pascale-Anne Brault and Michael B. Naas (Bloomington: Indiana University Press, 1992), 41, emphasis in original.

9. Elizabeth Grosz gives a slightly different but, I think, compatible reading of this "double gesture" in her contribution to this volume (Chapter 3), but see also the contributions by Peggy Kamuf and Ellen Armour (Chapters 4 and 9).

10. For instance, see Alice Jardine's *Gynesis: Configurations of Woman and Modernity* (Ithaca: Cornell University Press, 1985), which is also briefly discussed in Grosz's contribution to this volume (Chapter 3). Peg Birmingham raises the same issue, with regard to criticisms of poststructuralism by Linda Alcoff, in Chapter 5.

11. For one discussion of this problem, see Elizabeth V. Spelman, *Inessential Woman: Problems of Exclusion in Feminist Thought* (Boston: Beacon, 1988).

12. Some of these same points are covered in Elizabeth Grosz's discussion of the work of Rosi Braidotti below (Chapter 3), and in Chapter 4 by Peggy Kamuf. For an excellent discussion of how the same criticism can be extended to issues of race as well as gender, see Barbara Christian's "The Race for Theory," in *Cultural Critique* 6 (Spring 1987): 51–63, reprinted in *Gender and Theory: Dialogues on Feminist Criticism*, ed. Linda Kaufman (Oxford: Basil Blackwell), 225–37.

13. For full definitions of some of these categories, see Rosemarie Tong, *Feminist Thought* (Boulder, Colo.: Westview, 1989).

14. Jacques Derrida, *Edmund Husserl's Origin of Geometry: An Introduction*, ed. David B. Allison and trans. John P. Leavey (Stony Brook, N.Y.: Nicolas Hays, 1978), hereafter cited as OG with a page reference.

15. Jacques Derrida, *Speech and Phenomena*, trans. David Allison (Evanston: Northwestern University Press, 1973), hereafter in this section cited as SP with a page reference. Calling this "philosophy of language" begins with the preface by Newton Garver (ix). Peggy Kamuf discusses this text more fully in Chapter 4.

16. For more detailed discussions of the relationship between Husserl's work and Derrida's, see also *Derrida's Interpretation of Husserl*, ed. Lawrence Lawlor, The Spindel Conference 1993, *Southern Journal of Philosophy* 32, suppl.

17. Jacques Derrida, *Of Spirit: Heidegger and the Question*, trans. Geoffrey Bennington and Rachel Bowlby (Chicago: University of Chicago Press, 1989). For a feminist reading of this text, see my "Derrida and Feminism," *American Philosophical Association Newsletter on Feminism and Philosophy* 91, no. 2 (Fall 1992): 40–43.

18. For an excellent introduction to Heidegger's work, see Hubert L. Dreyfus, *Being-in-the-World: A Commentary on Heidegger's "Being and Time," Division I* (Cambridge: MIT Press, 1991).

19. Martin Heidegger, *Being and Time*, trans. John Macquarrie and Edward Robinson (New York: Harper, 1962).

20. Martin Heidegger, *Poetry, Language, Thought*, trans. Albert Hofstadter (New York: Harper, 1975), 91–142.

21. See Claude Lévi-Strauss, *The Elementary Structure of Kinship*, trans. James Harle Bell, John Richard von Sturmer, and Rodney Needham (Boston: Beacon, 1969). For Derrida's commentaries on the gift, Christie McDonald, in a footnote to "Choreographies," refers us to *Glas*, trans. John P. Leavey Jr. and Richard Rand (Lincoln: University of Nebraska Press, 1986); *Spurs*, trans. Barbara Harlow (Chicago: University of Chicago Press, 1979); and *The Post Card*. I would add, minimally, the more recent *Given Time: I. Counterfeit Money*, trans. Peggy Kamuf (Chicago: University of Chicago Press, 1992), which is discussed at some length in Kate Mehuron's essay (Chapter 8), and *The Gift of Death*, trans. David Wills (Chicago: University of Chicago Press, 1995).

22. But the issue is very much more complicated than that, of course. See, for instance,

Derrida's "How to Avoid Speaking: Denials," in *Languages of the Unsayable: The Play of Negativity in Literature and Literary Theory*, ed. Sanford Budick and Wolfgang Iser (New York: Columbia University Press, 1989), 3–70, as well as *The Gift of Death*.

23. Derrida, *Writing and Difference*, 79–153, hereafter in this section cited as *WD* with a page reference, "At This Very Moment in This Work Here I Am" and *The Gift of Death* already cited. While I shall focus primarily on "Violence and Metaphysics"; "At This Very Moment" is discussed in a long footnote to "Choreographies" (Chapter 1); as well as in Elizabeth Grosz's contribution (Chapter 3).

24. Emmanuel Levinas, *Totality and Infinity*, trans. Alphonso Lingis (Pittsburgh: Duquesne University Press, 1969).

25. About this questionable she, see "At This Very Moment," 39–48.

26. Derrida offers a rereading of this comment in "At This Very Moment," 40.

27. *The Post Card*, 411–96, hereafter in this section cited as *PC* with a page reference.

28. Jacques Lacan, "The Seminar on 'The Purloined Letter,' " in *Ecrits* (Paris: Le Seuil, 1966), partially translated by Jeffrey Mehlman in *Yale French Studies*, no. 48 (1972): 39–72.

29. An earlier version of this discussion, to which Spivak refers, was published as "The Question of Style," trans. Ruben Berezdivin, in David B. Allison's *The New Nietzsche* (Cambridge: MIT Press, 1985), 176–89.

30. To take just two examples, see "Restitutions" in Jacques Derrida, *The Truth in Painting*, trans. Geoff Bennington and Ian McLeod (Chicago: University of Chicago Press, 1987), 255–382, and "At This Very Moment In This Work Here I Am."

31. Jacques Derrida, *Acts of Literature*, ed. Derek Attridge (New York: Routledge, 1991).

32. Jacques Derrida, "The Force of Law: The 'Mystical Foundation of Authority,' " *Cardozo Law Review* 11, nos. 5–6 (July–August 1990): 919–1045 (in French and English on facing pages, except for additional material relative to part 2).

33. Derrida, "The Force of Law," 935.

34. J. L. Austin, *How To Do Things With Words*, ed. J. O. Urmson and Marina Sbisà (Cambridge: Harvard University Press, 1975). Derrida's discussion of Austin, "Signature Event Context," originally published in *Margins of Philosophy*, trans. Alan Bass (Chicago: University of Chicago Press, 1982), 307–330, is reprinted with a summary of John Searle's response to it and Derrida's rejoinder to Searle in *Limited Inc.*, trans. Samuel Weber (Evanston: Northwestern University Press, 1988).

35. On the use of this term, see Armour's essay (Chapter 9), and Derrida's *Of Grammatology*, trans. Gayatri Chakravorty Spivak (Baltimore: Johns Hopkins University Press, 1976).

36. Jacques Derrida, *Dissemination*, 61–171.

37. Derrida, *The Truth in Painting*, 15–147.

38. Immanuel Kant, *Critique of Judgment*, trans. Werner S. Pluhar (Indianapolis, Ind.: Hackett, 1987).

39. Jacques Derrida, "Economimesis," *Diacritics* 11, no. 2 (1981): 55–93.

1

Choreographies

Interview

Jacques Derrida and Christie V. McDonald

Question 1[1]

McDonald: Emma Goldman, a maverick feminist from the late nineteenth century, once said of the feminist movement: "If I can't dance I don't want to be part of your revolution." Jacques Derrida, you have written about the question of woman and what it is that constitutes 'the feminine.' In *Spurs/Eperons* (Chicago: University of Chicago Press, 1978), a text devoted to Nietzsche, style, and woman, you wrote that "that which will not be pinned down by truth [truth?] is, in truth, *feminine.*" And you warned that such a proposition "should not . . . be hastily mistaken for a woman's femininity, for female sexuality, or for any other of those essentializing fetishes which might still tantalize the dogmatic philosopher, the impotent artist or the inexperienced seducer who has not yet escaped his foolish hopes of capture."

What seems to be at play as you take up Heidegger's reading of Nietzsche is whether or not sexual difference is a "regional question in a larger order which would subordinate it first to the domain of general ontology, subsequently to that of a fundamental ontology and finally to the question of the truth [whose?] of being itself." You thereby question the status of the argument and at the same time the question itself. In this instance, if the question of sexual difference is not a regional one (in the sense of subsidiary), if indeed "it may no longer even be a question," as you suggest, how would you describe 'woman's place'?

DERRIDA: Will I be able to write improvising my responses as I go along? It would be more worthwhile, wouldn't it? Too premeditated an interview would be without interest here. I do not see the particular finality of such an endeavor, its proper end. It would be interminable, or, rather, with respect to these questions—which are much too diffi‑cult—I would never have even dared to begin. There are other texts, other occasions for such very calculated premeditation. Let us play surprise. It will be our tribute to the dance [in French the word dance, *la danse*, is a feminine noun requiring the use of a feminine pronoun, *elle*]: it should happen only once, neither grow heavy nor ever plunge too deep; above all, it should not lag or trail behind its time. We will therefore not leave time to come back to what is behind us, nor to look attentively. We will only take a glimpse. [In French, to take a glimpse is to look into the spaces between things, *entrevoir*, that is, inter‑view.]

It was a good idea to begin with a quotation, one by a feminist from the end of the nineteenth century maverick enough to ask of the feminist movement its questions and conditions. Already, already a sign of life, a sign of the dance.

One can question the repetition. Was the matrix of what was to be the future of feminism already there at the end of the last century? You smile, no doubt, as I do, at the mention of this word. [The word matrix in English like *matrice* in French comes from the Latin *matrix* meaning womb. In both languages it has taken on, among others, the following two meanings: (1) a situation or surrounding substance within which something originates, develops, or is contained; (2) in printing it means a metal plate used for casting typefaces.] Let us make use of this figure from anatomy or printing a bit longer to ask whether a program, or locus of begetting, was not already in place in the nineteenth century for all those configurations to which the feminist struggle of the second half of the twentieth century was to commit itself and then to develop. I refer here to their being in place at all levels—those of sociopolitical demands, alliances with other forces, the alternatives of compromise or various radicalisms, the strategies of discourses, various forms of writing, theory or literature, and so forth. One is often tempted to think of this program—and to arrive by way of conclusion at the stasis of a simple combinatory scheme—in terms of all that is interminable and exhausting in it. Yes, it is exhausting (because it always draws on the same fund of possibilities) and tedious because of the ensuing repetition.

This is only one of the paradoxes. The development of the present struggle (or struggles) is extraordinary not only in its quantitative extension within Europe—because of its progress and the masses that have been slowly aroused—but also, and this is a much more important phenomenon I believe, outside of Europe. And such progress brings with it new types of historical research, other forms of reading, the discovery of new bodies of material that have gone unrecognized or misunderstood up until now; that is to say, they have been excessively [*violemment*] concealed or marginalized. The history of different "feminisms" has often been, of course, a past "passed-over-in-silence." Now here is the paradox: having made possible the reawakening of this silent past, having reappropriated a history previously stifled, feminist movements will perhaps have to renounce an all too easy kind of progressivism in the evaluation of this history. Such progressivism is often taken as their axiomatic base: the inevitable or rather essential presupposition (*dans les luttes,* as we say in French) of what one might call the ideological consensus of feminists, perhaps also their "dogmatics" or what your "maverick feminist" suspects to be their sluggishness. It is the image of a continuously accelerated "liberation" at once punctuated by determinable stages and commanded by an ultimately thinkable telos, a truth of sexual difference and femininity, etc. And if there is no doubt that this theatre, upon which the progress of feminist struggles is staged, exists, it is a relatively short and very recent sequence within "extreme-Western" history. Certainly, it is not timely politically, nor in any case is it possible, to neglect or renounce such a view of "liberation." However, to credit this representation of progress and entrust everything to it would be to surrender to a sinister mystification: everything would collapse, flow, founder in this same homogenized, sterilized river of the history of mankind [man's kind in the locution *l'histoire des hommes*].

This history carries along with it the age-old dream of reappropriation, "liberation," autonomy, mastery, in short the *cortège* of metaphysics and the *tekhnē*. The indications of this repetition are more and more numerous. The specular reversal of masculine "subjectivity," even in its most self-critical form—that is, where it is nervously jealous both of itself and of its "proper" objects—probably represents only one necessary phase. Yet it still belongs to the same program, a program whose exhaustion we were just talking about. It is true that this is valid for the whole of our culture, our scholastics, and the trouble may be found everywhere that this program is in command, or almost everywhere.

I have not begun as yet to answer your question, but, if you will forgive me, I am going to try to approach it slowly. It was necessary to recall the fact that this "silent past" (as that which was passed-over-in-silence) could still reserve some surprises, like the dance of your "maverick feminist."

McDONALD: Yes, and in that respect, recognition of the paradox suggests that while nineteenth-century and late twentieth-century feminism do resemble each other, it is less because of their historical matrix than because of those characteristics which define them. True, the program was in place.[2] The resurgence in the United States during the nineteen sixties of anarchist-like attitudes, particularly within the feminist movement, attests to that. But Goldman was not before or behind the times. An admirer of Nietzsche as "rebel and innovator," she proclaimed that "revolution is but thought carried into action." She was an activist unable to support those forms of organized feminism that focused on merely contesting the institutionalizing of inequalities for women. Her stance was more radical—one that called for the restructuring of society as a whole. If she refused the vote, for example, it was because she deemed that behind standard forms of political action there lay coercion. As an anarchist-feminist she had no truck with statism.

DERRIDA: Perhaps woman does not have a history, not so much because of any notion of the "Eternal Feminine" but because all alone she can resist and step back from a certain history (precisely in order to dance) in which revolution, or at least the "concept" of revolution, is generally inscribed. That history is one of continuous progress, despite the revolutionary break—oriented in the case of the women's movement toward the reappropriation of woman's own essence, her own specific difference, oriented in short toward a notion of woman's "truth." Your "maverick feminist" showed herself ready to break with the most authorized, the most dogmatic form of consensus, one that claims (and this is the most serious aspect of it) to speak out in the name of revolution and history. Perhaps she was thinking of a completely other history: a history of paradoxical laws and nondialectical discontinuities, a history of absolutely heterogeneous pockets, irreducible particularities, of unheard of and incalculable sexual differences; a history of women who have—centuries ago—"gone further" by stepping back with their lone dance, or who are today inventing sexual idioms at a distance from the main forum of feminist activity with a kind of reserve that does not necessarily prevent them from subscribing to the movement and even, occasionally, from becoming a militant for it.

But I am speculating. It would be better to come back to your question. Having passed through several detours or stages you wonder how I would describe what is called "woman's place"; the expression recalls, if I am not mistaken, "in the home" or "in the kitchen." Frankly, I do not know. I believe that I would not describe that place. In fact, I would be wary of such a description. Do you not fear that having once become committed to the path of this topography, we would inevitably find ourselves back "at home" or "in the kitchen"? Or under house arrest, *assignation à résidence* as they say in French penitentiary language, which would amount to the same thing? Why must there be a place for woman? And why only one, a single, completely essential place?

This is a question that you could translate ironically by saying that in my view *there is no one place for woman*. That was indeed clearly set forth during the 1972 Cerisy Colloquium devoted to Nietzsche in the lecture to which you referred entitled *Spurs/Eperons*. It is without a doubt risky to say that there is no place for woman, but this idea is not antifeminist, far from it; true, it is not feminist either. But it appears to me to be faithful in its way both to a certain assertion of women and to what is most affirmative and "dancing," as the maverick feminist says, in the displacement of women. Can one not say, in Nietzsche's language, that there is a "reactive" feminism, and that a certain historical necessity often puts this form of feminism in power in today's organized struggles? It is this kind of "reactive" feminism that Nietzsche mocks, and not woman or women. Perhaps one should not so much combat it head on—other interests would be at stake in such a move—as prevent its occupying the entire terrain. And why for that matter should one rush into answering a *topological* question (what is *the* place of *woman* [quelle est *la* place de *la* femme])? Or an *economical* question (because it all comes back to *l'oikos* as home, *maison, chez-soi* ["at home," in this sense also means in French "within the self"], the law of the proper place, and so forth, in the preoccupation with a woman's place)? Why should a new "idea" of woman or a new step taken by her necessarily be subjected to the urgency of this topo-economical concern (essential, it is true, and ineradicably philosophical)? This step only constitutes a step on the condition that it challenge a certain idea of the locus [*lieu*] and the place [*place*] (the entire history of the West and of its metaphysics) and that it dance otherwise. This is very rare, if it is not impossible, and presents itself only in the form of the most unforeseeable and most innocent of chances. The most innocent of dances would thwart the *assignation à résidence,* escape those residences under surveillance; the dance changes place and above all changes *places.* In its wake they can no longer be recognized. The joyous disturbance of certain women's movements, and of some women in particular, has actually brought with it the chance for a certain risky turbulence in the assigning of places within our small European space (I am not speaking of a more ample upheaval en route to worldwide application). Is one then going to start all over again making maps, topographics, and so forth? Distributing sexual identity cards?

The most serious part of the difficulty is the necessity to bring the dance and its tempo into tune with the "revolution." The lack of place for [*l'atopie*] or the madness of the dance—this bit of luck can also compromise the political chances of feminism and serve as an alibi for deserting organized, patient, laborious "feminist" struggles when brought into contact with all the forms of resistance that a dance movement cannot dispel, even though the dance is not synonymous with either powerlessness or fragility. I will not insist on this point, but you can surely see the kind of impossible and necessary compromise that I am alluding to: an incessant, daily negotiation—individual or not— sometimes microscopic, sometimes punctuated by a pokerlike gamble; always deprived of insurance, whether it be in private life or within institutions. Each man and each woman must commit his or her own singularity, the untranslatable factor of his or her life and death.

Nietzsche makes a scene before women, feminists in particular—a spectacle that is overdetermined, divided, apparently contradictory. This is just what has interested me; this scene has interested me because of all the paradigms that it exhibits and multiplies, and insofar as it often struggles, sometimes dances, always takes chances in a historical space whose essential traits, those of the matrix, have perhaps not changed since then in Europe (I mean specifically in Europe, and that perhaps makes all the difference although we cannot separate worldwide feminism from a certain fundamental Europeanization of world culture; this is an enormous problem that I must leave aside here). In *Spurs/Eperons* I have tried to formalize the movements and typical moments of the scene that Nietzsche creates throughout a very broad and diverse body of texts. I have done this up to a certain limit, one that I also indicate, where the decision to formalize fails for reasons that are absolutely structural. Since these typical features are and must be unstable, sometimes contradictory, and finally "undecidable," any break in the movement of the reading would settle in a countermeaning, in *the meaning* that becomes countermeaning. This countermeaning can be more or less naive or complacent. One could cite countless examples of it. In the most perfunctory of cases, the simplification reverts to the isolation of Nietzsche's violently antifeminist statements (directed first against reactive, specular feminism as a figure both of the dogmatic philosopher and a certain relationship of man to truth), pulling them out (and possibly attributing them to me though that is of little importance) of the movement and system that I try to reconstitute. Some have reacted at times even more perfunctorily, unable to see beyond the end of phallic forms projecting into the text; beginning with style, the spur, or the umbrella, they take no account of what I have said about the difference between style and writing or the bisexual complication of those and other forms. Generally speaking, this cannot be considered reading, and I will go so far as to say that it is *to not read* the syntax and punctuation of a given sentence when one arrests the text in a certain position, thus settling on a thesis, meaning or truth. This mistake of hermeneutics, this mistaking of hermeneutics—it is this that the final message [*envoi*] of "I forgot my umbrella" should challenge. But let us leave that. The truth value (that is, Woman as the major allegory of truth in Western discourse) and its correlative, Femininity (the essence or truth of Woman), are there to assuage such hermeneutic anxiety. These are the places that one should acknowledge, at least that is if one is interested in doing so; they are the foundations or anchorings of Western rationality (of what I have called "phallogocentrism" [as the complicity of Western metaphysics with a notion of male firstness]). Such recognition should not make of either the truth value or femininity an object of knowledge (at stake are the norms of knowledge and knowledge as norm); still less should it make of them a place to inhabit, a home. It should rather permit the invention of an other inscription, one very old and very new, a displacement of bodies and places that is quite different.

You recalled the expression "essentializing fetishes" (truth, femininity, the essentiality of woman or feminine sexuality as fetishes). It is difficult to improvise briefly here. But I shall point out that one can avoid a trap by being precise about the concept of fetishism and the context to which one refers, even if only to displace it. (On this point, I take the liberty of alluding to the discussions of fetishism and feminine sexuality in *Spurs, Glas* or *La carte postale*, specifically in *Le facteur de la vérité*.) Another trap is more political and can only be avoided by taking account of the *real* conditions in which women's struggles develop on all fronts (economic, ideological, political). These conditions often require the preservation (within longer or shorter phases) of metaphysical presuppositions that one must (and knows already that one must) question in a later phase—or an other place—because they belong to the dominant system that one is deconstructing on a *practical level*. This multiplicity of places, moments, forms and forces does not always mean giving way either to empiricism or to contradiction. How can one breathe without such punctuation and without the multiplicities of rhythm and steps? How can one dance, your "maverick feminist" might say?

MCDONALD: This raises an important question that should not be overlooked, although we haven't the space to develop it to any extent here: the complicated relationship of a practical politics to the kinds of analysis that we have been considering (specifically the "deconstructive" analysis implicit in your discussion). That this relationship cannot simply be translated into an opposition between the empirical and the nonempirical has been touched on in an entirely different context.[3] Just how one is to deal with the interrelationship of these forces and necessities in the context of feminine struggles should be more fully explored on some other occasion. But let's go on to Heidegger's ontology.

DERRIDA: To answer your question about Heidegger, and without being able to review here the itinerary of a reading in *Spurs/Eperons* clearly divided into two moments, I must limit myself to a piece of information, or rather to an open question. The question proceeds, so to speak, from the end; it proceeds from the point where the thought of the gift [*le don*][4] and that of "propriation" disturbs without simply reversing the order of ontology, the authority of the question "what is it," the subordination of regional ontologies to one fundamental ontology. I am moving much too rapidly, but how can I do otherwise here? From this point, which is not a point, one wonders whether this extremely difficult, perhaps impossible idea of the gift can still maintain an essential relationship to sexual difference. One wonders whether sexual difference, femininity for example—however irreducible it may be—does not remain derived from and subordinated to either the question of destination or the thought of the gift (I say "thought" because one cannot say philosophy, theory, logic, structure, scene or anything else; when one can no longer use any word of this sort, when one can say almost nothing else, one says "thought," but one could show that this too is excessive). I do not know. Must one think "difference" "before" sexual difference or taking off "from" it? Has this question, if not a meaning (we are at the origin of meaning here, and the origin cannot "have meaning") at least something of a chance of opening up anything at all, however im-pertinent it may appear?

Question 2

McDonald: You put into question the characteristic form of women's protest, namely the subordination of woman to man. I shall attempt here to describe the direction of your argument, as I understand it, and then comment on it.

The new sense of writing (*écriture*) with which one associates the term deconstruction has emerged from the close readings that you have given to texts as divergent as those of Plato, Rousseau, Mallarmé and others. It is one in which traditional binary pairing (as in the opposition of spirit to matter or man to woman) no longer functions by the privilege given to the first term over the second. In a series of interviews published under the title *Positions* in 1972, you spoke of a two-phase program (phase being understood as a structural rather than a chronological term) necessary for the act of deconstruction.

In the first phase a reversal was to take place in which the opposed terms would be inverted. Thus woman, as a previously subordinate term, might become the dominant one in relation to man. Yet because such a scheme of reversal could only repeat the traditional scheme (in which the hierarchy of duality is always reconstituted), it alone could not effect any significant change. Change would only occur through the "second" and more radical phase of deconstruction in which a "new" concept would be forged simultaneously. The motif of *différance*, as neither a simple "concept" nor a mere "word," has brought us the now familiar constellation of attendant terms: trace, supplement, pharmakon and others. Among the others, two are marked sexually and in their most widely recognized sense pertain to the woman's body: *hymen* (the logic of which is developed in *La double séance*) and *double invagination* (a leitmotif in *Living On/Borderlines*).

Take only the term *hymen* in which there is a confusion or continuation of the term coitus, and from which it gets its double meaning: (1) "a membranous fold of tissue partly or completely occluding the vaginal external orifice" [from the Greek for *membrane*] and (2) marriage [from Greek mythology; the god of marriage]. In the first sense the hymen is that which protects virginity, and is in front of the uterus. That is, it lies between the inside and outside of the woman, between desire and its fulfillment. So that although (male) desire dreams of violently piercing or breaking the hymen (consummation in the second sense of the term), if that happens there is no hymen.

It seems to me that while the extensive play on etymologies (in which unconscious motivations are traced through the transformations and historical excesses of usage) effects a displacement of these terms, it also poses a problem for those who would seek to define what is specifically feminine. That comes about not so much because these terms are either under- or overvalued as parts belonging to woman's body. It is rather that, in the economy of a movement of writing that is always elusive, one can never decide properly whether the particular term implies complicity with or a break from existent ideology. Perhaps this is because, as Adam says of Eve in Mark Twain's satire, *The Diary of Adam and Eve*, not only does the "new creature name . . . everything" because "it looks like the thing," but—and this is the crux of the matter—"her mind is disordered [or, if you like, Nietzschean]—everything shows it."

In this regard there comes to mind a footnote to p. 207 of *La double séance*, concerning the displacement of writing, its transformation and generalization. The example cited is that of a surgeon who, upon learning of Freud's own difficulty in admitting to the possibility of masculine hysteria, exclaims to him: "But, my dear colleague, how can you state such absurdities? *Hysteron* means uterus. How therefore could a man be a hysteric?"

How can we change the representation of woman? Can we move from the rib where woman is wife ("She was called Woman because she was taken from man"—Genesis 2:23) to the womb where she is mother ("man is born of woman"—Job 14:13) without essential loss? Do we have in your view the beginning of phase two, a "new" concept of woman?

DERRIDA: No, I do not believe that we have one, if indeed it is possible to *have* such a thing or if such a thing could exist or show promise of existing. Personally, I am not sure that I feel the lack of it. Before having one that is new, are we certain of having had an old one? It is the word "concept" or "conception" that I would in turn question in its relationship to any essence which is rigorously or properly identifiable. This would bring us back to the preceding questions. The concept of the concept, along with the entire system that attends it, belongs to a precriptive order. It is that order that a problematics of woman and a problematics of difference, as sexual difference, should disrupt along the way. Moreover, I am not sure that "phase two" marks a split with "phase one," a split whose form would be a cut along an indivisible line. The relationship between these two phases doubtless has another structure. I spoke of two distinct phases for the sake of clarity, but the relationship of one phase to another is marked less by conceptual determinations (that is, where a new concept follows an archaic one) than by a transformation or general deformation of logic; such transformations or deformations mark the "logical" element or environment itself by moving, for example, beyond the "positional" (difference determined as opposition, whether or not dialectically). This movement is of great consequence for the discussion here, even if my formulation is apparently abstract and disembodied. One could, I think, demonstrate this: when sexual difference is determined by *opposition* in the dialectical sense (according to the Hegelian movement of speculative dialectics, which remains so powerful even beyond Hegel's text), one appears to set off "the war between the sexes"; but one precipitates the end with victory going to the masculine sex. The determination of sexual difference in opposition is destined, designed, in truth, for truth; it is so in order to erase sexual difference. The dialectical opposition neutralizes or supersedes [Hegel's term *Aufhebung* carries with it both the sense of conserving and negating. No adequate translation of the term in English has yet been found] the difference. However, according to a surreptitious operation that must be flushed out, one insures phallocentric mastery under the cover of neutralization every time. These are now well-known paradoxes. And such phallocentrism adorns itself now and then, here and there, with an appendix: a certain kind of feminism. In the same manner, phallocentrism and homosexuality can go, so to speak, hand in hand, and I take these terms, whether it is a question of feminine or masculine homosexuality, in a very broad and radical sense.

And what if the "wife" or the "mother"—whom you seem sure of being able to dissociate—were figures for this homosexual dialectics? I am referring now to your question on the "representation" of woman and such "loss" as might occur in the passage from man's rib to the womb of woman, the passage from the spouse, you say, to the mother. Why is it necessary to choose, and why only these two possibilities, these two "places," assuming that one can really dissociate them?

McDONALD: The irony of my initial use of the cliché "woman's place" which in the old saw is followed by "in the home" or "in the kitchen" leaves the whole wide world for other places for the same intent. As for the "place" of woman in Genesis, and Job, as rib (spouse) or womb (mother), these are more basic functional differences. Nevertheless, within these two traditional roles, to choose one implies loss of the other. You are correct in observing that such a choice is not necessary; there could be juxtaposition, substitution or other possible combinations. But these biblical texts are not frivolous in seeing the functional distinction that also has distinguished "woman's place" in Western culture.

DERRIDA: Since you quote Genesis, I would like to evoke the marvel-ous reading that Levinas has proposed of it without being clear as to whether he assumes it as his own or what the actual status of the "commentary" that he devotes to it is.[5] There would, of course, be a certain secondariness of woman, Ischa. The man, Isch, would come first; he would be number one; he would be at the beginning. Secondariness, however, would not be that of woman or femininity, but the division between masculine and feminine. It is not feminine sexuality that would be second but only the relationship to sexual difference. At the origin, on this side of and therefore beyond any sexual mark, there was humanity in general, and this is what is important. Thus the possibility of ethics could be saved, if one takes ethics to mean that relationship to the other as other which accounts for no other determination or sexual characteristic in particular. What kind of an ethics would there be if belonging to one sex or another became its law or privilege? What if the universality of moral laws were modeled on or limited according to the sexes? What if their universality were not unconditional, without sexual condition in particular?

Whatever the force, seductiveness or necessity of this reading, does it not risk restoring—in the name of ethics as that which is irreproachable—a classical interpretation, and thereby enriching what I would call its panoply in a manner surely as subtle as it is sublime? Once again, the classical interpretation gives a masculine sexual marking to what is presented either as a neutral originariness or, at least, as prior and superior to all sexual markings. Levinas indeed senses the risk factor involved in the erasure of sexual difference. He therefore maintains sexual difference: the human in general remains a sexual being. But he can only do so, it would seem, by placing (differentiated) sexuality beneath humanity, which sustains itself at the level of the Spirit. That is, he simultaneously places, and this is what is important, masculinity [le masculin] in command and at the beginning (the arkhē), on a par with the Spirit. This gesture carries with it the most self-interested of contradictions; it has repeated itself, let us say, since "Adam and Eve," and persists—in analogous form—into "modernity," despite all the differences of style and treatment. Isn't that a feature of the "matrix," as we were saying before? or the "patrix" if you prefer, but it amounts to the same thing, does it not? Whatever the complexity of the itinerary and whatever the knots of rhetoric, don't you think that the movement of Freudian thought repeats this "logic"? Is it not also the risk that Heidegger runs? One should perhaps say, rather, the risk that is *avoided* because phallogocentrism is insurance against the return of what certainly has been feared as the most agonizing risk of all. Since I have named Heidegger in a context where the reference is quite rare and may even appear strange, I would like to dwell on this for a moment, if you don't mind, concerned that I will be both too lengthy and too brief.

Heidegger seems almost never to speak about sexuality or sexual difference. And he seems almost never to speak about psychoanalysis, give or take an occasional negative allusion. This is neither negligence nor omission. The pauses coming from his silence on these questions punctuate or create the spacing out of a powerful discourse. And one of the strengths of this discourse may be stated (though I am going much too quickly and schematizing excessively) like this: it begins by denying itself all accepted forms of security, all the sedimented presuppositions of classical ontology, anthropology, the natural or human sciences, until it falls back this side of such values as the opposition between subject/object, conscious/unconscious, mind/body, and many others as well. The existential analytic of the Dasein opens the road, so to speak, leading to the question of being; the Dasein is neither the human being (a thought recalled earlier by Levinas) nor the subject, neither consciousness nor the self [le moi] (whether conscious or unconscious). These are all determinations that are derived from and occur after the Dasein. Now—and here is what I wanted to get to after this inadmissible acceleration—in a course given in 1928, Heidegger justifies to some degree the silence of Sein und Zeit on the question of sexuality [Gesamtausgabe, vol. 26, no. 10, p. 171ff.]. In a paragraph from the course devoted to the "Problem of the Sein und Zeit," Heidegger reminds us that the analytic of the Dasein is neither an anthropology, an ethics nor a metaphysics. With respect to any definition, position, or evaluation of these fields, the Dasein is neuter. Heidegger insists upon and makes clear this original and essential "neutrality" of the Dasein: "This neutrality means also that the Dasein is neither of the two sexes. But this a-sexuality (Geschlechtlosigkeit) is not the indifference of empty invalidity, the annuling negativity of an indifferent ontic nothingness. In its neutrality, the Dasein is not the indifferent person-and-everyone (Niemand und Jeder), but it is originary positivity and the power of being or of the essence, Mächtigkeit des Wesen." One would have to read the analysis that follows very closely; I will try to do that another time in relation to some of his later texts. The analysis emphasizes the positive character, as it were, of this originary and powerful asexual neutrality which is not the neither-nor (Weder-noch) of ontic abstraction. It is originary and ontological. More precisely, the a-sexuality does not signify in this instance the absence of sexuality—one could call it the instinct, desire or even the libido—but the absence of any mark belonging to one of the two sexes. Not that the Dasein does not ontically or in fact belong to a sex; not that it is deprived of sexuality; but the Dasein as Dasein does not carry with it the mark of this opposition (or alternative) between the two sexes. Insofar as these marks are opposable and binary, they are not existential structures. Nor do they allude in this respect to any primitive or subsequent bisexuality. Such an allusion would fall once again into anatomical, biological, or anthropological determinations. And the Dasein, in the structures and "power" that are originary to it, would come "prior" to these determinations. I am putting quotation marks around the word "prior" because it has no literal, chronological, historical, or logical meaning. Now, as of 1928, the analytic of the Dasein was the thought of ontological difference and the repetition of the question of being; it opened up a problematics that subjected all the concepts of traditional Western philosophy to a radical elucidation and interpretation. This gives an idea of what stakes were involved in a neutralization that fell back this side of both sexual difference and its binary marking, if not this side of sexuality itself. This would be the title of the enormous problem that in this context I must limit myself to merely naming: ontological difference and sexual difference.

And since your question evoked the "motif of difference," I would say that it has moved, by displacement, in the vicinity of this very obscure area. What is also being sought in this zone is the passage between ontological difference and sexual difference; it is a passage that may no longer be thought, punctuated, or opened up according to those polarities to which we have been referring for some time (originary/derived, ontological/ontic, ontology/anthropology, the thought of being/metaphysics or ethics, etc.). The constellation of terms that you have cited could *perhaps* be considered (for nothing is ever taken for granted or guaranteed in these matters) a kind of transformation of deformation of space; such a transformation would tend to extend beyond these poles and reinscribe them within it. Some of these terms, "hymen" or "invagination," you were saying, "pertain in their most widely recognized sense to the woman's body." Are you sure? I am grateful for your having used such a careful formulation. That these words signify "in their most widely recognized sense" had, of course, not escaped me, and the emphasis that I have put on resexualizing a philosophical or theoretical discourse, which has been too "neutralizing" in this respect, was dictated by those very reservations that I just mentioned concerning the strategy of neutralization (whether or not it is deliberate). Such resexualizing must be done without facileness of any kind and, above all, without regression in relation to what might justify, as we saw, the procedures—or necessary steps—of Levinas or Heidegger, for example. That being said, "hymen" and "invagination," at least in the context into which these words have been swept, no longer simply designate figures for the feminine body. They no longer do so, that is, assuming that one knows for certain what a feminine or masculine body is, and assuming that anatomy is in this instance the final recourse. What remains undecidable concerns not only but also the line of cleavage between the two sexes. As you recalled, such a movement reverts neither to words nor to concepts. And what remains of language within it cannot be abstracted from the "performativity" (which marks and is marked) that concerns us here, beginning—for the examples that you have chosen—with the texts of Mallamé and Blanchot, and with the labor of reading or writing which evoked them and which they in turn evoked. One could say quite accurately that the hymen *does not exist.* Anything constituting the value of existence is foreign to the "hymen." And if there were hymen—I am not saying if the hymen existed—property value would be no more appropriate to it for reasons that I have stressed in the texts to which you refer. How can one then attribute the *existence* of the hymen *properly* to woman? Not that it is any more the distinguishing feature of man or, for that matter, of the human creature. I would say the same for the term "invagination" which has, moreover, always been reinscribed in a chiasmus, one doubly folded, redoubled and inversed,[6] etc. From then on, is it not difficult to recognize in the movement of this term a "representation of woman"? Furthermore, I do not know if it is to a change in representation that we should entrust the future. As with all the questions that we are at present discussing, this one, and above all when it is put as a question of representation, seems at once too old and as yet to be born: a kind of old parchment crossed every which way, overloaded with hieroglyphs and still as virgin as the origin, like the early morning in the East from whence it comes. And you know that the word for parchment does not come from any "road" leading from Pergamus in Asia. I do not know how you will translate this last sentence.

McDONALD: It is a problem. In modern English usage the word for parchment no longer carries with it the sense of the French *parchemin,* on or by the road, as the Middle English *perchement* or *parchemin* did. The American Heritage Dictionary traces the etymology thus: "Parthian (leather) from *pergamina,* parchment, from Greek *pergamene,* from *Pergamenos,* or *Pergamun,* from *Pergamon.*" Lempriere's Classical Dictionary says further that the town of Pergamus was founded by Philaeterus, a eunuch, and that parchment has been called the *charta pergamena.*

DERRIDA: The Littré Dictionary which gives the etymology for French makes war responsible for the appearance of "pergamena" or "Pergamina." It is thereby a product of war: one began to write on bodies and animal skins because papyrus was becoming very rare. They say too that parchment was occasionally prepared from the skin of stillborn lambs.

And according to Pliny, it was out of jealousy that Eumenes, king of Pergamus, turned to parchment. His rival, Ptolemies, the king of Egypt, was so proud of his library that he had only books written on paper. It was necessary to find new bodies of or for writing.

McDONALD: I would like to come back to the writing of the dance, the choreography that you mentioned a while back. If we do not yet have a "new" "concept" of woman, because the radicalization of the problem goes beyond the "thought" or the concept, what are our chances of "thinking 'difference' not so much before sexual difference, as you say, as taking off 'from' " it? What would you say is our chance and "who" are we sexually?

DERRIDA: At the approach of this shadowy area it has always seemed to me that the voice itself had to be divided in order to say that which is given to thought or speech. No monological discourse—and by that I mean here monosexual discourse—can dominate with a single voice, a single tone, the space of this half-light, even if the "proffered discourse" is then signed by a sexually marked patronymic. Thus, to limit myself to one account, and not to propose an example, I have felt the necessity for a chorus, for a choreographic text with polysexual signatures.[7] I felt this every time that a legitimacy of the neuter, the apparently least suspect sexual neutrality of "phallocentric or gynocentric" mastery, threatened to immobilize (in silence), colonize, stop or unilateralize in a subtle or sublime manner what remains no doubt irreducibly dissymmetrical. More directly: a certain dissymmetry is no doubt the law both of sexual difference and the relationship to the other in general (I say this in opposition to a certain kind of violence within the language of "democratic" platitudes, in any case in opposition to a certain democratic ideology), yet the dissymmetry to which I refer is still let us not say symmetrical in turn (which might seem absurd), but doubly, unilaterally inordinate, like a kind of reciprocal, respective and respectful excessiveness. This double dissymmetry perhaps goes beyond known or coded marks, beyond the grammar and spelling, shall we say (metaphorically), of sexuality. This indeed revives the following question: what if we were to reach, what if we were to approach here (for one does not arrive at this as one would at a determined location) the area of a relationship to the other where the code of sexual marks would no longer be discriminating? The relationship would not be asexual, far from it, but would be sexual otherwise: beyond the binary difference that governs the decorum of all codes, beyond the opposition feminine/masculine, beyond bisexuality as well, beyond homosexuality and heterosexuality which come to the same thing. As I dream of saving the chance that this question offers I would like to believe in the multiplicity of sexually marked voices. I would like to believe in the masses, this indeterminable number of blended voices, this mobile of nonidentified sexual marks whose choreography can carry, divide, multiply the body of each "individual," whether he be classified as "man" or as "woman" according to the criteria of usage. Of course, it is not impossible that desire for a sexuality without number can still protect us, like a dream, from an implacable destiny which immures everything for life in the figure 2. And should this merciless closure arrest desire at the wall of opposition, we would struggle in vain: there will never be but two sexes, neither one more nor one less. Tragedy would leave this strange sense, a contingent one finally, that we must affirm and learn to love instead of dreaming of the innumerable. Yes, perhaps; why not? But where would the "dream" of the innumerable come from, if it is indeed a dream? Does the dream itself not prove that what is dreamt of must be there in order for it to provide the dream? Then too, I ask you, what kind of a dance would there be, or would there be one at all, if the sexes were not exchanged according to rhythms that vary considerably? In a quite rigorous sense, the *exchange* alone could not suffice either, however, because the desire to escape the combinatory itself, to invent incalculable choreographies, would remain.

Notes

1. The following text is the result of a written exchange carried on during the fall of 1981. Jacques Derrida wrote his responses in French, and I then translated them into English for publication. It should be noted that I do not ask the following questions in the name of any specific feminist group or ideology. I do nevertheless owe a debt to long-standing conversations on the subject of "Woman" and "Women" with, among others, A. Jardine, C. Lévesque, N. Miller, N. Schor and especially J. McDonald.

2. On 26 August 1970, a group of women calling themselves the Emma Goldman Brigade marched down Fifth Avenue in New York City with many other feminists, chanting: "Emma said it in 1910 / Now we're going to say it again."

3. See Rodolphe Gasché, "La bordure interne," and the response by Jacques Derrida, in *L'oreille de l'autre: Textes et débats avec Jacques Derrida*, ed. C. Lévesque and C. McDonald, (Montreal: VLB, 1982).

4. The *gift* is a topic that occurs in a number of recent texts, among others: *Glas, Eperons,* and *La carte postale*.

5. Jacques Derrida refers here to the text "En ce moment même dans cet ouvrage me

voici," in *Textes pour Emmanuel Lewis* (Paris: J. M. Place, 1980). Derrida interprets two texts in particular by Levinas: "Le judaïsme et le féminin," in *Difficile liberté*; and "Et Dieu créa la femme," in *Du sacré au saint*. In order to clarify this part of the discussion, I am translating the following passage from Derrida's text in which he quotes from and then comments upon Levinas's commentary: "The meaning of the 'feminine' will be clarified in this manner by beginning with the human essence; the female Isha [*la Isha*] begins with Ish: not that the feminine originates in the masculine, but rather the division into masculine and feminine—the dichotomy—starts with what is human. . . . Beyond the personal relationship established between two beings, each born of a discrete creative act, the specificity of the feminine is a secondary matter. It is not woman who is secondary; it is the relationship with woman as woman, and that does not belong to the primordial level of the human element. The first level consists of those tasks that man and woman each accomplishes as a human being. . . . In each of the passages that we are commenting upon right now, the problem lies in the reconciliation of men's and women's humanity with the hypothesis of masculine spirituality; the feminine is not the correlative of the masculine but its corollary; feminine specificity, as the difference between the sexes that it indicates, is not situated straightaway at the level of those opposites which constitute the Spirit. An audacious question, this one: How can equality of the sexes come from masculine "ownership" [*la propriété du masculin*]? . . . A difference was necessary that would not compromise equity: a difference of sex; and from then on, a certain pre-eminence of man, a woman whose arrival comes later and who is, as woman, the appendix of the human element. Now we understand the lesson. The idea of humanity is not thinkable from two entirely different principles. There must be a sameness [*le même*] common to others: woman was taken from man, but came after him: the very feminity of woman is in this inaugural after-thought." ("Et Dieu créa la femme," in *Du sacré au saint*). And Derrida follows up, commenting: "It is a strange logic, this 'audacious question.' " One would have to comment each step of the way and verify that the secondariness of sexual difference signifies the secondariness of the feminine in every case (but why indeed?). One would have to verify that the initialness of what is pre-differential is always marked by the masculine; the masculine should come, like all sexual marks, only afterward. Such a commentary would be necessary, but I prefer to first underscore the following, in the name of protocol: he himself is commenting and says that he is commenting; one must bear in mind that this is not literally the discourse of Levinas. He says, as he is discoursing, that he is commenting on doctors, at this very moment ("the passages upon which we are commenting at this moment," and further along: "I am not taking sides; today I am commenting"). However, the distance of the commentary is not neuter. What he comments upon is consonant with a whole network of his own assertions, or those by him, "him" (53–54).

6. This is an allusion to, among other things, all the passages on the so-called argument of the *gaine* (sheath, girdle; cognate with vagina), esp. 232ff. and 250ff. Furthermore, the word "invagination" is always taken within the syntax of the expression "Double invagination chiasmatique des bords" (in "Living On," in *Deconstruction and Criticism* [New York: Seabury, 1979]; and "The Law of Genre," *Glyph* 7).

7. This is an allusion to "Pas" (*Gramma: Lire Blanchot* 1, nos. 3–4 [1976]: 111–215); *The Truth in Painting*, trans. Geoff Bennington and Ian McLeod (Chicago: University of Chicago Press, 1987), French version *La verité en peinture* (Paris: Flammarion, 1978); "At This Very Moment in This Work Here I Am," trans. Ruben Berezdivin, in *Re-Reading Levinas*, ed. Robert Bernasconi and Simon Critchley (Bloomington: Indiana University Press, 1991), French version, "En ce moment même dans cet ouvrage me voici," included in *Psyche: Inventions de l'autre* (Paris: Galilée, 1987); *Cinders*, ed. and trans. Ned Lukacher (Lincoln: University of Nebraska Press, 1991), French version *Feu la cendre* (Paris: Des Femmes, 1987). TN

2

Displacement and the Discourse of Woman

Gayatri Chakravorty Spivak

When in *The Philosophy of Right* Hegel writes of the distinction between thought and object, his example is Adam and Eve.

> Since it is in thought that I am first at home (*bei mir*), I do not penetrate (*durchbohren*) an object until I understand it; it then ceases to stand over against me and I have taken from it its ownness (*das Eigene*), that it had for itself against me. Just as Adam says to Eve: "Thou art flesh of my flesh and bone of my bone," so mind says: "This is mind of my mind," and the alienness (*Fremdheit* as opposed to *das Eigene*; alterity as opposed to ownness) disappears.[1]

It would be possible to assemble here a collection of "great passages" from literature and philosophy to show how, unobtrusively but crucially, a certain metaphor of woman has produced (rather than merely illustrated) a discourse that we are obliged "historically" to call the discourse of man.[2] Given the accepted charge of the notions of production and constitution, one might reformulate this: the discourse of man is in the metaphor of woman.

Jacques Derrida's critique of phallocentrism can be summarized as follows: the patronymic, in spite of all empirical details of the generation gap, keeps the transcendental ego of the dynasty identical in the eye of the law. By virtue of the father's name the son refers to the father. The irreducible importance of the name and the law in this situation makes it quite clear that the question is not merely one of psycho-socio-sexual behavior but of the production and consolidation of reference and meaning. The desire to make one's progeny represent his presence is akin to the desire to make one's words represent the full meaning of one's intention. Hermeneutic, legal, or patrilinear, it is the prerogative of the phallus to declare itself sovereign source.[3] Its causes are also its effects: a social structure—centered on due process and the law (logocentrism); a structure of argument centered on the sovereignty of the engendering self and the determinacy of meaning (phallogocentrism); a structure of the text centered on the phallus as the determining moment (phallocentrism) or signifier. Can Derrida's critique provide us a network of concept-metaphors that does not appropriate or displace the figure of woman? In order to sketch an answer, I shall refer not only to Derrida, but to two of Derrida's acknowledged "creditors" in the business of deconstruction, Nietzsche and Freud.[4] I shall not refer to *La Carte postale*, which I have discussed elsewhere.[5]

The deconstructive structure of how woman "is" is contained in a well-known Nietzschean sentence: "Finally—if one loved them . . . what comes of it inevitably? that they 'give themselves,' even when they—give themselves. The female is so artistic."[6] Or: women impersonate themselves as having an orgasm even at the time of orgasm. Within the historical understanding of women as incapable of orgasm, Nietzsche is arguing that impersonation is woman's only sexual pleasure. At the time of the greatest self-possession-cum-ecstasy, the woman is self-possessed enough to organize a self-(re)presentation without an actual presence (of sexual pleasure) to re-present. This is an originary dis-

placement. The virulence of Nietzsche's misogyny occludes an unacknowledged envy: a man cannot fake an orgasm. His pen must write or
prove impotent.[7]

For the deconstructive philosopher, who suspects that all (phallogocentric) longing for a transcendent truth as the origin or end of semiotic
gestures might be "symptomatic," woman's style becomes exemplary, for
his style remains obliged to depend upon the stylus or stiletto of the
phallus. Or, to quote Derrida reading Nietzsche:

> She writes (herself) [or (is) written—*Elle (s')écrit*]. Style amounts
> to [or returns to (*revient à*)] her. Rather: if style were (as for Freud
> the penis is "the normal prototype of the fetish") the man writing
> would be woman.[8]

A lot is going on here. Through his critique of Nietzsche, Derrida is
questioning both the phallus-privileging of a certain Freud as well as the
traditional view, so blindly phallocentric that it gives itself out as
general, that "the style is the man." Throughout his work, Derrida asks
us to notice that *all* human beings are irreducibly displaced although, in
a discourse that privileges the center, women alone have been diagnosed
as such; correspondingly, he attempts to displace all centrisms, binary
oppositions, or centers. It is my suggestion, however, that the woman
who is the "model" for deconstructive discourse remains a woman
generalized and defined in terms of the faked orgasm and other varieties
of denial. To quote Derrida on Nietzsche again:

> She is twice model, in a contradictory fashion, at once lauded
> and condemned. . . . (First), like writing. . . . But, insofar as she
> does not believe, herself, in truth . . . she is again the model,
> this time the good model, or rather the bad model as good
> model: she plays dissimulation, ornament, lying, art, the artistic
> philosophy. (*Ep* 66)

At this point the shadow area between Derrida on Nietzsche and
Derrida on Derrida begins to waver. "She is a power of affirmation,"
Derrida continues. We are reminded of the opening of his essay:

> The circumspect title for this meeting would be
> *the question of style.*

> But woman will be my *subject*.
> It remains to wonder if that comes to the *same*
> (*revient au même*)—or to the *other*.
>
> The "question of style," as you no doubt have recognized, is a
> quotation. I wanted to indicate that I shall advance nothing here
> that does not belong to the space cleared in the last two years by
> readings that open a new phase in the process of deconstructive,
> *that is to say affirmative*, interpretation. (*Ep* 34, 36; my emphasis)

Quotation in Derrida is a mark of nonself-identity: the defining
predication of a woman, whose very name is changeable.[9] " 'Give
themselves' " is thus distinguished from "give themselves" in Nietzsche's
description of woman. The reader will notice the carefully hedged
articulation of the deconstructive philosopher's desire to usurp "the place
of displacement": between the reminder of an appropriate title and the
invocation of the complicity of the same and the other (philosophical
themes of great prestige), comes the sentence: "Woman will be my
subject." We give the "subject" its philosophical value of the capital I.
In the place of the writer's "I" will be woman. But, colloquially, "my
subject" means "my object." Thus, even if "le style" (man?) "revient à
elle" (returns or amounts to her) is an affirmation of "ce qui ne revient
pas au père" (that which does not return or amount to the father), the
author of *La question du style*—that displaced text that does not exist,
yet does, of course, as *Eperons*—having stepped into the place of
displacement, has displaced the woman-model doubly as shuttling between the author's subject and object. If, then, the "deconstructive" is
"affirmative" by way of Nietzsche's woman, who is a "power of affirmation," we are already within the circuit of what I call double displacement: in order to secure the gesture of taking the woman as model, the
figure of woman must be doubly displaced. For a type case of double
displacement, I turn to "Femininity," a late text of Freud certainly as
well known as the Nietzschean sentence.[10]

Freud's displacement of the subject should not be confused with Freud's
notion of displacement (*Verschiebung*) in the dream-work, which is one
of the techniques of the dream-work to transcribe the latent content of
the dream to its manifest content. The displacement of the subject that
is the theme of deconstruction relates rather to the dream-work in

general; for the dream *as a whole* displaces the text of the latent content into the text of the manifest content. Freud calls this *Entstellung* (literally "displacement"; more usually translated as "distortion").[11]

Freud expanded the notion of the displacement of the dream-work in general into an account of the working of the psychic apparatus and thereby put the subject as such in question. One can produce a reading of the "metapsychological" rather than the therapeutic Freud to show that this originarily displaced scene of writing is the scene of woman.[12] Let us consider Freud's description of woman's originary displacement.

"Psycho-analysis does not wish to describe (*nicht beschreiben will*) what the female (*das Weib*) is . . . but investigates (*untersucht*) how she comes into being, how the female develops out of the bisexually disposed child" (F 22:116 GW 15:125). The name of this primordial bisexuality is of course unisex. "We are now obliged to recognize," Freud writes, "that the little girl is a little man" (F 22:118; GW 15:126).

Here is the moment when woman is displaced out of this primordial masculinity. One of the crucial predications of the place of displacement—"the second task with which a girl's development is burdened"—is that the girl-child must change the object of her love. For the boy it never changes. "But in the Oedipus situation the girl's father has become (*ist geworden*) her love-object." The unchanged object-situation and the fear of castration allow the boy to "overcome (*überwinden*) the Oedipus complex":

> The girl is driven out of her attachment to her mother through the influence of her envy for the penis and she enters the Oedipus situation as though into a haven. . . . (She) dismantle(s) [*baut ab*] it late and, even so, imperfectly [*unvollkommen*]. (F 23:129; GW 15:138)

Through the subject-object topology of the I (ego) and the it (id), Freud displaces the structure of the psyche itself. The beginning of sexual difference is also given in the language of subject and object. The boy child is irreducibly and permanently displaced from the mother, the object of his desire. But the girl-child is doubly displaced. The boy is born as a subject that desires to copulate with the object. He has the wherewithal to make a "proper" sentence, where the copula is intention or desire. The sentence can be

$$S \text{ (subject)} \xrightarrow{\text{desires}} O \text{ (object)}$$

The girl child is born an uncertain role-player—a little man playing a little girl or vice versa. The object she desires is "wrong"—must be changed. Thus it is not only that her sentence must be revised. It is that she did not have the ingredients to put together a proper sentence in the first place. She is originarily written as

$$\text{(masquerading subject)} \xrightarrow{\text{desires (temporarily)}} \cancel{O} \text{ (wrong object)}$$

I have made this analysis simply to suggest that a deconstructive discourse, even as it criticizes phallocentrism or the sovereignty of consciousness (and thus seeks to displace or "feminize" itself according to a certain logic), must displace the figure of the woman twice over. In Nietzsche and in Freud the critique of phallocentrism is not immediately evident, and the double displacement of woman seems all the clearer: "There is no essence of woman because woman averts and averts herself from herself. . . . For if woman *is* truth, *she* knows there is no truth, that truth has no place and that no one has the truth. She is woman insofar as she does not believe, herself, in truth, therefore in what she is, in what one believes she is, which therefore she is not" (*Ep* 50, 52).

Here Derrida interprets what I call double displacement into the sign of an abyss. But perhaps the point is that the deconstructive discourse of man (like the phallocentric one) can declare its own displacement (as the phallocentric its placing) by taking the woman as object or figure. When Derrida suggests that Western discourse is caught within the metaphysical or phallogocentric limit, his point is precisely that man can problematize but not fully disown his status as subject. I do, then, indeed find in deconstruction a "feminization" of the practice of philosophy, and I do not regard it as just another example of the masculine use of woman as instrument of self-assertion. I learn from Derrida's critique of phallocentrism—but I must then go somewhere else with it. A male philosopher can deconstruct the discourse of the power of the phallus as "his own mistake." For him, the desire for the "name of woman" comes with the questioning of the "metaphysical familiarity which so naturally relates the *we* of the philosopher to 'we-men,' to the *we* in the horizon of humanity."[13] This is an unusual and courageous enterprise, not shared by Derrida's male followers.[14]

Yet, "we-women" have never been the heroes of philosophy. When it takes the male philosopher hundreds of pages (not to be able) to answer the question "Who, me?" we cannot dismiss our double displacement by saying to ourselves: "In the discourse of affirmative deconstruction, 'we' are a 'female element,' which does not signify 'female person.' " Women armed with deconstruction must beware of becoming Athenas, uncontaminated by the womb, sprung in armor from Father's forehead, ruling against Clytemnestra by privileging marriage, the Law that appropriates the woman's body over the claims of that body as Law. To the question: "Where is there a spur so keen as to compel to murder of a mother?" the presumed answer is: "Marriage appointed by fate 'twixt man and woman is mightier than an oath and Justice is its guardian." The official view of reproduction is: "the mother of what is called her child is not its parent, but only the nurse of the newly implanted germ."[15] This role of Athena, "the professional woman," will come up again at the end of the next section.

Let us consider briefly the problem of double displacement in Derrida as he substitutes undecidable feminine figurations for the traditional masculine ones and rewrites the primal scene as the scene of writing.

My first sample is the graphic of the hymen as it appears in *La double séance*, Derrida's essay on Mallarmé's occasional piece "Mimique."[16]

The hymen is the figure for undecidability and the "general law of the textual effect" (*Dis* 235) for at least two reasons. First, "metaphorically" it is the ritual celebration of the breaking of the vaginal membrane, and "literally" that membrane remains intact even as it opens up into two lips; second, the walls of the passage that houses the hymen are both inside and outside the body. It describes "the more subtle and patient displacement which, with reference to a Platonic or Hegelian idealism, we here call 'Mallarméan' by convention" (*Dis* 235; I have arranged the word order to fit my sentence). The indefinitely displaced undecidability of the effect of the text (as hymen) is not the transcendent or totalizable ideal of the patronymic chain. Yet, is there not an agenda unwittingly concealed in formulating *virginity* as the property of the sexually undisclosed challenger of the phallus as master of the dialectics of desire? The hymen is of course at once both itself and not-itself, always operated by a calculated dissymmetry rather than a mere contradiction or reconciliation. Yet if the one term of the dissymmetry is virginity, the other term is marriage, legal certification for appropriation in the interest of the passage of property. We cannot avoid remarking that marriage in *La double séance* remains an unquestioned figure of fulfilled identification (*Dis* 237–38).

We must applaud Derrida's displacement of the old feminine metaphor of the truth as (of) unveiling: "The hymen is therefore not the truth of unveiling. There is not *aletheia* (truth as unveiling), only a blink of the hymen."[17] Yet desire here must be expressed as man's desire, if only because it is the only discourse handy. The language of a woman's desire does not enter this enclosure:

> the hymen as a protective screen (*écran*), a jewel case (*écrin;* all reminders of writing—*écriture*—and the written—*écrit*) of virginity, virginal wall, most subtle and invisible veil, which, in front of the hysteron, holds itself *between* the inside and the outside of the woman, *therefore between desire and accomplishment.* (*Dis* 241; my emphasis)

Even within this sympathetic scene, the familiar topoi appear. The operation of the hymen is the "outmanoeuvering (*déjouante*—literally 'unplaying') economy of a seduction" (*Dis* 255). We are reminded of Nietzsche as we notice that, in commenting upon the pantomime of a hilarious wife-murder (Pierrot kills Columbine by tickling the soles of her feet) that Mallarmé comments on in *Mimique*, Derrida writes as follows:

> The crime, the orgasm, is doubly mimed. . . . Its author in fact disappears because Pierrot is (plays) also Columbine. . . . The gestures represent nothing that had ever been or could ever become present: nothing before or after the mimodrama, and in the mimodrama, a crime-orgasm that was never committed. (*Dis* 228, 238–39)

The faked orgasm now takes center stage. The Pierrot of the pantomime "acts" as the woman "is" ("Pierrot is [plays] Columbine") by faking a faked orgasm which is also a faked crime.

Derrida's law of the textual operation—of reading, writing, philosophizing—makes it finally clear that, however denaturalized and nonempirical these sexual images might be, it is the phallus that learns the trick of coming close to faking the orgasm here, rather than the hymen coming into its own as the indefinitely displaced effect of the text. Thus the hymen is doubly displaced. Its "presence" is appropriately deconstructed, and its curious property appropriated to deliver the signature of the philosopher. Hymen or writing "gets ready to receive the seminal jet (*jet*; also throw) of a throw of dice" (*Dis* 317; the last phrase—*un coup de dés*—is of course a reference to Mallarmé's famous poem; but, following Derrida's well-known signature-games, the passage can also read, "the hymen gets ready to receive the seminal *J*. of a blow of a *D*"). In terms of the custodianship of meaning, the philosopher no longer wishes to engender sons but recognizes that, at the limit, the text's semes are scattered irretrievably abroad. But, by a double displacement of the vagina, dissemination remains on the ascendant and the hymen remains reactive. It is "dissemination which *affirms* the always already divided generation of meaning" (*Dis* 300). Textual operation is back to position one and fireworks on the lawn with a now "feminized" phallus: "Dissemination in the fold (*repli*—also withdrawal) of hymen" (*Dis* 303).

One of the many projects of *Glas* is to learn the name of the mother.[18] There is an ideological phallocentrism in Freud that works to control some of his most radical breakthroughs. Derrida has traced this phallo-centrism in Lacan, who has written in the name of the "truth of Freud."[19] Now in Lacan's gloss on the Oedipus complex, it is through the discovery of the "name of the father" that the son passes the Oedipal scene and is inserted into the symbolic order or the circuit of the signifier. Upon that circuit, the transcendental signifier remains the phallus. Is it possible to undo this phallocentric scenario by staging the efforts of a critic who seeks to discover the name of the *mother?*

Within the argument from double displacement, this might still be a version of Freud's account of the right object-choice: the son's perennial longing for the mother. Whether interpreted this way or not, it remains the undertaking of the righthand column of *Glas*, where Derrida writes on some writings of Genet. He needs an eccentric occasion to ask the oblique question of the name of the mother: Genet is an illegitimate homosexual son whose name is—if such an expression can be risked—a matronymic.

(This particular concern, the name or status of the mother, remains implicit in the lefthand column of *Glas* as well. Explicitly, Derrida learns to mourn for fathers: his natural father, Hegel, Nietzsche, Freud. Yet the subject matter is the matter of the family, the place of mother, sister, wife in the Holy Family, in Greek tragedy, in the early writings of Hegel and Marx, in the story of Hegel's own life. Derrida comments repeatedly on the undisclosed homoeroticism of the official discourse of these phallogocentric philosophers—a discourse supported by the relegation of public homosexuals like Jean Genet to criminality.)

I shall not attempt an exhaustive description of this search. Let us consider two sentences toward the end of the Genet column: "I began to be jealous of his mother who could change phallus to infinity without details dividing herself. Hypothesis begodden father in (it)self (*en soi*; without gender differentiation in French) not being there" (GE 261b).

The best way to deal with these lines would be to gloss them as mechanically as possible. Derrida has not been able to articulate the name of Genet's mother. The most he has been able to do is a great L made by the arrangement of the type—"elle" being French for "she"—cradling or being penetrated by a wedge of emptiness.[20] The lines I quote follow almost immediately.

Derrida is jealous because she can *displace* herself ad infinitum. She has stolen a march on the false pride of the phallocentric Idea—which can merely repeat itself self-identically to infinity. She has taken the phallus out of the circuit of castration, dismemberment, cutting up (*détailler*). With her it is not a question of having or not having the phallus. She can change it, as if she had a collection of dildos or transvestite underwear. The Genet column of *Glas* has considered a phantasmagoria of such items, as evoked by Genet in his own texts.

Such a mother—the outcast male homosexual's vision of mother—is different from the phallic mother of fetishism. If Derrida is rewriting the text of Freud here by suggesting that the male homosexual is *not* caught in the fear of castration by regarding the phallus itself as a representation of what is not there—a theme of self-castration carefully developed in *Glas*—he must also suggest that the "feminization" of philosophizing for the male deconstructor might find its most adequate legend in male homosexuality defined as criminality, and that it cannot speak for the woman.

Such a recognition of the limits of deconstruction is in the admission that the shape of *Glas*, standing in here for the deconstructive project, might be a fetish, an object that the subject regards with superstitious awe. The book is divided into two columns—Hegel on the left, Genet on the right, and a slit in between. Derrida relates these two pillars with the fleece in the middle to Freud's reference "to the circumstance that the inquisitive boy sought out (*gespäht*) the woman's genitals from below, from her legs up" (F 11:155; GW 14:314). It is the classic case of fetishism, a uniquely shaped object (his bicolumnar book) that will allow the subject both to be and not to be a man—to have the phallus and yet accede to dissemination.

And indeed it is in terms of the concept-metaphor of fetishism that Derrida gives us a capsule history of the fate of dialectics. I can do no more here than mark a few moments of that "history." Hegel remarks on the fetishism of the African savage, who must eat the fetishized ancestor ceremonially. (*Glas* also is an act of mourning for fathers.) Hegel accuses Kant of a certain fetishism, since Kant sees the Divine Father merely as a jealous God, and must thus formulate a Categorical Imperative. (Derrida supplements the accusation by pointing out that, in French at least, the Categorical Imperative has the same initials as the fetishistic notion—saving the mother jealously from the father's phallus—of the Immaculate Conception: IC.)

The negation of the negation (*Aufhebung,* or sublation), at once denying a thing and preserving it on a higher level, Hegel's chief contribution to the morphology of the self-determination of the concept, was itself, Feuerbach suggested, the absolutely positive move. It may be called fetishistic because it allowed Hegel to keep both presence and its representation: "Marx then sets out the critical movement of Feuerbach. . . . The speculative unity; the secular complicity of philosophy and religion—the former being the truth and the essence of the latter, the latter the representation of the former . . . is the process of sublation [*la relève*]" (G 226a; GE 201a). Marx also relates *Aufhebung* to supporting the Christian "desire for maternity *and* for virginity" (G 228a; GE 203a).[21] The distance between deconstruction's project of displacement and the dialectic's project of sublation may be charted in terms of the son's longing for the mother. "And what if the *Aufhebung* were a Christian mother" (G 225a; GE 201a)—at once marked and unmarked by the phallus—deconstruction looks for a mother who can change her phallus indefinitely and has an outcast homosexual son. Crudely put, a quarrel of sons is not the model for feminist practice.[22]

The project of philosophy, Derrida continues, as each philosopher presents a more correct picture of the way things are, is not merely to locate the fetish in the text of the precursor, but also to de-fetishize philosophy. "If there were no thing"—the thing itself par excellence—(in this case the truth of philosophy), "the concept of fetish would lose its invariant kernel." For the fetish "is a substitute—for the thing itself"

(G 234a; GE 209a; I have modified the order of the sentences to make a summary). Rather than negating the thing itself—that would be merely another way of positing it—deconstruction gives it the undecidability of the fetish. The thing itself becomes its own substitute. Like the faked orgasm, the thing itself is its own fake. Yet the fetish, to qualify as fetish, must carry within itself a trace of the thing itself that it replaces. Deconstruction cannot be pure undecidability. It "constitutes an *economy* of the undecidable. . . . It is not dialectical but plays with the dialectic" (G 235a; GE 210a).

Thus *Glas* must end with an erection of the thing, not merely the oscillation of the phallus as fetish. The distance from the dialectic is measured simply by the fact that "the thing is oblique. It (*elle*) already makes an angle with the ground" (G 292b). Its relationship with the ground (of things) has the obliqueness of an originary fetish. The graphic of that angle can be that large *L* on page 290b. In French, the "it" of the second sentence above is "elle." Cradled in that angle between the fetish and the thing itself is the word *déjà* (already), separated out of the sentence by two commas. *Glas* makes clear that *déjà* is also a bilingual yes (*ja*) to the *D* (de)—the initial letter of Derrida's own patronymic—in reverse. It is the assent to the self that one must have already given (an assent at best reversed, never fully displaced). If the project of *La double séance* finally puts the phallus in the hymen, *Glas* is obliged to put the son with the patronymic in the arms of the phallic mother.

"Hypothesis begodden father in (it)self not being there" (*Hypothèse dieuvenue père en soi de n'être pas là*). This is the mother of whom, simply reversing Kant's position vis-à-vis the jealous father, Derrida begins to become jealous. As the possessor of the fetish, she carries a substitute of the thing itself—that father in himself; yet as the deconstructed fetish she also carries the trace of the thing itself; through not being there she *is*—one presumes, since the verb of being is strategically suppressed in the sentence—the father in himself. Here again that curious displacement—her separation from Athena or Mary. She allows the philosopher to question the concept of being by having no verb of being; she cannot be named. Yet she remains the miraculous hypothesis—"the supposition, i.e., a fact *placed under* a number of facts as their common support and explanation; though in the majority of instances these hypotheses or suppositions better deserve the name of *hypopoiesis* or suffictions."[23]

One must, then, remember *La double séance* and *Glas* as one reads *Eperons*. In the last the project to feminize philosophizing can be understood in the following way. If a man is obliged to perform by means of a single or singular style (stylus, phallus), he can at least attempt a plural style, always try to fake his orgasms, never speak for himself, be forever on the move away from a place that might be locatable as his own. Like the two other pieces, *Eperons* is an exercise in the plural style, a displaced reversal of what Nietzsche would call the "grand style." Ever complicit with his subject matter, Derrida tries this plural style to comment on the plurality of Nietzsche's style.

As in the case of *Glas*, my method here will be a mechanical decoding. As one attends to the stylistic orchestration in this decoding spirit, one notices among all the subtleties and indirections and ore-packed rifts a set of four triads:

1. *Le voile/tombe*
   L'érection tombe
   La signature/tombe
   (*Ep* 59, 105, 127)

2. He was, he dreaded such a castrated woman
   He was, he dreaded such a castrating woman
   He was, he loved such an affirming woman
   (*Ep* 100)

3. Perhaps it was cut out (*prelevée*) somewhere
   Perhaps it was heard here or there
   Perhaps it was the sense of a sentence to be written here or there
   (*Ep* 97)

4. the three final steps of the essay: *un pas encore*
   (yet another step; or, one not yet), P.S., and P.S. II
   (*Ep* 135, 138, 140)

Each of these triads stages a self-dislocation and thus connotes hetero-geneity. I have repeatedly pointed out that a structural (not natural or biological) description of heterogeneity (not being homogeneously "in place") in intention and signifying convention might be woman: "The heterogeneity of the text manifests it well. Nietzsche did not give himself the illusion, analyzed it on the contrary, of knowing anything of these effects, called woman, truth, castration, or of the *ontological* (being-related) effects of presence or absence" (*Ep* 94).

The second triad is a summary of what Derrida thinks "The History of an Error" (a chapter in Nietzsche's *The Twilight of the Idols*) reflects. The sentences describe three psychoanalytic "positions," three subject (man)—object (woman) relations. As Derrida explains (*Ep* 96), the first two sentences are reversals, the third a displacement. The displaced "position" sees the woman as "affirming." Deconstruction "affirms" (*Ep* 36). Deconstruction is or affirms the other (woman) after its simple alterity (otherness) has been reversed and displaced.

"How the 'True World' Finally Became a Fable: History of An Error" is Nietzsche's version of what I have called the feminization of philosophizing. In order to prove that the remark "she becomes female" within this chapter can be unpacked into the triad above, Derrida claims that Nietzsche's bitter thoughts are not about woman's essence, but about a historical change in it owing to the ambiguous status given it by Christianity, the ideology of the castrated. "Thus the truth has not always been woman nor is the woman always truth. They both have a history; together they both form a history" (*Ep* 86).

If one attended to the pronominal genders in the chapter, a different story is read. That so meticulous a reader as Derrida does not attend to them is in itself curious. This other story would be the story of the male philosopher's relationship to and birth from woman as such, the story of sexual difference retold.

Since the world—*die Welt*—is feminine in German, the first words to describe the philosopher's relationship to the true world—*die wahre Welt*—describe the child in the womb or at the breast (as if part of the mother's undifferentiated body): "he lives in her, *he is she* (*Er lebt in ihr, er ist sie*)." Next, this feminine world has become the *idea* (of the true world), and as such, progressing, "she becomes female (*Sie wird Weib*)." This is the first naming of the female as such. Before this she is merely *sie*, the pronominal referent to the true world. Here, at the moment of sexual differentiation, she is desexualized, she becomes neuter: *Weib* in German is not only contemptuous but neuter in gender. The rest of the chapter is the story of how to abolish "the true world" (Derrida reads the quotation marks as the mark of the woman). In the final paragraph this displaced and neutered woman is indeed abolished—and through a double displacement: both the true world and the apparent one (both the woman and her representation) are abolished. "Highpoint of mankind; INCIPIT ZARATHUSTRA" (*PN* 486; *CM* 75).

As usual in Nietzsche's plural style it is hard to decide if he is endorsing "truth" or "error," or indeed what perspective will allow us to make that distinction. The title of the chapter is subject to that well-recognized Nietzschean reversibility. "The history of an error" could be "the error of a history" just as "Zur Genealogie der Moral" could be "Zur Moral der Genealogie," or expressions like "die Bildung der Begriffe" (the growth of a concept) or "Das Erkennen erfanden" (invented understanding) could in context be read "der Begriff des Bildes" (the concept of the image) or "die Erfindung erkannten" (understood invention).[24] This is the gesture of putting the author's "place" in question.

If Hegel in the *Aufhebung* wishes to conserve both presence (philosophy) and representation (religion),[25] and if, at the end of *Glas*, Derrida wishes to keep a representation (fetish) that substitutes for a presence that is bent, Nietzsche's problematic desire here seems to be to abolish both the woman (the true world) and her representation (the differentiated female—"the true world"). That curious model of philosophizing he cannot practice but leaves rather for a Zarathustra who is merely announced. I have suggested that, paradoxically, when Derrida follows Nietzsche's lead, it results not in an abolishment but in a distanced embracing, of a doubly displaced woman.

If the pronominal charge of the chapter as a whole and especially of *Sie wird Weib* is noted, Zarathustra is seen to become possible through the desexualization of woman as truth or idea. Zarathustra does not speak in this chapter; the author's "place" is once again in question, for he may be no more than a foreshadower. Nietzsche displaces himself even as he doubly displaces the woman. It is this last move that Derrida presumably describes as "he was, he loved this woman."

I have shown and applauded how Derrida seeks to affirm through the (doubly displaced) figure of the woman. I should like, with some trepidation, to suggest that to keep that deconstructive affirmation intact, Derrida must ignore that the third psychoanalytic position in Nietzsche emerges as a violent negation. Whereas in the case of the other three triads in *Eperons* Derrida stages the heterogeneity and displacement in his text, this triad is given as a continuous one. The negation that would mark the heterogeneity between the first two positions and the third is not disclosed. Negation is a mark of the ego's desire to deny heterogeneity or discontinuity. As Freud writes:

> A negative judgment (*Verurteilung*) is the intellectual substitute for repression; the "no" is the hallmark of repression, a certificate of origin—like, let us say, "Made in Germany." With the help of (mediated by: *vermittelt*) the symbol of negation, thinking frees

> itself from the restrictions of repression and enriches itself with
> material that is indispensable for its proper functioning (*Leis-*
> *tung*). (F 19:236; GW 14:12–13)

If the peculiar and uncharacteristic nature of Derrida's protestation of
continuity is not noticed, the identification and love for the affirming
woman that Derrida finds in Nietzsche can be given a brutal reading.
One can then ask: is the displacement-affirmation of deconstruction
merely that the man-woman reversal, the scene of "castration," need no
longer be seen as a battleground? That "dread" can be turned into "love"
by realizing that the clitoridectomized/hysterectomized neuter woman
might just as well be an animal? (The woman whose sexual pleasure is
originarily self-(re)presentative in a way *different* from man's might just
as well not have a clitoris: the hymen that remains forever (in)violate,
upon which the seed is forever spilled afield in dissemination, has no use
for the hysteron.) Is this the scene of violence that is called love in the
transformation contained within our only perfect triad? If women have
always been used as the instrument of male self-deconstruction, is this
philosophy's newest twist?

One can then bring forward Derrida's explanation of the third position:

> Woman is recognized, beyond that double negation [the negation
> of negation in *Aufhebung*], affirmed as affirmative, dissimulative,
> artistic, dionysiac power. She is not affirmed by man, but affirms
> herself [or is affirmed—*s'affirme*—herself], *in herself and within*
> *man* [*en elle-même et dans l'homme*]. (*Ep* 97; my emphasis).

Further:

> And in truth, those women feminists so derided by Nietzsche,
> they are men. Feminism is nothing but the operation of a
> woman who wishes to resemble a man, the dogmatic philosopher,
> claiming truth, science, objectivity, that is to say all the virile
> illusions, and the castration-effect that attaches to them. Femi-
> nism wishes castration—also of the woman. Loses the style.
> (*Ep* 64)[26]

The scene changes if one notices Derrida's rider to the consequence
of the "indeterminability of castration" if woman is identified with "the

question of style" and opposed to "the strict equivalence between the affirmation and the negation of castration": "To be developed later, perhaps, in terms of the argument of the *athletic support-belt* [*gaine*—an extremely important theme in *Glas*] in Freud's text on fetishism."[27] Perhaps Derrida speaks from the irretrievably compromised position of a man with a self-diagnosed fetish (can there be such a thing?) that substitutes nothing but the trace of a truth (if there could be such a thing). Under the guise of a description of the problematics of being a feminist woman, he might be describing the problematics of being a "woman's man." Then we might remark that, in the lines immediately preceding our passage, where man and woman are within quotation marks, if the woman is predictably described as elusive, the man is given the full blast of the critique of phallocentrism. It is at least within that frame that feminists are derided as women who wish to resemble men. It is at least possible to read this as a lament that in the place of phallocentrism a mere hysterocentrism should be erected:

> The "woman" takes so little interest in truth, she believes in it so little that the truth of her proper subject no longer even concerns her. It is the "man" who believes that his discourse on woman or truth *concerns*—such is the topographical problem that I sketched, which also slipped away, as usual, earlier, relating to castration's undecidable contours—the woman. (*Ep* 62)

The voice is at least not given as disinterested or Olympian. As much as at the end of *Glas*, this is a son caught in the desire for the mother, a man for the woman:

> The questions of art, of style, of truth do not let themselves be dissociated from the question of the woman. But the simple formation of this common problematic suspends the question "what is woman?" One can no longer seek her, no more than one could search for woman's femininity or feminine sexuality. At least one cannot find them according to a known mode of concept or knowledge, even if one cannot escape looking for them. (*Ep* 70)

This might indeed be a bold description of the feminist's problem of discourse after the critique of the old ways of knowing. To avoid the problem is to "make a mistake." Yet, with respect, we cannot share in the mysterious pathos of the longing: for a reason as simple as that the question of woman in general, asked this way, is *their* question, not *ours.*

Perhaps because we have a "different body" the fetish as woman with changeable phallus is *on her way to* becoming a transcendental signifier in these texts. As the radically other she does not *really exist,* yet her name remains one of the important names for displacement, the special mark of deconstruction. The difference in the woman's body is also that it exists too much, as the place of evidence, of the law as writing. I am not referring to the law in general, the Logos as origin, Speech as putative identity of voice and consciousness, "all the names of the foundation, of the principle, or of the center (that) have always desig-nated the invariant of a presence (*eidos, archē, telos, energeia, ousia* [essence, existence, substance, subject] *aletheia,* transcendentality, con-sciousness, God, man, and so forth."[28] I am speaking in the narrow sense, of the law as the code of legitimacy and inheritance.

One version of this "simple" law is written on the woman's body as an historical instrument of reproduction. A woman has no need to "prove" maternity. The institution of phallocentric law is congruent with the need to prove paternity and authority, to secure property by transforming the child into an alienated object named and possessed by the father, and to secure property by transforming the woman into a mediating instrument of the production and passage of property.[29] In this narrow but "effective" and "real" sense, in the body of the woman as mother, the opposition between displacement and logocentrism might itself be deconstructed. Not merely as the undecidable crease of the hymen or envied place of the fetish, but also as the repressed place of production can the woman stand as a limit to deconstruction.

My attitude toward deconstruction can now be summarized: first, decon-struction is illuminating as a critique of phallocentrism; second, it is convincing as an argument against the founding of a hysterocentric to counter a phallocentric discourse; third, as a "feminist" practice itself, it is caught on the other side of sexual difference.[30] At whatever remove of "différance" (difference/deferment from/of any decidable statement of the concept of an identity or difference)[31] *sexual difference is thought,* the sexual *differential* between "man" and "woman" remains irreducible. It is within the frame of these remarks that I hope the following parable will be read.

Within this frame, let us imagine a woman who is a (straight) deconstructivist of (traditional male) discourse. Let us assume that her position vis-à-vis the material she interprets is "the same" as that of the male deconstructivist. Thinking of the irreducible sexual differential, she might say: in order to have used the discourse of the phallus as a sign of my power, I was obliged to displace myself from what has been defined as my originary displacement by that very discourse and thus (re)-present for myself a place. Should my gesture of deconstructive practice be a third-degree displacement so that, on the other side of the sexual differential, I can "be myself"? Yet, the project of the critique of phallocentrism-logocentrism is an exposure of the ideology of self-possession—"being myself"—in order to grasp the idea—"the thing itself." Should I not have an attitude parallel to the deconstructive philosopher's attitude to the discourse of the phallus toward any discourse of the womb that might get developed thanks to the sexual differential? What about the further problem of creating "purposively" a discourse of the woman to match an official discourse of the man whose strength is that it is often arbitrary and unmotivated? Deconstruction puts into question the "purposive" activities of a sovereign subject.

A certain historical "differential" now begins to suggest itself. Even if all historical taxonomies are open to question, a minimal historical network must be assumed for interpretation, a network that suggests that the phallocentric discourse is the object of deconstruction because of its coextensivity with the history of Western metaphysics, a history insepa-rable from political economy and from the property of man as holder of property. *Whatever their historical determination or conceptual allegiance, the male users of the phallocentric discourse all trace the itinerary of the suppression of the trace.* The differential political implications of putting oneself in the position of accomplice-critic with respect to an at best clandestinely determined hysterocentric subtext that is only today becoming "authoritative" in bourgeois feminism, seems to ask for a different program. The collective project of our feminist critic must always be to rewrite the *social* text so that the historical and sexual differentials are operated together. Part of it is to notice that the argument based on the "power" of the faked orgasm, of being-fetish, and hymen, is, all deconstructive cautions taken, "determined" by that very political and social history that is inseparably coextensive with phallocentric discourse and, in her case, either unrecorded in accessible ways, or recorded in terms of man.[32] Since she has, indeed, learned the lesson of deconstruction, this rewriting of the social text of motherhood cannot be an establishment of new meanings. It can only be to work away at concept-metaphors that deliberately establish and cast wide a different system of "meanings."

If she confines herself to asking the question of woman—What is woman?—she might merely be attempting to provide an answer to the honorable male question: What does woman want? She herself still remains the *object* of the question. To reverse the situation would be to ask the question of woman as a subject: What am I? That would bring back all the absolutely convincing deconstructive critiques of the sovereign subject.

The gesture that the "historical moment" requires might be to ask the "question of man" in that special way: What is man that the itinerary of his desire creates such a text? Not, in other words, simply, What is man? All the texts in the world are at our disposal, and the question cannot flounder into the delusions of a pure "What am I?" Yet it restores to us the position of the questioning *subject* by virtue of the question-effect, a position that the sexual differential has never allowed woman à propos of men in a licit way. This gesture must continue to supplement the collective and substantive work of "restoring" woman's history and literature.[33] Otherwise the question "what is man's desire?" asked by women from the peculiar *sub rosa* position of the doubly displaced subject will continue to preserve masculinity's business as usual and produce answers that will describe themselves, with cruel if unselfconscious irony, as "total womanhood."

As a literary critic she might fabricate strategic "misreadings," rather than perpetrating variations on "received" or "receivable" readings, especially upon a woman's text. She might, by the superimposition of a suitable allegory, draw a reading out of the text that relates it to the historicosocial differential of the body. This move should, of course, be made scrupulously explicit. Since deconstruction successfully puts the ideology of "correct readings" into question, our friend is content with this thought.[34] Even more content because, since she has never been considered a custodian of truth anyway (only its mysterious figure), this move seems to possess the virtue of turning that millennial accusation into a place of strength. To undo the *double* displacement, as it were, and to operate from displacement as such, if there can be such a thing. To produce useful and scrupulous fake readings in the place of the passively active fake orgasm.

In the recently published "Law of Genre," Derrida/Blanchot (the identities are, as usual, blurred) steps into the Mother/Daughter relationship.[35] The daughter is the Law (*la loi*), in French always in the feminine. Instead of the Law being of the Father, the irreducible madness of the Law-as-daughter is seductive ("one time she had me touch her knee," writes Blanchot) of the male mother, who by this means accedes to a "neuter" voice that is "doubly affirmative," "guarding the opportunity of being woman (*garder la chance d'être femme*) or changing sex" ("LG" 194, 196, 222, 223).

The Law's proffered knee (*genou*) provides the first person with a bisexual "I/we" (*je/nous*)—the rewriting of the "we-men of the total horizon of humanity" that was sought in 1969 in "Ends of Man." All the verbs of seeing and saying at the end of Derrida's essay are given to an "I" within quotation marks. The crucial verb of being lets the *je/nous* enter the story "where I/we are (*ou je/nous somme*)." What this "I," on its knees (*à genoux*), but also as I/we (*je/nous*), sees is indeed the Law, in sum. But, playing with *somme* ("sum" as well as "are" in the first person plural), the previous sentence would allow the *je/nous* to be in the place of the Law: *la loi en somme*. If the situation of the Law is written into the situation of father-daughter incest, Athena the Law (giving) daughter can be produced, and the phallic mother circumvented; especially if, changing sex, I myself become a mother:

> he wishes to seduce the law to whom he gives birth [there is a hint of incest in this] and . . . he makes the law afraid. . . . The law's female element [which does not signify a female person] has thus always appealed to: me, I, he, we. ("LG" 225, 198, 197)

The female element does not signify female person. There is no *elle* among the *je, nous,* and *ils* who accede to voice and being at her expense in the last paragraph.

The father-daughter fantasy is not to be found in the companion piece "Living On/*Border Lines*."[36] There the narrator operates the hymen "or the alliance *in the language of the other*" ("LO" 77) by "speak(ing) his *mother tongue* as the language of the other" ("LO" 153).

Mixing of the sexes is one of the chief concerns of "The Law of Genre." Before actually beginning his commentary on Blanchot's *La folie du jour*, Derrida reminds us that "in French, the semantic scale of *genre* is much larger and more expansive than in English, and thus always includes within it the gender" ("LG" 221; not in the French version). On the next page we are shown how, by invoking "beautiful creatures" who are "almost always" (but not invariably)—"there is no natural or symbolic law, universal law, or law of a genre/gender here"—women, the man accedes to a bizarre quasi-performative:

> In this risky (*aléatoire*) claim that links affirmation almost always to women, beautiful ones, it is then more than probable that, as long as I say yes, yes, I am a woman and beautiful. Grammatical sex (anatomical as well, in any case, sex submitted to the law of objectivity), the masculine genre (gender) is thus affected by the affirmation through a risky drift that could always make it other. ("LG" 223, 195–96)

Let us remind ourselves that when this sex-change seems to go the other way, from woman to man, the fetishized phallic mother causes a good deal of anguish, as at the end of *Glas*. We might also say, following Derrida in "Limited Inc," that there is "something like a relationship" between such a point of view about becoming a woman at the stroke of a word and the men who legislate and adjudicate against abortion because they believe they can speak for the woman and her body.[37]

The name of the double displacement that allows the double affirmation is now not merely hymen but double invagination, a double turning-inside-out. This creates a space that is larger than the whole of which it is a part, and allows "participation without belonging" (to the female sex?). As in the customary illustrations of the set theory, Venn diagrams, where the men- and the women-sets intersect, there is the left-handed-people set, which is larger than either the men-set or the women-set.

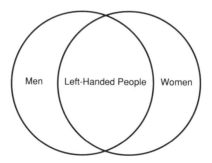

Only here we have fake-frame accounts and fake-interior accounts intersecting (invaginating) to form a "left-handed-people" set where the account-effect can both be and not be a legally answerable account by virtue (if that is the word) of the seductive daughter-law.

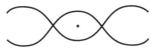

("LG" 218, 191)

However stubbornly Derrida might insist that female personhood must be reduced out of the female element or the female silhouette, that the vagina has only a figural connection with invagination, the strength of his own methodology will not allow such a totalizing exclusion and binary opposition to stand. "The opposition of fact and principle . . . in all its metaphysical, ontological, and transcendental forms, has always functioned within the system of what *is*."[38] It is not the question of "a feminist leader" finding it "hard . . . to bear that a 'man' should have dared (such a) 'mad hypothesis' " ("LO" 167). It is rather that other question: What is man that he should, even as he argues deconstruction of the substance-form opposition, need so vehement a negation of woman?

The mathematico-sexual metaphorics of invagination seem even to supersede the self-diagnosed "fetishism" of *Glas*. The telegraphic language allows for great indeterminacy in syntactic connections:

> no piece, no metonymy, no integral corpus. *And thus no fetishism.* Everything said here about double invagination can be brought to bear—a labor of translation—on what is worked out in *Glas*, for example, on the subject of fetishism as the argument of the *gaine* [to be translated "vagina"?]. ("LO" 137–38; my emphasis)

To want to speak for the phallus would, of course, be hopelessly mystified. Fetishism can apparently be circumvented by the morphology of set theory. Perhaps the indefinitely trans-sexual I/we can still not speak for the clitoris as the mark of the sexed subject.

Is it too fanciful to claim that, at the end of "Living On," when Derrida begins the discussion of the "*arrêt* between the two deaths," one can discern a vague legend of the doubly vaginated clitoris ("LO" 163)? "Of course, nothing [or very little] on the manifestly readable surface of the *récits* makes it possible to sustain such a mad hypothesis" ("LO" 170).[39] Yet, it is not the first time Derrida has coupled writing and masturbation

> *at the very place* where the *relationship* of the "book" *to itself*, in its fragile binding, is formed, the *relationship* of the "I" *to himself*, his alliance with himself, his ring, his anniversary, the *alliance* that joins him to himself. This *very* place, the very *same* place, being the place, the locus, of interruption, is also the place where double invagination gathers together what it interrupts in the strange *sameness* of this place ("LO" 166)

But perhaps this is circular reasoning. I might see this vague clitoral legend because the space between these two women, two vaginations, or two folds, when the man is not there, has a "terrifying *figura*, figure, face . . . inter-dicted in the quasi-middle of it, over above beyond its double inner border" ("LO" 166), and is an "uncrossable glass partition" ("LO" 169). Perhaps I am thinking back from passages such as the following and remarking upon the calculable impact of a "different body":

> But the woman touches herself by and in herself without the necessity of a mediation, and before all possible decisions between (*départage entre*) activity and passivity. A woman "touches herself" all the time, without anyone being able to forbid her to do so, in fact, for her sex is composed of two lips which embrace continually. Thus, in herself she is already two—but not divisible into ones (un[e]s)—who affect each other.
>
> The uncertainty (*suspens*) of this auto-eroticism is effected (*s'opère*) in a violent break-in: the brutal spreading apart of this two lips by a violating penis.[40]

I haven't a different conclusion to offer. Although, I must repeat, it is a bold and helpful thing to restore the female element when it is buried in gender conventions (I remain surprised that Derrida does not do it in *Eperons*), the displacement of the originarily faked orgasm into the mark of the double affirmation in the interest of man's accession to provisional androgyny cannot lead us very far. It is excellent to posit this female element as the irreducible madness of truth-in-law, but we are daily reminded that a little more must be undertaken to budge the law's oppressive sanity. It is not really a question of the "institution" being able to "bear" our more "apparently revolutionary ideological sorts of 'content' " ("LO" 95) because we do not threaten its institutionality.[41] It is rather an awareness that even the strongest personal goodwill on Derrida's part cannot turn him quite free of the massive enclosure of the male appropriation of woman's voice, with a variety of excuses: this one being, it is not *really* woman.

If my present conviction is that to sublate the natural or physiological evidence of motherhood into a prospective historical or psychological continuity is the idealist subtext of the patriarchal project, what then do I propose? I have discussed this question at length in "French Feminism in an International Frame."[42] Here suffice it to indicate the line of my argument somewhat cryptically:

> The clitoris escapes reproductive framing. In legally defining woman as object of exchange, passage, or possession in terms of reproduction, it is not only the womb that is literally "appropriated"; it is the clitoris as the signifier of the sexed subject that is effaced. All historical and theoretical investigation into the definition of woman as legal *object*—in or out of marriage, or as politico-economic passageway for property and legitimacy— would fall within the investigation of the varieties of the effacement of the clitoris.

The social text of motherhood is inscribed within this inquiry. For if an "at least symbolic clitoridectomy has always been the 'normal' accession to womanhood and the unackowledged name of motherhood, why has it been necessary to plot out the entire geography of female sexuality in terms of the imagined possibility of the dismemberment of the phallus?"[43]

And when we ask, What is man that the itinerary of his desire creates such a text? it will help us to remember that the text (of male discourse) gains its coherence by coupling woman with man in a loaded equation and cutting the excess of the clitoris out.

I began this essay with an invocation of great passages. I shall end by going back to the classics as well, and summarize my suggestions as an undoing of the *Eumenides*. I have already written of the immaculate Athena finding against Clytemnestra. Now I speak of another part of her judgment: her defeminating of the Furies, pursuing Orestes the matricide, and bidding them be "sweet-voiced" (Eumenides) by the stroke of a word. If we take the discourse of the "patriarchy" as a straw monster, and pursue it mightily, our role as Furies will lead to little more than self-congratulation and euphoria. We must use and attend to "the patriarchy's" own self-critique even as we recognize that it is irreducibly determined to disable us. It was after all a man who pointed out that the real charge in Hegel's picture of the subject appropriating the object—sweetly metaphorized by Adam and Eve—was a deep hostility:

> The appropriation (*die Aneignung*) of estranged objective being on the sublation (*die Aufhebung*) of objectivity in the determination (*Bestimmung*) of *estrangement*—which must proceed from indifferent alienness (*Fremdheit*) to real hostile estrangement—has for Hegel at the same time or even principally the significance of the sublation (*aufzuheben*) of *objectivity*, since it is not the *determinate* (*bestimmte*) character of the object but its *objective* character which constitutes the offense and the estrangement for self-consciousness. The object is therefore negative, self-sublating (*sich selbst Aufhebendes*), a nullity.[44]

Although Derrida and deconstruction, because of their overt critique of phallocentrism, rather than Marx and materialism, have been my example, the entire business of my essay might still be summed up (1) in the suggestion that a feminist reader would see in Marx's correction of Hegel a gesture useful for feminism, and (2) in the definition of such a reader, such uses.

Notes

    1. Georg Willhelm Friedrich Hegel, *Sämtliche Werke* (Leipzig: F. Meiner, 1920–55), 7:47; Hegel, *Philosophy of Right*, trans. T. M. Knox (Oxford: Clarendon Press, 1942), 226. Throughout the essay I have modified all quotations from texts in translation when necessary.
    2. I do not use the word "patriarchy"—the rule of the father—because it is susceptible to biologistic, naturalistic, and/or positivist-historical interpretations, and most often provides us with no more (and no less) than a place of accusation. I am more interested in the workings of a certain "discourse"—language in an operative and abyssal heterogeneity. I should add

that the absence of Marxist issues in this paper signifies nothing that cannot be explained by the following conviction: as women claim legitimation as agents in a society, a congruent movement to redistribute the forces of production and reproduction in that society must also be undertaken. Otherwise we are reduced to the prevailing philosophy of liberal feminism: "a moralistically humanitarian and egalitarian philosophy of social improvement through the re-education of psychological attitudes" (Charnie Guettel, *Marxism and Feminism* [Toronto: Women's Press, 1974], 3). As a deconstructivist, my topic in the present essay is: Can deconstruction help? That should not imply that I am blind to the larger issues outlined here.

3. For literary critics, the most recent articulation of this "official philosophy" is in the concept of the hermeneutic circle. Digests can be found in Sarah N. Lawall, *Critics of Consciousness: The Existential Structures of Literature* (Cambridge: Harvard University Press, 1968); and Robert R. Magliola, *Phenomenology and Literature: An Introduction* (West Lafayette: Purdue University Press, 1977).

4. See Jacques Derrida, "Speculations on 'Freud,' " in *La Carte postale* (Paris: Aubier-Flammarion, 1980), 237–437; translated as "To Speculate—On 'Freud,' " in *The Post Card: From Socrates to Freud and Beyond,* trans. Alan Bass (Chicago: University of Chicago Press, 1987), 257–409.

5. Spivak, "Love Me, Love My Ombre, Elle," *Diacritics* 14 (Winter 1984): 19–36.

6. Friedrich Wilhelm Nietzsche, *Werke: Kritische Gesamtausgabe*, ed. Georgio Colli and Mazzino Montinari (Berlin: de Gruyter, 1970), 2:291, hereafter cited in the text as CM; Nietzsche, *The Gay Science,* trans. Walter J. Kaufmann (New York: Vintage, 1974), 317. Translations are taken from *The Portable Nietzsche,* trans. Walter J. Kaufmann (New York: Viking, 1954) when possible and cited in the text as PN.

7. I do not believe Nietzsche's passage is necessarily read this way by everyone.

8. Jacques Derrida, *Éperons: Les Styles de Nietzsche; Spurs: Nietzsche's Styles,* trans. Barbara Harlow (Chicago: University of Chicago Press, 1979), 56, hereafter cited in the text as Ep. This is a bilingual edition of *Éperons;* I have used my own translations.

9. For a discussion of "citationality," see Jacques Derrida, "Limited Inc," trans. Samuel Weber, *Glyph* 2 (1977): 102–254. For a discussion of citationality in Derrida, see Spivak, "Revolutions That As Yet Have No Model: Derrida's *Limited Inc*," *Diacritics* 10 (Winter 1980): 29–49.

10. Sigmund Freud, *Standard Edition of the Complete Psychological Works,* trans. James Strachey, vol. 22 (London: Hogarth, 1964), hereafter cited in the text as F; *Gesammelte Werke,* vol. 15 (Frankfurt am Main: S. Fischer, 1940), hereafter cited in the text as GW. Citations indicate volume and page number.

11. For definitions of psychoanalytic terms, consult Jean Laplanche and J.-B. Pontalis, *Le Vocabulaire de la psychanalyse* (Paris: Presses Universitaires de France, 1967); *The Language of Psycho-Analysis,* trans. Donald Nicholson-Smith (New York: Norton, 1973). For a cautionary viewpoint against such a sourcebook, see Derrida, "Moi-la psychanalyse," introduction to Nicolas Abraham, *L'Écorce et le noyau* (Paris: Aubier-Montaigne, 1978); "Me-Psychoanalysis: An Introduction to the Translation of *The Shell and the Kernel* by Nicolas Abraham," trans. Richard Klein, *Diacritics* 9 (March 1979): 4–12.

12. Derrida produces such a reading, using *Beyond the Pleasure Principle* as his occasion, in "Speculer-sur 'Freud.' "

13. Jacques Derrida, "Les fins de l'homme," in *Marges de la philosophie* (Paris: Minuit, 1972), 137; "Ends of Man," trans. Alan Bass, in *Margins of Philosophy* (Chicago: University of Chicago Press, 1982), 116.

14. This essay was composed in 1979. A considerable literature on deconstruction and feminism has appeared since then. See Michael Ryan, *Marxism and Deconstruction: A Critical Articulation* (Baltimore: Johns Hopkins University Press, 1982), 194–212; and Jonathan

Culler, *On Deconstruction: Theory and Criticism after Structuralism* (Ithaca: Cornell University Press, 1982).

15. *Aeschylus*, trans. Herbert W. Smyth (London: Heinemann, 1936), 2:311, 293, 335.

16. Jacques Derrida, "La double séance," in *La Dissémination* (Paris: Seuil, 1972); *Dissemination*, trans. Barbara Johnson (Chicago: University of Chicago Press, 1981), hereafter cited in the text as *Dis*. Page references are to the French edition, and the translations are my own.

17. *Dis*, 293. The hymen is also substituted here for the imperious eye, whose blink measures the self-evident moment (in German, *Augenblick*; literally, the blink of an eye), in Husserlian philosophy as in the general Western tradition; see "Le Signe et le clin d'oeil," in *La Voix et le phénomène* (Paris: Presses Universitaires de France, 1967); "Signs and the Blink of an Eye," in *Speech and Phenomena*, trans. David Allison (Evanston: Northwestern University Press, 1973).

18. Jacques Derrida, *Glas* (Paris: Galilée, 1974); hereafter cited in the text as *G*. Translated as *Glas*, trans. John P. Leavey Jr. and Richard Rand; hereafter cited in text as *GE*.

19. Jacques Derrida, "Le Facteur de la vérité," *Poétique* 21 (1975): 96–147; in *The Post Card*, 410–96.

20. This particular reading of the capital L has been independently developed by Geoffrey Hartman in *Saving the Text* (Baltimore: Johns Hopkins University Press, 1981), 75.

21. In "Freud and the Scene of Writing," in *Writing and Difference*, and in *La double séance*, Derrida suggests that both in Freud and in Mallarmé the desire is to find a surface both marked and virgin. In *De la grammatologie* (Paris: Minuit, 1967); *Of Grammatology*, trans. Gayatri Spivak (Baltimore: Johns Hopkins University Press, 1976), he suggests that Rousseau wanted a category that was both transcendental (virgin) and supplementary (marked). An interpretation of Derrida's interpretation of the intellectual history of European men, in terms precisely of sons' longing for mothers, can perhaps be made.

22. I should make it clear that Derrida himself, like the Nietzsche of *Ecce Homo*, is, at least in theory, suspicious of discipleship. This particular "feminist" charge would probably seem a mark of excellence to him.

23. Samuel Taylor Coleridge, *Biographia Literaria*, ed. J. Shawcross (London: Oxford University Press, 1907), 1:72.

24. The last two examples are from "Über Wahrheit and Lüge im äußermoralischen Sinne," CM III (Berlin, 1973), 2:373, 369; "Of Truth and Falsity in an Extramoral Sense," in *Essays on Metaphor*, ed. Warren Shibles (Whitewater, Wis.: Language Press, 1972), 41.

25. This could be related to the idea that Marx saw in Hegel "A double inversion" (first of subject and predicate, and next of idealism and an unexamined empiricism), which Lucio Colletti develops in *Marxism and Hegel* (London: New Left Books, 1973).

26. "The style," of course, continues to allude to the phallus, whose status in Derrida is precarious precisely because castration cannot be taken as the all-or-nothing threat, and the question of the style (phallus) remains "the question of woman."

27. For elaboration upon Derrida's argument from the *gaine*, see my "*Glas*-piece: A Compte Rendu," *Diacritics* 7 (1977): 22–43.

28. Jacques Derrida, "La Structure, le signe et le jeu," in *Écriture et la différence*, 411; "Structure, Sign, and Play," in *The Structuralist Controversy: The Languages of Criticism and the Sciences of Man*, ed. Richard Macksey and Eugenio Donato (Baltimore: Johns Hopkins University Press, 1970), 249; in *Writing and Difference*, 279–80.

29. Although Engels's strict progressivist-dialectical account of the stages of marriage with matching sexual relations of production would be indefinitely complicated by a deconstructivist analysis, his pioneering statement is worth quoting here: "The first class antagonism which appears in history coincides with the development of the antagonism between man and woman in monogamian marriage, and the first class opposition with that of the female sex by

the male." In Friedrich Engels, *The Origin of the Family, Private Property, and the State* (New York: Pathfinder Press, 1972), 75. The distinction between patrilineage as passage of property and so-called matrilineage would also be open to a deconstructive reading. It should also be remembered that much of Engels's work in this book owes an unacknowledged debt to Flora Tristan.

30. From this point of view, it is worth noting that in Julia Kristeva's more mainstream or masculist celebration of motherhood, the child remains male; "Hérethique de l'amour," *Tel Quel* 74 (Winter 1977): 30–49. "Maternité selon Giovanni Bellini" and "Noms de lieu," in *Polylogue* (Paris: Seuil, 1977); "Motherhood According to Bellini" and "Place Names," in *Desire in Language: A Semiotic Approach to Literature and Art*, trans. Thomas Gorz et al. (New York: Columbia University Press, 1980).

31. Derrida, "La Différance," in *Marges*; "Differance," *Margin of Philosophy*.

32. I have tried to develop such a program since this essay was written. See especially Spivak, "Feminism and Critical Theory," in Spivak, *In Other Worlds: Essays in Cultural Politics* (New York: Methuen, 1987), 77–92.

33. Elizabeth Fox-Genovese has written a pathbreaking essay on the subject that appeared after my own essay was completed. See her "Placing Women's History in History," *New Left Review* 133 (May–June 1982).

34. I have attempted to use this method of criticism in "Unmaking and Making in *To the Lighthouse*," in Spivak, *In Other Worlds*, 30–45.

35. Jacques Derrida, "The Law of Genre," trans. Avital Ronell, *Glyph* 7 (1980). Both English and French versions appear in *Glyph*; hereafter cited in the text as "LG," with page reference to the English version followed by reference to the French.

36. Jacques Derrida, "Living On: Border Lines," trans. James Hulbert, in *Deconstruction and Criticism*, ed. Harold Bloom et al. (New York: Seabury, 1979), hereafter cited in the text as "LO."

37. In "Limited Inc," *Glyph* 2 (1977), Derrida points to the relationship between the normativity of speech act theory and the repressive state apparatus of official psychiatry.

38. Derrida, *Grammatologie*, 110; *Grammatology*, 75.

39. My apologies to David Carroll, who has quite appropriately chastised me for my tendency to imitate Derridian gestures: "Spivak's attempt (and failure) to imitate Derrida's style is precisely the problem with her very long 'Translator's Preface' to *Of Grammatology*, which I would advise any reader not totally familiar with Derrida's writing simply to ignore." Cf. "History As Writing," *Clio* 7 (Spring 1978): 460.

40. Luce Irigaray, *Ce sexe qui n'en est pas un* (Paris: Minuit, 1977), 24; trans. in *New French Feminisms*, ed. Elaine Marks and Isabelle de Courtivron (Amherst: University of Massachusetts Press, 1980), 100.

41. Roland Barthes brought a comparable charge against "a group of revolutionary students," in "Ecrivains, intellectuels, professeurs," *Tel Quel* 47 (Autumn 1971): 8, translated by Stephen Heath as "Writers, Intellectuals, Teachers," in *Image/Music/Text* (New York: Hill and Wang, 1977), 198–99. Given the tradition of academic radicalism in France, and our experiences with the old New Left, "feminist" should not be taken as a subset of "revolutionary."

42. Spivak, "French Feminism in an International Frame," in *In Other Worlds*, 134–53.

43. This passage and the preceding one are modified quotations from "French Feminism in an International Frame."

44. Karl Marx and Friedrich Engels, *Werke* (Berlin, 1960–68), *Ergänzungsband*, part 1:579–80; *Early Writings*, trans. Rodney Livingstone and Gregor Benton (New York: Random House, 1975), 391.

3

Ontology and Equivocation
Derrida's Politics of Sexual Difference

Elizabeth Grosz

The Politics of Equivocation

Only a political or theoretical commitment that can confront its own internal paradoxes, its inherent or constitutive inconsistencies, and its necessary if changeable limits can be said to have come of age.* I believe that, after considerable struggle and often great reluctance, feminist theory has finally reached the stage when it can not only defend itself from outside incursions and external criticism—from positions committed to antifeminism, phallocentrism, patriarchalism—but is prepared to speak up against some of its own commitments, some of the stages and positions that were perhaps historically necessary for its current forms but to which it can now no longer adhere. Feminist theory must be prepared to accept that any position has its limits, that no position can encompass the entire field, and that to present a position, to provide a strategy, to make specific claims is always to exclude, to deny and to problematize other, competing positions. As part of its coming-to-maturity, feminism (and indeed any political movement with theoretical aspirations and commitments) must be prepared as it were, to air dirty laundry, to make public as well as private criticisms of other feminists, to be seen to disagree with other feminists or feminisms. This may well prove confusing, unsettling, and disappointing to outsiders (who may like to believe in generally agreed-upon base issues and platforms, who may be shocked that feminists can disagree with each other at least as strongly as they may disagree with phallocentric or male positions), but it is something that most feminists themselves have probably long recognized and that many have evaluated as one of the positive strengths of feminist politics, its diversity, its commitment to multiplicities and specificities, its nonunified functioning.

Postmodern theory in general and Derridean deconstruction in particular have posed a series of the most difficult challenges to the selfconception of feminist theories, challenges—and not simply critiques or objections—that have raised serious questions about the status of subversion, the position of subordination, and the possibilities of transgression, transformation, and upheaval that feminists now need to address if feminism is to remain a viable and effective political force into the twenty-first century. The general suspicion that many feminists have of that work now most easily categorized as postmodern,[1] the wariness of different projects to decenter subjectivities, sexualities, agencies, political platforms, and revolutionary goals has caused many feminists to cling steadfastly to humanist and enlightenment values, or to naturalist and essentialist commitments that may ultimately harm more than help feminist aims and strategies. My goal here, though, is not to provide some general defense of the broadly conceived movements of postmodernism. I do not believe that the phenomenon of postmodernism—conceived in its absolute generality—has anything to offer feminism; it is already an abstraction of and distancing from any of the particular positions that may prove very useful in their concrete details. Instead, here I hope to provide something of a feminist revaluation of some of the writings of Jacques Derrida, a revaluation that will function as a mode of criticism of both those feminists who have resolutely attacked deconstruction (often in the name of postmodernism) without any familiarity with his writings[2] and those feminists who have actively struggled with his texts (anyone who has read Derrida must be aware of this irreducible feature of the struggle of reading, which necessarily involves struggling, grappling with the complexities of his writings) only to reject it as outside of or hostile to feminist concerns. My purpose here, though, is not to criticize other feminists (although I no longer want to shy away from this necessity when it occurs); it is to demonstrate that feminist demands for a clear-cut position, for answers, for unequivocal boundaries and divisions, and certainties in political judgment can afford to learn much from deconstruction.

I do not suggest that Derrida's works are feminist in themselves; nor do I make the contrary claim that his writings are antifeminist in any straightforward sense. His position defies ready-made categories and clear-cut characterizations. It is perhaps this apparently slipperiness, this refusal to state or stay within a singular definitive position, more than anything else that may explain the suspicion his work seems to generate among feminists and political activists of various kinds. His work cannot be assigned a definitive position on one side or the other of a divide separating feminist from antifeminist positions—indeed, it problematizes this very dividing line—and is not easily assimilable into a kind of feminist appropriation that would or could re-read his works to absorb or ingest them, making them feminist in this movement of incorporation.[3] Nonetheless I believe that deconstruction provides a series of challenges and insights that may serve to make feminist theory more self-critical, more aware of necessary conceptual and political investments and the cost of these investments, and thus more effective and more incisive in its struggles than it may have been before or beyond deconstruction. Moreover, deconstruction provides a way of rethinking our common conceptions of politics and struggle, power and resistance by insisting that no system, method, or discourse can be as all-encompassing, singular, and monolithic as it represents itself. Each is inherently open to its own undoing, its own deconstruction (deconstruction is not imposed from outside a discourse or tradition but emerges from its own inner dynamics). And resistance too cannot be conceived as simply outside or beyond dominant regimes but is conditioned and made possible by them. They do not have a relation of exteriority; each is the other's internal condition of effectivity. It is for this reason that, rather than deconstruction's being construed as a system of critique, of destruction, Derrida insists over and over that it must be understood as a mode of affirmation, indeed as a mode of double affirmation.[4] In a feminist context this means that discourses influenced by or in some way involved with deconstruction are committed to *both* an affirmation, a saying-yes to patriarchy (the gesture of phallocentrism), *and* an affirmation of feminism, an affirmation of the overcoming of patriarchy. The first affirmation is perhaps the one many feminists wish, hope, is unnecessary: that they can simply and resoundingly say no to patriarchy. Yet, the inherited nature of feminist discourse, a discourse that is not, or not yet, a discipline, and its location within "patriarchal" institutions, knowledges, and languages; the ways in which feminist self-help projects and equal opportunity commitments must negotiate with patriarchal institutions of the capitalist state for funding, the implication of Western feminism in neocolonialism, indeed the very investment of all of us in the West to a kind of cannibalization of the imperialized other—all illustrate our necessary, indeed constitutive immersion in the very systems from which we seek to distance, and against which we seek to position, ourselves. Without both moments in this affirmative investment, however, feminism remains in danger of repeating and being unable to recognize the very implications it believes it has repudiated.

Derrida does not question the mistakes, errors, or false assumptions of feminist theory as some philosophers have attempted without too much success:[5] he is not really interested in how to correct or improve any particular theory (indeed, such a notion presupposes that deconstruction somehow knows what a theory means to say and can say it better, more rigorously, or more accurately than the theory it corrects, a commitment that, as Derrida acknowledges, is necessarily bound up with notions of teleology and truth in ways that he himself, more than anyone, has problematized). Rather, his work raises difficult, possibly irresolvable questions regarding the internal and essential implications of feminist theory and practice in an oft-unrecognized complicity with the very forces feminists have commonly identified as outside of, as other to, and as different from feminism itself: patriarchy, phallocentrism, racism, forces from which feminists have, they believe, separated themselves in order to see feminism as beyond or outside their laws of operation. Here Derrida is not addressing an error that, by ingenuity or careful rethinking, could somehow be rectified, but a constitutive binding, the *always already* implication of feminism or any oppositional mode of political struggle to the law it undertakes to subvert or displace. He poses the necessary implication of feminism in phallogocentrism, of antiracism in racism, of philosophical texts (most particularly Nietzsche's, Heidegger's, and de Man's, no less than his own) in Nazism and fascism, of the "revolution" in what it revolts against—possibly the most unsettling and disquieting charge that can be leveled at any political position that strives to ameliorate or transcend given situations and power relations.[6] This is *not* the claim that feminism is doomed from the start, that it cannot hope to accomplish its aim; but rather, the more limited claim that feminism can only hope to succeed insofar as it is implicated in and part—admittedly a recalcitrant part—of patriarchy itself.

By way of a counterbalance to this pessimism that denies the possibility of a definitive break with traditions and social norms, is the claim Derrida directs to those traditions and social norms. He poses the inherent or necessary investment of the proponents of the canon and of tradition in their own undermining and undoing, the constitutive "openness" of every theoretical and textual position to its own outstripping. It is not as if one has the luxury of either remaining faithful to a given, settled, finalized, and "objective" history that passively accepts its textual reconstitution in truth (as conservatives and traditionalists assume); nor that we have any control over the kind of future that will necessarily rewrite our present in the historical terms and frames we ourselves choose (this is what such control implies) as the revolutionary, feminist or otherwise, hopes. This question of complicity is probably the most forceful and disturbing challenge—I cannot call it a critique, because there can be no correction, no truth, no supersession of this complicity—that can be posed for any discourse or practice that regards itself as oppositional: the claim that one's struggles are inherently *impure*, inherently bound up with what one struggles against, that even as one struggles against a system or position, its force and power are actively reaffirmed. This assertion of complicity, while certainly not the claim of a conscious collusion, is nonetheless the refusal of a space beyond or outside, the refusal of the fantasy of a position safe or insulated from what it criticizes and disdains. If feminism does not occupy a space outside of patriarchy and phallocentrism, if it is implicated in the interstices of patriarchal functioning, then the security of its identity, the definitiveness of its borders as other than and outside of patriarchy, its very self-representations as a bounded position separable from patriarchy are all problematized. I do not see this as an antifeminist gesture, but as a measure of the maturity of feminism to accept its internal limits and to use them in enabling and productive ways.

In this essay, I shall explore a number of feminist positions regarding Derrida's work, most of which remain highly critical of his various interventions into and speculations on femininity. I propose to defend Derrida against common feminist reactions and resistances to his deconstructive strategies, by showing that they have misunderstood and misrepresented his position. But I do not suggest only that Derrida's work is simply misread; I maintain that this misreading is systematic and is structurally related to his equivocal position regarding feminism. I shall then examine his account of the ontology of sexual difference, in order to show what a more positive feminist relation to deconstruction may look like.

Feminisms Wary of Deconstruction

With the exception of only a very few feminists (Drucilla Cornell, Gayatri Spivak, Barbara Johnson, Vicki Kirby, Peggy Kamuf), Derrida's work has been regarded almost uniformly with great suspicion, even by those feminists who find themselves attracted to other postmodern discourses and commitments. Lacanian, psychoanalytic, and Foucauldian feminisms are no longer required to provide elaborate self-justifications or accounts of their political acceptability.[7] It can now be safely presumed that such feminisms do not necessarily compromise their feminist commitments in order to accommodate the works of these male theorists; instead, the latter may enhance and make them more incisive. However, the same kinds of assurance are not so readily found—indeed they have yet to be forged—in the case of Derrida's relation to feminist concerns, which remains of ambiguous status. However, it may be this very ambiguity that seems to me to offer feminists something of value.

In this context Rosi Braidotti may serve as representative of a more general feminist hostility toward Derrida's work—a hostility that she by no means reserves especially for Derrida, but directs to a number of (male) "postmodernists." Derrida too, she claims, forms part of a tendency within contemporary theory to use the metaphor of woman to question the status of truth, knowledge, and subjectivity at the expense of women's concrete social struggles. Woman has become the metaphor for the undoing of truth, knowledge, and subjectivity, while never herself being accorded access to these deemed social goods. Braidotti sees Derrida as part of a general tendency within postmodernism to borrow from femininity while effacing its specificity and its links to "real" women. This opposition between (male) representations of women and femininity and "real" women seems both oversimplified and assumes what it needs to argue. I am not suggesting that men's representations of women necessarily accord with or refer to "real" women without residue or resistance: on the contrary "real" women are themselves the products and effects of discursive practices that cannot be confined simply to misogynist (mis)representations. "Real" women are as much an effect of women's discourses as men's, especially seeing that the dividing line between feminist discourses and patriarchal ones can no longer be drawn with any a priori certainty.[8] At the same time, however, it is also the case that any assumption of the independent existence of "real" women outside of or before representation, able to rise against it, must be invested in certain unnegotiable essentialisms. I am not, of course, claiming that there are no real women, but that real women are the consequences or effects of systems of representation and inscription.

> The zero value of the feminine in the system of representation is confirmed [in Derrida's work]; but in this instance, the feminine is used by the (male) thinker so as to avoid confronting the problem of the reality of women and their relation to truth, both of which have been declared fluid and indefinable. . . . Not only is woman undefinable, but she becomes, besides, the sign of unrepresentability itself; definitively other than the system of truth. . . . Historically, . . . truth has become woman at the moment when philosophy can only survive in the becoming woman of the idea, that is in the affirmation of the non-truth of truth, in the acceptance of its lack.[9]

Elsewhere, Braidotti questions the timing of what she (mistakenly) sees as a Derridean reveling in the fragmentation and destabilization of identities provoked by postmodernism: at precisely the moment that women for the first time in history are about to claim an identity, a voice, a politics, a series of positions as their own, men such as Derrida find ever more devious ways of robbing women of these new found gains:

> Well may the high-priests of postmodernism preach the decon-
> struction and fragmentation of the subject, the flux of all identi-

ties, based on phallocentric premises; well may they keep reading into feminism the image of the crisis of their own acquired perceptions of human consciousness. The truth of the matter is: one cannot deconstruct a subjectivity one has never been fully granted; one cannot diffuse a sexuality which has historically been defined as dark and mysterious. In order to announce the death of the subject one must first have gained the right to speak as one; in order to demystify metadiscourse one must first gain access to a place of enunciation. [10]

A self-righteous tone is usually an index of the degree to which one has projected outward, in anger, the very points of uneasiness one feels in one's own position. My point here is Braidotti is herself here invoking a certainty, a clarity and definitive position that she must elsewhere and in other terms deny or disavow. One cannot simply adjudicate the matter by stating, as she does that she has "the truth of the matter." Is it unequivocally "the truth of the matter" to claim that women *do not* have a subjectivity, a position of enunciation, a sexuality? If this were simply "the truth of the matter," feminism itself, including Braidotti's position, would not be possible. It is only if women are ambiguously *both* subjects *and* deprived of a socially recognized subjective position, are *both* speaking beings *and* beings whose words have not been heard; and beings who have a sexuality but whose sexual specificities are ignored, denied, or covered over that women can undertake feminist politics. In a certain sense, women must be accredited with precisely the qualities patriarchal practices attempt to deprive them of or leave unacknowledged, in order to account for the very possibility of feminism, of women overcoming these patriarchal constrictions. In any case, even given this ambiguous inclusion and exclusion of women in the patriarchal order, Braidotti seems to criticize Derrida for the kinds of claims he himself criticizes: she mistakes his position as an affirmation rather than a contestation of the views he is reading. This is quite striking in her discussion of *Spurs*. [11] For Derrida, there is no question of simply decentering the subject once and for all, [12] or simply moving beyond metaphysics or logocentrism into a somehow pure deconstructive space; there is no question that deconstruction, rather than being beyond logocentrism, always remains implicated in it. Braidotti accuses Derrida of attempting to eliminate the very attributes feminists have so long sought for women, when in fact, he questions the very possibility of such an elimination.

Braidotti is certainly not the only feminist to raise such objections. Although Alice Jardine is considerably more careful in her analysis of Derrida's texts, she too seems, in the end, to share Braidotti's suspicions of Derrida's appropriations of the radicality of feminist theory and politics:

> Might there be a new kind of desire on the part of (Modern) Man to occupy all positions at once (among women, among texts?) Are we here only brushing up against a new version of an old male fantasy: that of escaping the laws of the fathers through the independent and at the same time dependent female? Are men projecting their own "divisions" onto their primordial interlocutors—women? Do they hope to find a way of depersonalizing sexual identity while maintaining the amorous relation through women?
>
> How can we emphasize the political stakes of those questions without betraying the necessity of asking them knowingly—even "academically"?[13]

Jardine implies that the danger of deconstruction is its attempt to be all-pervasive, to occupy all specific positions—to speak as woman, as man, as decentered, as centered—opportunistically seeking any position momentarily or strategically while remaining committed to none. This signals a kind of disavowal of his position as masculine that Braidotti has also suggested, a refusal to be located, to make a definite statement—of being evasive when he should be straightforward.

Significantly, Margaret Whitford accuses Derrida of precisely the opposite maneuver: not of disavowing the masculinity of his position (she claims that "he makes it possible to address the question of the *maleness* of the speaking subject/the subject of philosophy"); on the contrary, Whitford is concerned with what he does not do, which is "to make it possible to address the question of how one might be a woman speaking subject/philosopher."[14] For Whitford, Derrida does not adequately speak "in his own voice" he hides his own position behind a web of quotations and readings of other texts. She describes his position as "elusive," "feminine," difficult to locate, for he does not own up to any position:

> Discourse is citation; meaning is ultimately elusive (feminine). Where is Derrida's place of enunciation if he is always quoting

> someone else? In a sense he wants to make his position impregna-
> ble, ultimately undecidable, ultimately "feminine." Deconstruc-
> tion enables him to speak indefinitely, to hold the floor. . . .
> [H]e "masters" feminist discourse by speaking about it. (130)

Several questions arise for me here. Surely a position of enunciation
is not simply hidden behind the apparent neutrality of all citation. It
has been Derrida who has claimed that an enunciative position, the
possibility of (provisional or temporary) contextualization, the possibility
of a parergonal framing of any utterance is always a matter, not simply
of citation, but also of a citation-situating activity, which is itself
amenable to other citations and thus other resituatings (as Whitford
herself demonstrates in critically repeating/reframing Derrida's work in
the context of the Irigarayan affirmation of sexual difference). Far
from hiding behind a system of citationality that makes his position
"impregnable" (the implication being that he hides his "real" position
behind citations; that there is a discourse, concept or view-point "hidden," but logocentrically "present," like the signified, behind mere
words), his, or any other position, only emerges as such within the
structure of citationality or iteration, as one provisional destination of
the cited text. In any case, there seems to be no attempt on his part to
"master feminist discourse," because feminist discourses do not provide
the texts he cites and are not the objects of his investigations. These are
usually derived from what are often considered the most misogynist of
male writers: Nietzsche, Heidegger, Levinas, Freud.[15] Derrida cannot
naively pretend to master feminist discourse through a careful reading of
Nietzsche et al., largely because they are not themselves writers of
feminist texts.

I have offered here some typical and well-worn objections to or
reservations about the relevance of deconstruction for feminist theory.
They are merely the tip of a veritable iceberg of criticisms generally
directed at the incursions of postmodern thought on the "authenticity"
and political efficacy of feminism. While not wishing to engage too
much in the general demeaning of postmodern thought in the works of
a number of feminists,[16] I nonetheless find it worthwhile to outline in
schematic form a few of the more common and serious objections that
may be and have been leveled at Derrida by feminists and other
political activists.

First, that Derrida speaks in the name of, for, or as a feminine subject in a mode of male appropriation of women's right to speak. Just at that moment in history when speaking as a woman finally has some political and theoretical credibility, Derrida, along with Deleuze and others, wants to occupy just the very speaking position that women have finally produced for themselves. This is a claim Irigaray articulates very clearly:

> What I am able to say without any hesitation is that when male theoreticians today employ women's discourse instead of using male discourse, that seems to me a very phallocratic gesture. It means: "We will become and we will speak a feminine discourse in order to remain the master of discourse." What I would want from men is that, finally, they would speak a masculine discourse and affirm that they are doing so.[17]

While this plea is an understandable one, it rests on two problematic assumptions: (a) that one can, through a conscious avowal, acknowledge what one's position is. This seems to be a basic assumption in much of what is at present called "identity politics," which commonly functions in a publicly confessional mode; and in antiracist calls for an authentic native voice, a voice that can speak only for and as it is. Can one *admit* what one's position is? Is a position definitively present, not only to a subject's self-representation, but for all others to avow and accept? Does any subject or position have the stability to definitively state what-it-is? It seems, first, that texts, speaking positions, identities cannot anchor themselves so readily in a definite moment of articulation where their "consciousness" exactly coincides with their existence. And (b) the assumption that there is a clear-cut distinction between talking as a man and talking as a woman. We may be able to presume (possibly without clear-cut justification) a ready distinction between men and women; but even if we do, it is not clear how any one can contain men and women to speak only in their own voice or as their sex. This is to ignore or misunderstand that language itself is the endless possibility of speaking otherwise. This is the irremediably fictional orientation of language, which makes not only fictional but theoretical production possible.

Second, that Derrida has placed deconstruction in a position oppositional to feminism, a position of structural domination over feminist concerns, able to adjudicate the merits and radicality of feminism without in turn being judged by it. This is a claim that Whitford makes explicitly: "there is in practice a 'violent hierarchy' at work in which deconstruction is the privileged term. In the opposition which he sets up between deconstruction and feminism, there is no question for Derrida of privileging the subordinate term, since it could leave him without a place to speak."[18]

This claim seems to misunderstand the commitment Derrida has to undermining oppositional thought and structures precisely through the assertion of difference. The relations between deconstruction and feminism cannot be regarded as oppositional: deconstruction does not affirm what feminism denies; feminism is not the denial or negation of deconstruction, because their relations do not occupy the same intellectual space, because they are not mirror doubles, because the ongoing possibility of their incommensurability must be affirmed, because their difference must be acknowledged.[19] It is only on the basis of an acceptance, not of an oppositional relation, but of a possibly antagonistic and possibly allied set of struggles that any *relation* between feminism and deconstruction may be possible. Feminism is other to deconstruction; as indeed deconstruction remains one of feminism's others. It is only this that makes them of possible use to use each without having to face the fear of the immersion or absorption of the one in and by the other. It is this that makes productive relations between them possible.

Third, a number of those openly committed to political activism—Ryan, Braidotti, Fraser, Brodrib—claim that while deconstruction may help to problematize certain philosophical and intellectual practices, it remains both elitist and unrelated to power struggles that function in more mundane and everyday terms. Ryan, for example, in agreement with a number of feminists, claims that Derrida's work is limited by the absence of any social, political, or economic understanding of the more "real" pressing issues of day-to-day struggle. This claim is not unrelated to a common lament of those who discuss Derrida's position without having read or having badly read his works: it is too textually bound, it is too enclosed within language, it is hermetically sealed from the real world and real politics.

This oft-made claim seems to miss the point entirely. Only two kinds of response are possible here: the first is to point out, as has been done many times before by Derrida and others, that this objection too closely identifies writing as textuality with the Book, with writing in its vulgar or oppositional sense, as the opposite of speech. Derrida talks of the writing of a world, the production of reality by the trace, by difference. Such a notion of writing cannot be understood literally; it makes the world, objects, and relations possible; it structures and gives the world and its contents meaning and value. Writing cannot be confined to the safe pages of formal texts but must be seen to underlie and to exceed the very structure of oppositional thought—whether "real" (the male/female opposition) or "textual" (for example, the pervasive functioning of oppositional forms within the history of Western philosophy). Indeed, the notion of writing Derrida develops underlies this very opposition that activism itself relies on to distinguish itself: the opposition between the real and the text. A second response, again developed by Derrida himself, is to problematize the presumed finality and givenness of what qualifies as politics, to ask what presumptions have already been made about what politics is and must be, to position politics as somehow outside of, beyond or other than deconstruction (and equally, what presumptions about deconstruction have set it up as somehow apolitical).[20] Deconstruction is a preeminently political set of maneuvres, as capable of taking as its object the primary political concerns of the present—nuclear arms, the bomb, the environment, the reorganization of Europe, the struggles of indigenous peoples, of women, of lesbians and gays—as any discourse, even if one does not always necessarily agree. Disagreement is itself a mode of political engagement.

If these claims represent serious misunderstandings of the deconstructive project associated with Derrida's name, it is perhaps now time to turn more directly to a couple of Derrida's central texts on the question of the ontological status of sexual difference, to see more precisely what he has to offer feminist theory and to what extent the general feminist nervousness surrounding his position is justified.

The Ontology of Sexual Difference

The question of the ontological status of sexual difference is one of the most central issues facing feminist theory today: at its center lies a whole series of issues that occupy the major concerns of feminism in the 1990s. It provides probably the broadest way of raising the more "regional" questions of the status of the "given" in feminist thought, whether this is conceived in terms of the status of the female body, the origins of patriarchy, or the power of phallocentric discourses. To take the body as a particular example, in other recent work[21] I have asked the question central to any corporeal feminism: What is the ontological status of the sexed body? Is the sexed body (a body presumably given by biology) the raw materials of modes of social inscription and production? Or do modes of social inscription produce the body as sexually specific? Which comes "first"—sexed bodies or the social markers of sexual difference? Similarly, if feminists take patriarchy as a given term in feminist analysis, the question can always be asked, What is the origin of patriarchy? Is it men's natural strength, aggression, and competitiveness that produced a system of patriarchal domination over women? Or, rather, did a system of patriarchal domination produce men's strength, and so forth, as the relevant explanatory factor in the devaluation of women's attributes? How could such questions be resolved? How could one decide what a suitable answer to these questions might be? It is these constitutive types of feminist question that Derrida's analysis of the ontology of sexual difference may help to resolve or at least understand.

Derrida deals with the question of sexual difference largely indirectly, through his readings of various texts in which woman, femininity, or sexual difference function either as invisible but traceable supports (Heidegger) or as the explicit objects of secondarization or derision in a philosophical system (Levinas, Nietzsche). He does talk more directly about contemporary feminist movements, admittedly rather reluctantly and evasively, in some interviews.[22] His position must be teased out; it resists any reading that seeks to place him firmly on either side of a divide between a pure, a-, or pre-sexual ontology and an ontology that takes sexual difference as its first presumption or defining characteristic. In the following, I shall present a highly selective reading of some of Derrida's key texts on the ontology of sexual difference.

In his elaboration of Heidegger's relation to the question of sexual difference in "Geschlecht: Sexual Difference, Ontological Difference," one purpose, among others, is to raise the question, "How do you think by those words [sexual difference] or through them?" (66). What does it mean, for example, to say that Heidegger speaks little (less than other philosophers) of sexual difference? How is one to recognize what it means to speak of sexual difference, especially if sexual difference is not reducible to the sexual identities of male and female? What is its referent if it is difference and not an identity that is articulated? If Heidegger does not speak of sexual difference as such, it may nonetheless pervade his text, in spite of his attempts to keep it contained and beyond the scope of Dasein, despite his ambition to render Dasein neutral, clean, unbounded with the complications of sexuality and anthropological specificity. Basically Heidegger seems committed to two positions that sit uneasily together, and whose tension will provoke a reexploration and reinterpretation of both.

On the one hand, Heidegger insists that Dasein is a neutral term, a term that must be stripped of its humanist, egoist, anthropomorphic associations and characteristics in order to be understood in terms of fundamental ontology, in terms prior to any concrete specification, at the origin of any particularity:

> The peculiar *neutrality* of the term "Dasein" is essential, because the interpretation of this being must be carried out prior to every factual concretion. . . . Neutrality is not the voidness of an abstraction, but precisely the potency of the *origin*, which bears in itself the intrinsic possibility of every concrete factual humanity.[23]

Dasein is thus construed as outside or beyond the reach of sexual difference, preceding it. It is being minus its sexual, cultural, historical, ethical, and political determinations, a pure relation, involving nothing but Dasein's relation to itself: "This neutrality also indicates that *Dasein* is neither of the two sexes" (136).

On the other hand, in making Dasein the origin of things, of every concrete existence, including the human, through a kind of scattering or dispersion, in insisting that Dasein is not a negativity or abstraction, but is itself capable of corporeality, facticity, concreteness, Heidegger also acknowledges for Dasein its inherent openness to sexual specificity and the centrality of sexual difference to Dasein in its very neutrality. Heidegger affirms that Dasein is the well or source of all concreteness, the "intrinsic possibility of every factual humanity" (137):

> Neutral Dasein is never what exists; Dasein exists in each case only in its factical concretion. But neutral Dasein is indeed the primal source of intrinsic possibility that springs up in every existence and makes it intrinsically possible. . . . Dasein harbors the intrinsic possibility for being factically dispersed into bodiliness and thus into sexuality. . . . As factical, Dasein is, among other things, in each case disunited in a particular sexuality. (137)

Dasein in its neutrality, free of any predetermination, in its "pure" relations to itself, is nonetheless implicated in the dispersion or dissemination that comes later to constitute the specificity, determinacy, and sexual coding of any (human) being. Sexual difference cannot spring from nothing; it is not an artificial imposition from outside that, like logocentrism itself, can have no outside. Dasein contains within itself the very possibility of its dispersion into multiplicity, the very condition of the attribution or acquisition of any qualities or properties, including a sexual specification. Dasein is both what neutralizes all determination, including that implied by sexual difference while at the same time providing the precondition and possibility of the sexual determination of things, humans. Derrida suggests that Dasein is not simply *neuter*, without trace of sexual markings, but rather that it neutralizes a prior sexual marking, that of the oppositional or binarized model of sexuality.

Derrida is very careful, in a number of key texts, to distinguish (as he or we may not in fact be capable of doing so clearly as he suggests) between sexual opposition and sexual difference, between a binary structuring of the relations between the sexes into a model of presence and absence, positive and negative, and a nonbinarized *differential* understanding of the relations between the sexes, in which no single model can dictate or provide the terms for the representation, whether negative or positive, of all sexes. His reading stresses that Heidegger (and presumably Derrida himself) actively distances himself from the model of sexual binarity, through the neutralizing activity of Dasein:

> Whether a matter of neutrality or asexuality, the words accentuate strongly a negativity. . . . By means of such manifestly negative predicates there should become legible what Heidegger doesn't hesitate to call a "positivity," a richness, and, in a heavily charged code, even a power. Such precision suggests that the a-sexual neutrality does not desexualize, on the contrary, its *ontological* negativity is not unfolded with respect to *sexuality itself* (which it would instead liberate), but on its differential marks, or more strictly on *sexual duality* . . . asexuality could be determined as such only to the degree that sexuality would mean immediate binarity or sexual division. . . . If Dasein as such belongs to neither of the two sexes, that doesn't mean that its being is deprived of sex. On the contrary, here one must think of a predifferential, rather a predual, sexuality—which doesn't

necessarily mean unitary, homogeneous or undifferentiated. Then, from that sexuality, more originary than the dyad, one may try to think to the bottom a "positivity" and a "power."[24]

In short, Derrida wants to claim that there is a sexuality more primordial than the binarized opposition between the sexes, a sexual difference that is neutral with respect to the sexes as they are currently or have been historically represented, a "raw material" out of which, through dispersion and splitting, sexual difference is rendered concrete and specific. This primordial sexuality *is*, as it were, Dasein, an order before sexual determination that is in itself sexual. There is, on the one hand, the indebtedness of sexual opposition to a neutral Dasein; on the other hand, Dasein is the primordial status of sexuality before its determination in concrete form:

> There is not properly a sexual predicate: there is none at least that does not refer, for its sense, to the *general* structures of *Dasein*. So that to know what one speaks of, and how, when one names sexuality, one must indeed rely upon the very thing described in the analytic of *Dasein*. Inversely, if this be allowed, that disimplification allows the general sexuality or sexualization of discourse to be understood: sexual connotations can only mark discourse, to the point of immersing it in them, to the extent that they are homogeneous to what every discourse implies.[25]

The same sort of interests and concerns that appear in "Geschlect" are also evident in Derrida's reading of Levinas in "At this Very Moment in This Work Here I Am" (1991). Here he again interrogates the relations between a foundational concept—no longer Dasein but now the Levinasian absolute Other as articulated in *Totality and Infinity*—with the question of sexual difference. The same sorts of questions remain appropriate in this new context: Is the absolute Other beyond or before sexual determination? Or is sexual determination part of the very establishment of the concept of the Other (the Other as feminine)? Is sexual difference and femininity (and even the collapsing of sexual difference into femininity, as if only the feminine side of the opposition can represent difference) primary or secondary? As with his analysis of Heidegger, Derrida's goal is not to criticize or punish the Levinasian double-take on the question of sexual difference, but to show its unacknowledged reliance on precisely that which his model must refuse, deny, or cover over.

While on the one hand, unlike virtually an entire history of Western philosophy, Levinas seems prepared to write as a masculine, as a man, an "I-he" as Derrida describes it, to sign (with) his masculine signature, to own up to the position of authority and articulation usually unmarked as man, but occupiable only by men; on the other hand, he participates in a certain effacement of the question of sexual difference, a certain investment in the phallocentric covering of women under the generic human:

> I interrogate the link, in E.L.'s work, between sexual difference— the Other as the other sex, otherwise said as otherwise sexed— and the Other as wholly other, beyond or before sexual difference. To himself, his text marks its signature by a masculine "I-he." . . . His signature thus assumes the sexual mark, a remarkable phenomenon in the history of philosophical writing, if the latter has always been interested in occupying that position without re-marking upon it or assuming it on, without signing its mark. But as well as this, E.L.'s work seems to me to have always rendered secondary, derivative, and subordinate, alterity as sexual difference, the trait of sexual difference, to the alterity of a sexually non-marked wholly other.[26]

Derrida recognizes in the well-known gesture of neutralization, or humanization, the ruses of a masculine domination that leaves itself unmarked as such. The emptying out of particular determinations is a prerogative of the masculine position: where one says "it doesn't matter if it is he or she," the he is always already privileged as unmarked, a mode of prior determination of the she. Derrida raises one of the central questions of feminist theory: "How can one mark as masculine the very thing said to be anterior, or even foreign, to sexual difference?" (40). Elsewhere he reformulates this question as a question of the relation of primacy between sexual difference and difference: "Must one think 'difference' 'before' sexual difference or taking off 'from' it? Has this question, if not a meaning (we are at the origin of meaning here, and the origin cannot 'have meaning') at least something of a chance of opening up anything at all, however im-pertinent it may appear?"[27]

It is never clear, Derrida claims, if Levinas is simply commenting on or affirming certain biblical passages, such as those, for example, who claim that woman, *Ichah* is derived from man, *Iche*. This equivocation runs through the whole of Derrida's reading: Is there a clear-cut division between description and affirmation? Levinas *describes* (let us for the moment give him the benefit of the doubt) the attribution of a secondariness to woman. Man is prior to and generic of—before the division of the man-human from the woman-human—not of woman, but rather, of sexual difference itself, which woman now comes to represent. Humanity in general, before its division into the two sexes, is sexually neutral; that is, masculine. With the later advent of sexual difference, comes woman. But like Heidegger's gesture of removing all trace of sexual difference from Dasein only to restore a (different) notion of sexual difference, so too does Levinas both remove all traces of sexual specificity from his ontology while at the same time seeking to retain an ontological base that is the ground or prior condition for sexuality:

> Levinas indeed senses the risk factor involved in the erasure of sexual difference. He therefore maintains sexual difference: the human in general remains a sexual being. But he can only do so, it would seem, by placing (differentiated) sexuality beneath humanity, which sustains itself at the level of Spirit. That is, he simultaneously places . . . masculinity in command and at the beginning, on a par with the Spirit. This gesture carries with it the most self-interested of contradictions.[28]

If the wholly Other is beyond all determination, then the wholly Other cannot identify with the other sex, with femininity. The indifference of the relation with the Other, the relation that, for Levinas, precedes ontology, and founds the domain of ethical difference, is prior to and the precondition of sexual difference. Now, on the one hand, this gesture of the neutralization of the domain of the Other is perhaps a necessary condition for the very existence of an ethics. Can there be an ethics between men and women that does not rely upon or presume a common or neutral ground, a ground of what the sexes (or races) share in common, a ground that ethics fills? Does it even make sense to talk of an ethics for women and an ethics for men as two different projects, if one of the implications of an ethics is that it regulates relations between the different sexes? (This is indeed the kind of ethics Irigaray seeks: she is not looking for a women's ethic, a feminist ethic, a set of principles or prescriptions governing women's behavior, because such an ethics leaves women's relations to the men, and men's relations to each other and to women completely untouched; instead she is seeking an ethics of sexual difference, an ethics that is cognizant of the specificity and autonomy of each sex.) On the other hand, the attribution of the masculine pronoun to mark the wholly Other, to mark the domain of the ethical, is clearly an attempt to master and control, not simply the terms by which sexual difference is thought but the very conceptions of the feminine and of woman, which now have to take their place under the label of the "he." The problem here is not simply that Levinas encloses the feminine in a masculine/universal model that cannot but privilege the masculine at the expense of the feminine; but also that this entails that even the masculine subject has effaced the wholly other status of the Other, the fundamental openness to alterity that he also attributes to the masculine. In defining the Other in the terms of the masculine, Levinas in effect reduces this otherness, converting it into a version of the same, thus obliterating the very possibility, in his terms, of an ethics.[29]

A different version of his analysis of the relations between sexual binarity and sexual difference has also marked Derrida's much-observed and contested interviews on the question of femininity, feminism, and sexual difference. Instead of, as some have been tempted to do, affirming women's specificity through some reference to a kind of independent authenticity, or positing women's subversive powers and capacities in some inarticulable beyond of language (as psychoanalysis tends to), Derrida refers both to the historical tenacity of the binary dividing the sexes that prioritizes the masculine at the expense of the feminine (the implication being that it is not so easy to dislodge the privileged masculine term in order to put the feminine in its place) and to the logical openness of our capacity to understand sexual difference in terms other than the binary type of model. Drucilla Cornell, for one, seems to actively affirm Derrida's advocacy of a sexuality outside or independent of the sexual duality:

> [I shall] argue that the deconstruction of the conventional struc-
> tures of gender identity as either biologically necessary or as
> culturally desirable not only does not erase the "reality" of
> women's suffering, but demands instead the affirmation of femi-
> nine sexual difference as irreducible to the dominant definition
> of the feminine within the gender hierarchy as man's other or

his mirror image. In other words, sexual difference and more specifically feminine sexual difference, is not being erased; instead the rigid structures of gender identity which have devalued women and identified them with the patriarchal conventions of the gender hierarchy are being challenged.[30]

It seems to me that Derrida is indeed interrogating the very conditions under which women have been attributed a secondary social status on the basis of biological, natural, or essential qualities; he is suggesting a fundamental indeterminacy of sexuality before the imposition of sexual difference (and presumably he must also be committed to the claim that this indeterminacy is not quite captured by the sexual identities of males and females, that it exerts a kind of resistance to its reduction to binarization). In doing so, he is not simply or straightforwardly speaking as a woman or appropriating women's right to speak. Unlike the vast majority of other male philosophers, particularly those labelled postmodern,[31] Derrida takes seriously feminist issues; he doesn't dismiss them as minor or regional problems reducible to or subsumable by the resolution of other problems. But neither does he (nor could he) provide solutions for these issues insofar as feminism is not resolvable through the acquisition of certain specific rights and values, or through the enactment of a program or specific path. Indeed, with and through his reading of Nietzsche in *Spurs* (1979), he remains generally critical of an egalitarian feminism in which women seek formal and legal equality with men. Such a feminism, as he rightly suggests, aspires to make women like men; it is inherently reactive. In his by now famous interview with Christie McDonald, Derrida is quite explicit about differentiating this kind of reactive feminism, which aspires no further than the emulation of men's accomplishments and positions, from other, more active and positive forms:

> Can one not say, in Nietzsche's language, that there is a "reactive" feminism and that a certain historical necessity often puts this form of feminism in power in today's organized struggles? It is this kind of "reactive" feminism that Nietzsche mocks, and not woman or women. Perhaps one should not so much combat it head on—other interests would be at stake in such a move—as prevent its occupying the entire terrain.[32]

This is not, however, to suggest that Derrida's work should be accepted wholesale as feminist or as readily compatible with and amenable to feminism. Two factors make this a difficult assertion: first, Derrida has a good deal to offer feminist theory that is not generally there in feminist works. His work mounts a productive challenge to many of the underlying assumptions, values, and methods in much feminist writing, and insofar as he provides insights into what might be called the "politics of representation," his work is both other than but useful for feminist theory. And second, perhaps more problematic, there remain residual feminist problems with Derrida's work, problems that are less serious than those raised by the feminists I discussed earlier but that nonetheless mitigate any too easy identification and acceptance of his position.

I have in mind here a certain strategic ambiguity in Derrida's use of the notion of an indeterminate or undecidable sexuality, a sexuality before the imposition of dual sex roles, a sexuality that is somehow ontological but entirely without qualities and attributes. I believe that Derrida is hovering between two uses of the notion of sexuality, sometimes using one to evade the implications of the other. It is clear that sexuality, in the sense of "pleasurable drive," could quite valuably be understood as a mode of prior indeterminacy that gains its specific form and qualities a posteriori, and largely as an effect of binary polarization. It is not so easy to see how sexuality, in the sense of sexed subjectivity, male and female, can be understood as indeterminate.[33] By this I do not want to suggest that a ready division can be made between these two conceptions. They are clearly bound up with each other: how one lives one's sexuality in the first sense, depends on how one is sexed in the second sense. This is what I presume that the framework of sexual difference implies: that there is an irreducible specificity of each sex relative to the other, that there must be (at least, but necessarily not only) two sexes. In short, one lives one's sexual indeterminacy, one's possibilities for being sexed otherwise differently depending on whether one is male or female. This is not, however, to predetermine how one "is" male or female, but simply to suggest that there is an ineradicable rift between the two, in whatever forms they are lived.[34] Unless such a presumption is made, sexual difference remains in danger of collapsing into a sexual neutrality of precisely the kind Derrida problematizes in Heidegger and Levinas. Derrida's dream of a multiplicity of "sexually marked voices" seems to me worthy of careful consideration, as long as the question of the limits of possibility of each (sexed) body is recognized. Each sex has the capacity to (and frequently does) play with, become, a number of different sexualities; but not to take on the body and sex of the other:

> The relationship would not be a-sexual, far from it, but would be sexual otherwise; beyond the binary difference that governs the decorum of all codes, beyond the opposition feminine/masculine, beyond bisexuality as well, beyond homosexuality and heterosexuality which come to the same thing . . . I would like to believe in the multiplicity of sexually marked voices. I would like to believe in the masses, this indeterminate number of blended voices, this mobile of non-identified sexual marks whose choreography can carry, divide, multiply the body of each "individual," whether he be classified as "man" or as "woman" according to the criteria of usage.[35]

Deconstructive Politics

Derrida does not offer any political solutions for either feminism or any other politics. This has tended to evoke suspicion. If he does not offer any solutions, if his goal is to demonstrate the complex and paradoxical nature of any political commitment—or for that matter any conceptual commitment either—then it is commonly and naively assumed that his work is nonpolitical, apolitical, or, worst of all, aligned with the forces of conservatism or even fascism. What is usually not recognized is that his work has the effect of rethinking entirely the ways in which politics and theory have been considered. This does not amount to the creation of a new political theory or epistemology, but the reordering—or perhaps the disordering—of the ways in which politics and theory have been understood. Politics can no longer be understood in terms of clear-cut heroes and villains, the politically correct position and its incorrect alternatives; that is, on the polarized model of pro or contra that has dominated and continues to dominate so much of feminist and Marxist politics. Instead, things are now murkier: saying no to a political or conceptual structure can no longer remain unequivocal, unilaterally opposed to any (conservative) yes. It is implicated in a yes; it is implicitly *also* a yes. One cannot say no to the law, to requirement, to history, to power, without being committed at the same time to affirmation of precisely that which one wishes to deny.

Derrida is concerned with complicating politics, with making it no longer simply readable as the setting out of a clear-cut, unambiguous, solid set of guarantees. This necessarily disturbs those who seek to be reassured of the rightness of their positions, who seek to be sure that, in all contexts and in all situations, they have a position that remains on the "right" side. Indeed, I suspect that this was precisely the appeal of a vulgar Marxism or feminism that claimed to provide a position, a perspective, from which to judge other political positions and claims without accepting the right in turn to be judged by them, to submit to their perspectives, to be assessed in terms of their adequacy or relevance to the situation. This amounts, fundamentally and in effect, to a wish to end politics, to stop contestation, to have an answer that admits of no complications and ramifications.[36] To know, to be right.

Such a will to silence others, to prevent contestation, to adjudicate once and for all and with definitive status, the rightness, the appropriateness, the truthfulness or justice of any position is not a will that can be readily repudiated. In claiming a position, one must remain committed to its ability to explain, enact, produce, and outperform its alternatives; that is, in a certain sense, to its "rightness," its "truth," its value over and above others. This is what it is to have a position. Yet at the same time, this will to overpower, to master, to control, must undermine itself, must remain bound up with the very disturbances, and to what is unsettling to, uncontainable by it, its others. The no is always committed to a (prior and stronger) yes. And in turn, the yes always contains within a maybe, a quivering of uncertainty, an acknowledgment that even as one commits oneself to a position (whatever it might be) at the same time one is also committed to its undoing and surpassing. Such a yes cannot be said once and for all, to make room for a later no but must remain continuous, an eternal return to the yes, even as one is inclined, propelled to repudiation and the movement beyond. (It is in this sense that Derrida openly acknowledges his responsibility for and implication in the views not simply of his acolytes and faithful followers, those who follow in his spirit, who remain within his orbit of influence, but also, and more significant, for the misreadings generated by his work.)

Derrida's complication of the political thus involves not only the acknowledgment of the complexities and ambiguities of any position (this formulation still implies the possibility of resolving or at least clarifying these complexities) but of the aporias, the irresolvably contradictory tensions within each claim, the impossibility of assigning a singular assessment and a definitive and settled value. This may explain why those who have pretensions to any political certainty, or of having answers for political issues seem so hostile to what deconstruction may offer in rethinking the political. They see Derrida's work as an alternative that competes with their own positions without having anything commensurable to offer by way of political solutions. All he offers are complications, modes of unsettling.

To return, finally, to the question of the ontological status of sexual difference. To presume either the one or the other side of this question—that is, the claim that ontology is sexually neutral and thus precedes sexual difference and the claim that sexual difference is ontological—necessarily involves the implication of the one in the other. If ontology is claimed to be sexually neutral, then it has to be shown how, out of such a neutrality it is nevertheless able to generate sexual difference; how, in short, there must always already be a trace of sexual difference even within the postulation of an indifference. And equally, if sexual difference is an, if not the, ontological bedrock, nonetheless, it must also be clear that sexual difference takes the forms in which we recognize it today only through a later inscription or production (a binary ordering) that both contains and retranscribes it. The ontological status of sexual difference implies a fundamental indeterminacy, such that it must explain its openness, its incompleteness and its possibilities of being completed, supplemented, by a (later) reordering. The question remains inherently undecidable, which is not to say that it is unintelligible. One cannot opt for one side of an opposition without at the same time (whether wittingly or not) remaining implicated in and complicit with its opposite. This does not mean one must accept both sides as equal in value, or that one must abandon the opposition altogether and produce a middle or compromise path between them. None of the binary oppositions structuring logocentric and phallocentric thought can be simply avoided, and no compromise between them is possible. One must accept the tangible and singular irresolvability of oppositions in their concrete contexts, and in contexts to come. I believe that this remains one of the great strengths rather than a weakening of feminist theory: not its closure of certain positions with which it disagrees, but its openness to its own retranscriptions and rewritings.

Notes

*My thanks to Pheng Cheah for his helpful comments and suggestions on my reading of Derrida.

1. This general label of postmodernism has always seemed to me to be a shorthand formula of dismissal for the various—and highly disparate—positions thus categorized. It is not at all clear that writers like Lacan, Derrida, Deleuze, Foucault, and Lyotard, not to mention Kristeva and Irigaray, share a common denominator that could be called postmodern. This label designates the giving up of certain features that characterize the project of modernity, including the opposition between structuralism and humanism; beyond this shared negative concern, however, the names thus lumped together seem to me to share little in common. The label of postmodernism has helped serve as a justification for treating these figures together without paying any particular attention to their specific contributions, to their major differences and inconsistencies, to the various debates and disagreements that have marked their complex and often uneasy relations. And perhaps more alarmingly, postmodernism has functioned as a marketing label to designate what is new, difficult, and hip, to mark the contemporaneity of the various academic or intellectual "products" or "commodities" thus being marketed—a book, a conference, a seminar, a program.

2. The best that can be said of such a position is that it is intellectually dishonest, even if politically well intentioned. To criticize any position on the basis of hearsay, or rumor or gossip is to abrogate one's intellectual responsibility to ensure that criticism is justified, that it hits its mark, that it is "fair." Such a position is exactly analogous of the attitude of the popular or commercial press in the face of the complexity of feminist theory and politics at present. At best, a caricature can be drawn, but any broad understanding is precluded.

3. This is what seems to make up the fraught yet highly productive relations between feminism and psychoanalysis: feminism sees itself as capable of ingesting psychoanalytic discourse in order to make it over into a feminist discourse, absorbing and excreting those elements antithetical to or in tension with explicit feminist commitments.

4. As Derrida himself affirms, the issue of the yes, what yes is, what it means, what it designates, has preoccupied all of his writings: "For a very long time, the question of the *yes* has mobilized or traversed everything I have been trying to think, write, teach or read"; see "Ulysses Gramophone," in his *Acts of Literature*, ed. Derek Attridge (New York: Routledge, 1992), 256–309; quotation on 287. The yes is for him the condition of all language, representation, and thus intimately tied to the trace, writing, pharmakon, and so forth; it functions in the modality of the promise and the signature (and hence also requires countersignature, doubling); in itself it always calls forth its repetition, a double affirmation; and finally (though not exhaustively), it is linked to, and echoed by the figure of "a certain kind of woman" (in Joyce, in Nietzsche, in Blanchot): "the relationship of a *yes* to the Other, of a *yes* to the other and of one *yes* to the other *yes*, must be such that the contamination of the two *yeses* remains inevitable. And not only as a threat: but also an opportunity. With or without a word, a *yes* demands *a priori* its own repetition, its own memorizing, demands that a *yes* to the *yes* inhabit the arrival of the 'first' yes, which is never therefore simply originary. We cannot say *yes* without promising to confirm it and to remember it, to keep it safe,

countersigned in another yes, without promise and memory, without the promise of memory, Molly remembers (and recalls herself). The memory of a promise initiates the circle or appropriation, with all the risks of technical repetition, of automatized archives, of gramo-phony, of simulacrum, of wandering deprived of an address and destination. A *yes* must entrust itself to memory. Having come already from the other, in the dissymmetry of the request, and from the other of whom it is requested to request a *yes*, the *yes* entrusts itself to the memory of the other, of the *yes* of the other and of the other yes. All the risks already crowd around from the first breath of yes" ("Ulysses Gramophone," 305).

5. I am thinking here of the attempt on the part of a few women philosophers (I hesitate to call them feminists) to correct the bad arguments and inconsistencies of feminist theory with a good dose of philosophical thinking, which is capable of rewriting feminist propositions in more rigorous and accurate form—but at the expense of certain major feminist political commitments. Janet Radcliffe Richards, for example, rewrites feminist notions of women's oppression in terms of a broader, human concern with issues of social justice; see her *Sceptical Feminist* (Harmondsworth: Penguin, 1982).

6. On the relations between Derrida's reading of Heidegger and the latter's implication in the discourses of National Socialism on the one hand, and Derrida's relation to feminist theory on the other, see Nancy J. Holland, "Derrida and Feminism," *APA Newsletter* 91, no. 2 (Fall 1992): 40–43.

7. Although I do believe that feminist resistance to Deleuze's work is even stronger than to Derrida's. See my "A Thousand Tiny Sexes: Feminism and Rhizomatics," in *Gilles Deleuze and The Theater of Philosophy*, ed. Constantin V. Boundas and Dorothea Olkowski (New York: Routledge, 1994). For feminist evaluations of Foucault, see Irene Diamond and Lee Quinby, eds., *Feminism and Foucault: Reflections on Resistance* (Boston: Northeastern University Press, 1988); Jana Sawicki, *Disciplining Foucault: Feminism, Power, and the Body* (London: Routledge, 1991); and Lois McNay, *Foucault and Feminism* (Oxford: Polity, 1993).

8. This claim is addressed in considerably more detail in my "Sexual Signatures: Feminism after the Death of the Author," in Elizabeth Grosz, *Space, Time, and Perversion: Essays on the Politics of Bodies* (New York: Routledge, 1995).

9. Rosi Braidotti, *Patterns of Dissonance* (Oxford: Polity, 1991), 103.

10. Braidotti, "Envy: Or With Your Brains and My Looks, " in *Men in Feminism*, ed. Alice Jardine and Paul Smith (New York: Routledge, 1989), 233–41; quotation on 237.

11. Derrida, *Spurs: Nietzsche's Styles = Eperons: Les styles de Nietzsche*, trans. Barbara Harlow (Chicago: University of Chicago Press, 1979).

12. As Derrida himself explicitly states, his goal has never been to eliminate or decenter the subject: "I have never said that the subject should be dispensed with. Only that it should be deconstructed. To deconstruct the subject does not mean to deny its existence. There are subjects, operations, or effects of subjectivity. This is an incontrovertible fact. To acknowledge this does not mean, however, that the subject is what it says it is. The subject is not some meta-linguistic presence; it is always inscribed in language. My work does not, therefore, destroy the subject; it simply tries to resituate it." "Deconstruction and the Other," in *Dialogues with Contemporary Continental Thinkers—The Phenomenological Heritage: Paul Ricoeur, Emmanuel Levinas, Herbert Marcuse, Stanislas Breton, Jacques Derrida*, by Richard Kearney (Manchester: Manchester University Press, 1984), 105–26.

13. Alice Jardine, *Gynesis: Configurations of Women and Modernity* (Ithaca: Cornell University Press, 1985), 207.

14. Margaret Whitford, *Luce Irigaray: Philosophy in the Feminine* (London: Routledge, 1991), 129.

15. Indeed, this is the ground of a quite different objection to Derrida's work articulated by Braidotti—that he is ignorant of feminist writings and has generally ignored them, and

that consequently his conclusions regarding feminism remain intellectually sloppy: "[Derrida's] disconcerting conclusions [that feminism wants the castration of women] emanate from a misunderstanding and downright ignorance of feminist texts, of the history of women's struggles, and from a carelessness as regards the theoretical aspects of feminism, coupled with a determination to denigrate them." Braidotti, *Patterns of Dissonance*, 105.

16. Possibly the starkest example of this is given by Somer Brodrib, who takes it upon herself to criticize wholesale the general field of postmodern; see her *Nothing Mat(t)ers: A Feminist Critique of Postmodernism* (Melbourne: Spinifex, 1992).

17. Irigaray, quoted in Whitford, *Luce Irigaray*, 132.

18. Whitford, *Luce Irigaray*, 130.

19. Derrida himself, in "Deconstruction and the Other," distinguishes his project's fascination with the question of femininity from a feminist impulse toward "liberation" for women, while acknowledging their interimplications: "The philosophical and literary discoveries of the feminine—and even the political and legal recognition of the status of women—are all symptoms of a deeper mutation in our search for meaning which deconstruction attempts to register. . . . One could describe the transformation effected as good without positing it as an a priori goal or telos. I hesitate to speak of liberation in this context because I don't believe that women are liberated any more than men are. They are of course no longer enslaved in many of the old socio-political respects but even in the new situation woman will not be any freer than man. One needs another language besides that of political liberation to characterize the deconstructive import of the feminine as an uprooting of our phallogocentric culture" (121–22).

20. See Derrida's response in James Creech, Peggy Kamuf, and Jane Todd, "Deconstruction in America: An Interview with Jacques Derrida," *Critical Exchange* 17 (Winter 1985): 1–33.

21. This is one of the central concerns I address in *Volatile Bodies: Toward a Corporeal Feminism* (Sydney, Australia: Allen and Unwin, 1994).

22. See Derrida, *Spurs;* "Geschlecht: Sexual Difference, Ontological Difference," trans. R. Berezdvin, in *Research in Phenomenology* (1983), 13:65–83; "Otobiographies," in *The Ear of the Other: Otobiography, Transference, Translation,* ed. Christie McDonald (Lincoln: University of Nebraska Press, 1985), 3–38; "Women in the Beehive," in *Men and Feminism*, ed. Jardine and Smith, 189–203; "At This Very Moment in This Work Here I Am," in *Re-Reading Levinas*, ed. Robert Bernasconi and Simon Critchley (Bloomington: Indiana University Press, 1991), 11–48; and Derrida and Christie McDonald, "Choreographies," in *The Ear of the Other*, ed. McDonald, 163–85 (reprinted with revisions in this volume, Chapter 1).

23. Martin Heidegger, *The Metaphysical Foundations of Logic*, trans. Michael Heim (Bloomington: Indiana University Press, 1984), 136–37.

24. Derrida, "Geschlecht," 71–72.

25. Ibid., 82.

26. Derrida, "At This Very Moment," 40. Christie McDonald provides a detailed and convincing explanation of this point of resistance or inconsistency in Levinas's work; see Derrida and McDonald, "Choreographies."

27. Derrida and McDonald, "Choreographies," 172.

28. Ibid., 178.

29. See Simon Critchley's analysis of this text:

> One might say that sexual difference is Levinas's "blind spot." But what economy governs this blind spot? . . . Two *enclosures* can be detected in Levinas's work: 1) By making sexual difference secondary and by seeking to master the un-said alterity of the feminine, the "il" of the wholly other would risk *enclosing* itself within the economy of the same. 2) By seeking the enclosed sexual difference within ethical difference, the feminine is *enclosed* within the economy of the same.

. . . Levinas's work encloses the trace of illeity within the economy of the same and encloses the feminine within a crypt. . . . Levinas's work can only go unto the wholly other on the condition that feminine alterity is circumscribed and inhumed. The strange consequence of the latter is that Levinas's work is itself engaged in a denial of (feminine) alterity and thus remains enclosed within the economy of the same which it has constantly striven to exceed.

Critchley, " 'Bois'—Derrida's Final Word on Levinas," in *Re-Reading Levinas*, ed. Robert Bernasconi and Simon Critchley (Bloomington: Indiana University Press, 1991), 162–89.

30. While there is much with which I agree in Cornell's general defense of deconstruction from largely misconstrued feminist objections, I do have one major point of disagreement with her analysis: her ongoing commitment to the basic terms in which the sex/gender distinction is framed by feminists. The sex/gender opposition must be read as simply another version of the opposition between nature and culture or mind and body that Derrida has elsewhere taken great pains to challenge. One cannot understand the structures of sexual privilege simply in terms of a gender hierarchy that somehow hangs, unanchored to any sexual terms, as if the opposition between masculine and feminine makes no sense without its implicit or explicit reliance on the opposition between men and women. Cf. Cornell, *Beyond Accomodation: Ethical Feminism, Deconstruction, and the Law* (New York: Routledge, 1991), 281.

31. I believe that an exception to this generalization is probably Jean-François Lyotard, who has also addressed the question of sexual difference and the struggles of women in what I believe is a sensitive and productive way; see his "One of the Things at Stake in Women's Struggles," *Sub-Stance* 20 (1978): 9–18.

32. Derrida and McDonald, "Choreographies," 168.

33. Here I do not want to suggest simply that there are not individuals of indeterminate sex—so-called intersexed individuals—who are ambiguously neither clearly male nor female, but have characteristics of both. Such individuals cannot be understood as indeterminate, except in the sense that they do not conform to the binary division of the sexes into two clear-cut categories. Nonetheless, such individuals remain concrete, determinate, specific in their morphologies.

34. This rift need not, indeed should not, be understood simply in anatomical or biological terms, for these themselves are in constant social transformation, as Derrida acknowledges: " 'hymen' and 'invagination,' at least in the context into which these words have been swept, no longer simply designate figures for the feminine body. They no longer do so, that is, assuming that one knows for certain what a feminine or masculine body is, and assuming that anatomy is in this instance the final recourse" (Derrida and McDonald, "Choreographies," 181).

35. Ibid., 184.

36. See also Geoffrey Bennington's similar justification of what might be understood as Derrida's politics: "That there is political concern among Derrida's readers does not worry us, on the contrary: but it could easily be shown that this 'worry' claims in fact to resolve politics in such a way that one should no longer have to worry about it, so that nothing should happen in it, so there should be no more politics. . . . It is precisely where one protests most against a supposed lack of political reflection that such reflection is most sorely lacking." Bennington and Derrida, *Jacques Derrida* (Chicago: University of Chicago Press, 1993), 197.

4

Deconstruction and Feminism
A Repetition

Peggy Kamuf

Othello, act 3, scene 4: Emilia is putting Desdemona on guard against her husband's jealousy while the latter seeks to explain Othello's "strange unquietness" to herself as surely "something of state" that has "puddled his clear spirit." "Pray heaven it be state matters, as you think, / And no conception nor no jealous toy / Concerning you," says Emilia. Desdemona protests: "Alas the day, I never gave him cause," to which Emilia then rejoins with this observation about "jealous souls": "But jealous souls will not be answered so. / They are not jealous for the cause, / But jealous for they're jealous. It is a monster / Begot upon itself, born on itself." Here, then, the older, married woman speaks of a monstrousness that the new bride, in her virginal innocence, has never conceived: a self-begetting that turns on itself and returns to itself in a tautological repetition without cause and therefore, it is implied, without end: "they're jealous for they're jealous." This is no natural birth, but a production, if we can call it that, without any other parent than itself, a parent that is also its own monstrous child.

Women speaking together, in private, apparently of a man's jealousy. Yet Emilia speaks of "jealous souls" without distinguishing men from women, even if everything else about the scene seems to override this equivocation. She then shifts the referent altogether when she says "It is a monster," speaking now of neither men, nor women, nor perhaps even anything human. It is, we understand, jealousy itself that she is evoking in the traits of a certain monstrousness. But "jealousy itself," begotten upon and from itself as "it"—neither man nor woman—is that not precisely what is monstrous? Therefore, do we not seek to contain the self-begotten monster with a sex, and only one sex? And to define such a monstrosity as we define one sex over against the other? For if jealousy is monstrous because it suspends or effaces the difference called sexual, if only in its desire or its phantasm, then to contain it thus is to suspend that suspension and give it a human face, perhaps all too human.

These questions about Shakespeare's monster may serve to introduce a reflection on jealousy, which is taken here as the angle of entry into the all-too-bewildering and perhaps monstrous topic of "deconstruction and feminism." This choice is prompted by what seems to be an avoidance or a silence somewhere close to the heart or the soul of feminist theory regarding this subject—presuming that theory to be unified and unified around something like a heart or a soul. The silence has followed on the critique of the Freudian theory of *Penisneid*, penis envy, a critique one may justifiably take to be indispensable to feminist thought of the last seventy-five years. The critique accompanied from the first Freud's elaboration of the theory; indeed, his most succinct formulations of penis envy—in the "lecture" on femininity in *New Introductory Lectures on Psychoanalysis* (1933) and the essay "Female Sexuality" (1931)—are responses to objections already raised by members of the first generation of psychoanalysts: Karen Horney, Helene Deutsch, Ernest Jones among the most prominent of them.[1] That critique has been reelaborated by, among others, Luce Irigaray and Sarah Kofman. Their similar but competing studies of the lecture "Femininity" have had a significant influence on a certain thinking about women's sexuality and subjectivity that we cannot document here. Rather, we take merely as a point of departure the sense that this thinking has assumed or assimilated the deconstruction of *Penisneid* to the benefit of a notion of the feminine subject that would be, in theory or in principle, free of any *constitutive* envy or jealousy, and most particularly of that constitutive formation Freud called penis envy. In other words, envy or jealousy (and we will say something further below about this apparent semantic distinction) would be thought of as accidental or contingent states that can characterize this subject at any given moment or in certain circumstances; its manifestations, however, would remain essentially external to the subject's own constitution before and beyond jealousy. This idea of a feminine subject would grant no essential place to jealousy or envy, would recognize or allow for no effects of jealousy in the constitution of a subject by sexual difference as feminine. To the extent, therefore, that jealousy operates as a constitutive, irreducible determinant in sexual differentiation, it is a masculine determinant and a determining factor of masculinity. Unlike contingent feminine jealousy, unlike the historically conditioned feminine resentment of masculine privilege that Freud, for example, would have all but ignored and neglected to take into account, there would be an essential masculine jealousy that is the effect of the thwarted drive to possess or appropriate feminine difference. Such a theory of the nonjealous feminine subject would therefore have to answer our earlier question, Does the self-begotten monster have a sex and only one sex? in the affirmative: Yes, and it is masculine.

This assertion and the preceding ones are attributed less to some feminist discourse than, as already mentioned, to a silence observed or imposed there around the topic or topos of jealousy. On the one hand, this silence closes out the Freudian account of penis envy, that unconscious formation to which women would owe virtually all affective, social, and intellectual development, including, as Sarah Kofman recalls, feminism itself. From the essay "The Psychogenesis of a Case of Homosexuality in a Woman," she cites this description of Freud's patient:

> The analysis showed, further, that the girl had suffered from childhood from a strongly marked "masculinity complex." A spirited girl, always ready for romping and fighting, she was not at all prepared to be second to her slightly older brother; after inspecting his genital organs she had developed a pronounced envy of the penis, and the thoughts derived from this envy continued to fill her mind. She was in fact a feminist; she felt it

to be unjust that girls should not enjoy the same freedom as boys, and rebelled against the lot of woman in general.[2]

Elsewhere, in the "Taboo of Virginity," Freud writes: "Behind this envy for the penis, there comes to light woman's hostile bitterness against the man, which never completely disappears in the relations between the sexes, and which is clearly indicated in the strivings and the literary productions of 'emancipated' women."[3] From this perspective, therefore and on the other hand, current feminist analysis of the subject would be anything but silent on the topic of jealousy: On the contrary, jealousy speaks loudly there and nothing but jealousy. Yet, it is, of course, precisely the imposition of this perspective that has led many to conclude that what is going on in the psychoanalytic account is itself a jealous defense of the privilege accorded the phallus. Thus, when Freud affirms, for example, in the lecture "Femininity" that women are in general more jealous than men and the reason for this supplemental jealousy is the lack of a penis,[4] with the very performance of that assertion he can be understood as confirming the contrary: men are more jealous inasmuch as they impute to women an envy of the penis. And with this we circle back to the feminist theoretical position already described: man is constitutively jealous (of the phallic privilege and its privileged relation to his own penis) whereas a woman's jealousy is secondary, derived, contingent, historically conditioned. Phallocentrism is structured by jealousy, whereas woman as such, considered before or beyond phallocentrism's rule, is herself before or beyond jealousy. And if feminism is the thinking of woman outside the jealous rule of phallo-centrism, then it is not jealous; rather it thinks (masculine) jealousy on the basis of a position without jealousy.[5]

Can this position or supposition be put in question without giving merely another instance of reversal within the pattern of reversal just outlined? This is what we are asking.

But first, we have invoked envy and jealousy as if they were the same or interchangeable. Classically, however, a distinction is drawn between them: One is said to be envious of that which one does not possess, but would like to possess, and jealous of that which one does possess and fears losing. Descartes, for example, in his *Passions de l'âme*, makes this distinction:

Jealousy is a species of fear that relates to the desire to remain in possession of some good [*quelque bien*]; and it does not arise so much from the strength of the reasons that lead one to judge it might be lost as from the great esteem in which it is held; that is why one examines the least causes for suspicion and takes them to be persuasive reasons.

Envy . . . is a species of sadness mixed with hatred that derives from our seeing something good happen to those whom we think do not deserve it; and this can only reasonably be said of goods of fortune since concerning those of the soul or even the body, inasmuch as they are endowed at birth, it is enough to deserve them that they are received from God before one was capable of committing any wrong.[6]

We could remark here that Freud inscribes sexual difference at least in part in this tradition of the distinction between jealousy and envy: Jealousy of what one has and fears losing would describe the boy's castration anxiety, whereas envy for what others have and one does not would describe the girl's penis envy. But this difference is also erased when, as already mentioned, Freud attributes the excess of a woman's jealousy (*Eifersucht*) to an envy (*Neid*) of what she never possessed.[7]

This tendency to subsume all these possible relations to some object—possession, dispossession, nonpossession, desire for possession—under a single heading, called indifferently jealousy or envy, has been justified by the French psychoanalyst Daniel Lagache in his monumental clinical study of amorous jealousy. He first notes the tradition we have just cited, quoting both a succinct formulation by d'Alembert—"One is jealous of what one possesses and envious of what others possess"—as well as one of La Rochefoucauld's many maxims concerning jealousy: "Jealousy is in a certain way just and reasonable since it tends only toward preserving something that belongs to us; whereas envy is a frenzy that cannot abide what belongs to others."[8] But Lagache then comments that these distinctions "are difficult to maintain."

Jealousy does not exclude envy, because I am jealous of that which I possess inasmuch as it can be desired and possessed by others; and the fear at least puts the jealous person *fictively* in the situation of the envious one; the jealous lover is jealous of his mistress and envious of the *real or fictive* success of his rival. Moreover, one is not jealous only of what one possesses, but also of what one desires, of the goods or beings over which desire has already cast the shadow of possession. Inversely, by envying others' possessions, one envisions them inasmuch as they can be desired and possessed by oneself, and it is precisely the impossibility of substituting oneself for others that makes envy intolerable. (ibid.; my emphasis)

Although Lagache does not proceed to draw the interference here, all these crossings between the two states called envy and jealousy would only be possible if there were no such thing as assured possession or property. Jealousy (or envy) defines a relation to that which one "possesses" in the mode of an always possible, always imminent, and therefore already effected dispossession. One never really possesses what one has. If it can be lost or stolen or expropriated, then to a degree it already has been, if only in a "fictive" projection onto a future rival. Likewise, one can be jealous rather than just envious of that which one only desires to possess, as if the shadow of possession cast by desire, in Lagache's phrase, were already its substantialization or realization. But this is to confirm that between this shadow and this substance, between the "fictional" possession and the "real" one, there is no effective difference: proper or "real" possession is a shadow figure always ready to fade away.[9]

It seems but a step from this insubstantial link that cannot guarantee proper possession (of something or someone else) to the loosening of the tie that binds the self to itself, in a relation of self-possession or "ownness." From the jealousy (or envy) that marks the relation to some-other-than-the-self, who or which can never be possessed or appropriated beyond the fictive projections of desire, one is led to evoke envy (or jealousy) as a mark within the self or the "own," a mark that accuses therefore a similar space of always possible "dis-ownment" in the very self that would appropriate others to itself. Both Descartes and Lagache, for example, recall the common usage in French (but the same use may be found in English) of the adjective jealous to denote a zealous defense of some abstract quality or attribute. One is said to be jealous of one's reputation, honor, good name, and so forth. "Thus, for example," writes Descartes, "a captain who holds a highly placed position has the right to be jealous of it, that is, to be on guard against any means by which it might be taken away [*surprise*]; and an honest woman is not blamed for being jealous of her honor, that is to say not only for guarding herself from any wrongdoing but also for avoiding even the least causes for gossip" (776). Lagache, for his part, goes to Corneille, La Fontaine, and Bossuet for occurrences similar to the examples given by Descartes (368–69). His citations evoke the zeal with which certain predicates or attributes—honor and freedom—are defended as one defends one's very life by the person who claims them as his or her own. What both these examples recall is a jealous relation of the self to itself, that by means of which it guards itself intact, keeps its own possession of itself but in the mode of an always possible dispossession. "An always possible dispossession": in other words, an irreducible expropriability at the heart of this strange relation to self in which one may be jealous of oneself.

Because Descartes also distinguishes a morally righteous (or as he says "honnête") jealousy from a wrongful one, he may once again be seen as relaying Freud in a long tradition. Freud too speaks of a normal, as distinct from a pathological jealousy. "Jealousy," he writes, "is one of those affective states that may be described as normal. If anyone appears to be without it, the inference is justified that it has undergone severe repression and consequently plays all the greater part in his unconscious mental life. . . . It is easy to see that essentially [normal jealousy] is compounded of grief, the pain caused by the thought of losing the loved object, and of the narcissistic wound, *in so far as this is distinguishable from the other wound.*"[10] The wound that occasions normal jealousy may not be distinguishable from the narcissistic wound. This suggestion, planted at the beginning of an essay on jealousy, paranoia, and homosexuality, is not followed up. If it were, would we find that "normal" jealousy is rooted in the narcissism one has always, already, had to give up, the narcissism one only enjoys in the mode of its loss? And then would one not have to speak of a primary jealousy, alongside and indissociable from the structure of that primary narcissism Freud so tentatively outlined? Following up this suggestion, therefore, would have to take us back to the essay "On Narcissism" that Sarah Kofman has re-read so persuasively as a short ceasefire within Freud's prolonged war against the feminine, a kind of cameo appearance put in by the Nietzschean affirmative woman that briefly upstages those three caskets in which Freud reads only death behind each of woman's guises.[11] The question that might be asked is whether the affirmative figure discerned by Kofman is also supposed to be exempt from jealousy or whether this affirmation must be understood altogether differently, as a movement that at once both inscribes jealousy and displaces it—an affirmation, therefore, of self-love *as* other- or object-love that suspends their opposition and retraces their boundaries.[12] Is such a configuration even possible?

This latter question is essentially a reformulation of the one we posed above: Can the position or supposition of a feminine subject beyond a constitutive jealousy—the project of feminist theories of the subject—be put in question without giving thereby merely another instance of reversal within a pattern of reversal? This question is certainly not new: It has defined for some time now the principal stakes of the often fraught relation between Derridean deconstruction and these same feminist theories of the subject. To put it in deceptively simple terms: what has been so long at stake is the very category or analytical term of *subject,* which deconstruction seems so effectively to do without and which feminist theory is largely concerned with preserving *in a certain form.* The latter qualification is central to feminist subjectivist analysis, since it is a contestation of the *generality* of the structure of subjectivity that that analysis undertakes to effect. As a general structure, the subject—whether described in terms of the Cartesian *cogito,* the subject of phenomenology, the Foucauldian subject of power, or the grammatical subject of structural linguistics[13]—can be made to display the more or less violent effacement of difference(s) whereby it lays claim to that very generality. This generality, it is argued, is therefore but a masked particularity; in particular it masks the effacement of the difference that is the feminine. Rather than give up altogether on the generalizing category of "subject," however, much feminist thought has sought to preserve it, albeit in a relativized, particularized, or differentiated form. Hence, the tendency to speak of a feminine subject, a masculine subject, a colonized and a colonizing subject, etc.[14] This kind of particularization, in other words, points to the general failure of the general subject to attain the generality of its concept except as an ideal or ideality. In its material inscription, which is to say wherever a body "lends" its singular articulation to the featureless, mute, pure idea of the "I," the general concept falls back into particularity or specificity.

Feminist subjectivism has been very effective in pointing out the repeated failure of the general subject to inscribe itself beyond the specificity of its material inscription. At the same time, nevertheless, it has argued to preserve the category of subject, understood now as a *limited* generality. One might see in this double gesture a kind of compromise formation: on the one hand, there is recognition of the general structure or ideality of the subject, which necessarily fails to materialize itself; on the other hand, there is a certain disavowal of that recognition, as if the necessary failure could all the same be overcome. This makes it sound like a version of fetishism, the fetishism of the subject who, in saying "I," believes it is fully itself, not "castrated," despite what it knows. It is here that the stakes of a deconstruction of the fetishistic subject become apparent. To return to the terms we elaborated above, what is put in question by this deconstruction is the subject as beyond- or without-jealousy, a subject that can fully appropriate or possess itself. Deconstruction remarks a certain irreducible and constitutive nonreturn of the subject to itself,[15] an ineradicable force of difference—exteriority, materiality, otherness—within the very relation and the jealous zeal with which the same allies with itself, affects and effects itself in a *movement* of appropriation that is never simply given in the present but must be performed, posed, invented, or traced. Jealousy, then, would be the movement of the same back to itself, a movement ceaselessly driven by the mark of noncoincidence, of impossible appropriation. "They're jealous for they're jealous": the monster of self-begetting returns to a same that is not the same as itself, but already is jealous of a nonappropriable marking or spacing that sends the movement off again.

Before considering what it might mean specifically for feminism to affirm (rather than disavow) the inappropriability of its own subject, one needs to say something more about the latter. This because it is too often assumed, not only by feminist subjectivists but by many others as well, that the deconstruction of the subject is not based on much more than a kind of willful play for power within the discursive field loosely called "theory." Rather than get mired in such a projection, however, we can look briefly at an early text in which Derrida most clearly lays out the conditions in which and by which the signifying subject says—or writes—"I."[16]

La Voix et le phénomène, one of the inaugural texts of deconstruction, is a reading of Husserl's phenomenological description of language in the first of his *Logical Investigations*.[17] It opens with an epigraph from that text: "When we read this word 'I' without knowing who wrote it, it is perhaps not meaningless, but is at least estranged from its normal meaning." Derrida's reading of Husserl's theory of the sign will in large measure be oriented by this statement, or rather against it, since, as he writes when he comes to quote the statement again toward the end of his reading, "Husserl's premises should authorize us to say exactly the contrary" (107; 96). That is, an anonymous written "I" is not at all "estranged from its normal meaning"; on the contrary, the condition of anonymity or estrangement is the very soul, so to speak, of the normal meaning of "I" whenever it is spoken or written. Indeed, it is only on the condition of this estrangement that "I" can ever have any meaning whatsoever. How can that be?

It has to do first of all with the structure of the linguistic sign as repetition:

> A sign is never an event, if by event we mean an irreplaceable and irreversible empirical unicity. A sign which would take place but "once" would not be a sign; a purely idiomatic sign would not be a sign. A signifier (in general) must be recognizable in its form in spite of and through the diversity of empirical characteristics which may modify it. It must remain the *same*, and be repeatable as such despite and across the distortions that what is called the empirical event necessarily makes it undergo. . . . [I]t can function as a sign, and in general as language, only if a formal identity enables it to be issued again and recognized again. This identity is necessarily ideal. (55–56; 50).

"Identity" here means self-identity, identity to and with itself, the nondifference and immediacy of the sign as both formal characteristic (signifier) and meaning (signified). As such, this identity is "necessarily ideal" because no single occurrence, no empirical particular achieves it—only repeats it. By ideality, however, one must understand that which has no existence either in this or some other "metaphysical" world; rather, it is "but the name for the permanence of the same and the possibility of its repetition." The ideality (of the identity of the sign) is but the possibility of the repetition of the same, that is, it "depends entirely on the possibility of acts of repetition. It is constituted by that possibility" (58; 52). This amounts to effecting a reversal of the conventional, metaphysical derivation of the sign as re-presentation of an original presence: as pure ideality, that presence derives from the possibility of repetition and not the reverse. Or rather, as Derrida will put it later, idealization, repetition, and signification "are thinkable, in their pure possibility, only on the basis of one and the same opening"

(104; 93). There is, however, a fourth term in this series of possibilities: death. What is opened up, with language and repetition and idealization, is a relation to death, and specifically to "my" death, the death of the one who says "I." How so?

The sense of any discourse depends on the possibility of a repetition of the same, on the movement, therefore, of an idealization that can traverse all the variants of empirical existence, contingency, factuality, and so forth. This sense does not depend on any actual presence; indeed, the condition of discourse is that it be intelligible *in the absence* of its object. The notion that meaning does not essentially imply the intuition or perception of the object of discourse is worked out by Husserl and illustrated by Derrida as follows:

> I say, "I see a particular person through the window" while I really do see him. It is structurally implied in my performance that the content of this expression is ideal and that its unity is not impaired by the absence of perception *hic et nunc*. Whoever hears this proposition, whether he is next to me or infinitely removed in time or space, should, by right, understand what I mean to say. Since this possibility is the possibility of discourse, it must structure the very act of him who speaks while perceiving. My nonperception, my nonintuition, my absence *hic et nunc* are said by that very thing that I say, by *that* which I say and *because* I say it. . . . The absence of intuition—and therefore of the subject of the intuition—is not only *tolerated* by speech; it is *required* by the general structure of signification, when considered *in itself*. It is radically requisite: the total absence of the subject and object of a statement—the death of the writer and/or disappearance of the objects he may have described—does not prevent a text from "meaning-to-say." On the contrary, this possibility gives birth to the meaning-to-say as such, gives it be heard and read. (103–4; 92–93)

Up to this point, Derrida has been drawing out to their radical conclusions Husserl's analyses. But with the next step, this radicalization overturns an important and very symptomatic limit that Husserl attempts to place on the possible absence from intuition of the elements of discourse. That limit is the first person pronoun. When "spoken" by the self to itself and referring to itself—in solitary speech or internal monologue—Husserl affirms that "the meaning of 'I' is essentially realized in the immediate idea of one's own personality" (106; 95). In other words, there is at least one situation in which the object of discourse is *never* absent from the intuition of the speaker/listener: when the "I" says "I" to itself. The meaning of that speech act is "essentially realized" by the speaker in an "immediate idea of [his/her] own personality." When I say "I" to myself, not only do I know immediately what I mean, but I know the "object" of my meaning to be present in the moment I speak. It is this immediacy of self-presence that Derrida puts in question in the same terms used above for the person seen through the window. This move has as its consequence the uncovering of the essential relation to "my own death" inscribed in the very possibility of discourse. "I," like any other sign, can have meaning only if it "remains *the same* for an I-here-now in general, keeping its sense even if my empirical presence is eliminated or radically modified" (ibid.). Radicalizing from there, Derrida will affirm that if the "I" must be able to function with the same meaning in my absence, then that absence—my death—is structurally inscribed in the possibility of its repetition, the ideality of its meaning.

> My death is structurally necessary to the pronouncing of the *I*. That I am also "alive" and certain of being alive comes over and above the meaning-to-say. And this structure is operative, it retains its original efficiency even when I say "I am alive" at the very moment when, if such a thing is possible, I have a full and current intuition of it. . . . The statement "I am alive" is accompanied by my being-dead, and its possibility requires the possibility that I be dead; and conversely. This is not an extraordinary tale by Poe but the ordinary story of language. (108; 96–97)

"My death is structurally necessary to the pronouncing of the *I*." This statement not only propounds a rule, it also performs under the imposition of that rule: the phrase "my death" has to have *the same* meaning in the absence of whoever first pronounced it and whoever may subsequently quote it (as we are doing here) or otherwise repeat it. "My death," therefore, does not say *my* death or absence because it says the (necessary) absence of any empirical singularity, my own or anyone else's. Thus, without naming my death and only mine, and precisely because it does not do so, it also enacts my disappearance; that is, the disappearance of the singular, finite instance of its pronouncing. And it does so through the very figure of my finitude, which here assumes the general aspect of "my death." My death, as mine, is structurally absent from "my death" and therefore it is signified as the limit on which I can signify anything whatsoever. That limit inscribes the finitude of meaning as appropriated by any act of signification, the limit, in other words, whereby nothing finally can be signified as mine and only mine, not even or especially not "my death."[18]

Deconstructive thought largely proceeds from this de-propriating force of repetition that is the ground of possibility of meaning. This ground of possibility may also therefore be described as a certain impossibility: the impossibility of a subject that has fully appropriated its own meaning, its own being, in a state—however momentary—of self-presence. Now, too often this latter, critical thrust of deconstruction is mistaken as its principal or even sole "insight"; that is, it is understood as merely a critique of the grounds of meaning and the subject of meaning. This is the version of "deconstructionism" that has been widely consecrated by a certain journalism and has served all sorts of dubious ends, including for some supposedly nonjournalist academics. What this version cannot reckon with, however, is an *affirmative* deconstruction for which the critique of presence does not exhaust the resources of thought. On the contrary, for deconstruction the impossibility of a fully self-present meaning is that which opens the possibility of any relation to meaning, indeed of any relation whatsoever to and within difference(s). The impossible reappropriation of the self to itself, the irreducible difference or gap within the relation-to-self is what calls for affirmation and not merely recognition or confirmation. It is not enough, in other words, to offer a critique that demonstrates this impossibility or that negates the possibility of the full presence of the self or the subject. It is not enough because it confirms and leaves intact the valence of negativity that has always attached itself to the inevitable failure of the self to master or appropriate its own meaning, to have the last word, so to speak. Deconstructive practice, on the other hand, affirms the necessary dispersion through repetition of the "I" as the chance and the possibility, not just the negation, of a signifying act or an inscription that, without belonging to or being appropriable by any identity, would nevertheless be marked as *singular* or *idiomatic*.

In an interview published in 1983, Derrida put it this way when prompted by a question about the anxiety aroused by the undecidability of meaning:

> When one writes, one is always trying to outsmart the worst. Perhaps so as to prevent it from taking everything away, but the last word, you know, always belongs to non-mastery, for both the reader and oneself. And it's good that this is the way it is. The living desire to write keeps you in relation to a terror that you try to maneuver with even as you leave it intact, audible in that place where you may find yourself, hear or understand yourself, you and whoever reads you, beyond any partition, thus at once saved and lost.[19]

One could be tempted to see in this brief passage a somewhat off-guard characterization of three essential elements of Derrida's deconstructive practice portrayed in the aspect of its desiring motivation. The affirmation "And it's good that this is the way it is [Et c'est bien ainsi]" follows on the constatation of ultimate nonmastery (finitude as necessary limit) and ushers in a possibility: a writing or practice of inscription where perhaps "you may find yourself, hear or understand yourself, you and whoever reads you, beyond any partition, thus at once saved and lost." The impossibility of appropriation is affirmed, which overturns a hierarchical opposition between mastery and nonmastery, self and other, but the desire that had maintained that hierarchy is not thereby negated or denied as desire (there is perhaps no more futile exercise than to attempt to destroy the narcissistic desire in question); rather, it is displaced as the possibility of another *entente*, that of the other, precisely, and of oneself as other. The possibility of being "beyond any partition, thus at once saved and lost," is not a possibility for the self, which is but a figure of its own impossible appropriation, but for an idiomatic singularity, which in the same interview Derrida glosses as follows:

> A property that one cannot appropriate; it signs you without belonging to you; it only appears to the other and it never comes back to you except in flashes of madness that bring together life and death, that bring you together dead and alive at the same time. You dream, it's unavoidable, about the invention of a language or of a song that would be yours, not the attributes of a "self," rather the accentuated paraph, that is, the musical signa-

ture, of your most unreadable history. I'm not talking about a *style* but an intersection of singularities, habitat, voices, graphism, what moves with you and what your body never leaves. (119)

This dreamed-of, desired inscription of a singularity, "beyond any partition," would save from ultimate erasure a nonrepeatable idiom, but only by losing it for any "self" since "it appears only to the other." Nevertheless, it is as an almost unhoped-for chance that this "loss" is solicited from the other, infinitely desired.

We began by asking what it might mean for feminism to affirm the inappropriable subject. One thing is already clear: it could not mean a simple evacuation or negation of the "I" as instance of the inscription of difference. Rather than that of the subject, however, this instance would be that of a singular force of insistence, a singularity. Singularity is not the subject, which, as we have seen, is but the possibility of a repetition. The singular is not repeatable *as such,* but is precisely the impossible presentation of an "as such." The singular remains in excess of—before or beyond—representation, the difference between the subject and an unpresentable *I.* The latter is finite, determined by the singular events of birth and death, whereas the former is infinitely or indefinitely repeatable, having no origin nor end other than in that repetition.[20] The notion of the singular cannot, by definition, be accommodated by any generality, be it the sort of limited generality we discussed above. Instead, it has to lead us to consider the possibility, the desirability of *something like* autobiography.

That resemblance must immediately be qualified so as not to blur a number of important distinctions that set a recognizable and consecrated *genre* of writing, such as autobiography, apart from that "invention of a language" that Derrida evokes in the passage just cited ("You dream, it's unavoidable, about the invention of a language or of a song that would be yours, not the attributes of a 'self' "). Beginning with the distinction of genre (or gender): the idiomatic singularity in question cannot in any simple sense *belong* to a generality without disappearing altogether, leaving no trace. For it to appear at all (always only to the other), it must remain unrepeatable, ungeneralizable, without genre or gender. At the same time, however, and just as necessarily, for it to appear at all, for it to have even the chance of the other's arrival, it must unfold out of its silence and its secret; that is, it must also be repeatable. Thus, if it is saved in its absolute singularity, then it can never appear before the "last word" of finitude; on the other hand, saved from "my death" through repetition, it is lost as singular idiom. Now, this double bind structure may be ineluctable, but, in theory at least, there are no limits on the forms of negotiations with its constraints—what Derrida calls above "trying to outsmart the worst."

Which brings up the second reason one should hesitate to invoke the category of autobiography. It is not at all certain that the most "successful" negotiations result in a manifestly "autobiographical" text, according to conventional criteria, nor even, of course, in what we commonly think of as a written text. Practices of the most diverse, infinitely varied kinds, from the moment they appear to the other, including, indeed especially, the most inadvertent gestures, the unreflected corporality and materiality of a life (that which is the always singular domain of love and jealousy)—all may bear traces of the inappropriable signature, singularity saved and lost, repeated in its unrepeatability.

Finally, however, it is perhaps the "auto" of autobiography that most dissimulates what is at stake in this inscription of singular differences. The "auto" would refer the "-graphy" back to a single life, "bio," and thereby close it up in a circle of self-reference. Not only does this model suggest a closed relation-to-self and therefore an appropriation in place of what "appears only to the other," but in so doing it also leaves wholly unaccounted for the paradoxical problematic we have been describing: that of repetition of the unrepeatable in a general language. It is this problematic, by contrast, that is brought out, consistently and insistently, in deconstruction. More precisely, deconstruction "happens" because of the necessarily unfinished and interminable articulation of singularity with the structures of repetition of the same. Which is to say that singular differences (material, corporal, historical, linguistic, sexual, and so forth; the list is, by definition, without end), to the extent they do not disappear without a trace, reserve the possibility for these structures to transform themselves, to deconstruct. Deconstructive thought, and most singularly the work of Jacques Derrida, attempts to formalize *to a certain extent* this possibility held in reserve by the greatest formalizing tradition in the West, the philosophical tradition; it bears down on those places where, precisely, that tradition cannot formalize itself completely or entirely, therefore where it must open itself not only to other traditions or genres (the literary or the autobiographical, for example), but to that which as yet has no tradition, no convention, and no recognizable form: to the force of something other, to the other-than-the-same, to the possibility of invention or the invention of the possible.[21]

"Feminism" and "deconstruction": two terms that designate sites of theoretico-practical intervention. When these terms have been taken up in recent and ongoing "theory wars" in the university, a certain trivial-ization has worked to prevent an understanding of what is at stake between them. Those stakes are said to be political. And indeed they are: the stakes are political because it is the very sense of the political that is at stake. A deconstruction of subjectivisms (including feminist subjectivism) has necessarily to entail a *different* sense of the political, one that does not project the eventual realization of a fully present (appropriated) subject that would be at the same time fully representa-tive, one that is not itself shaped and determined by the version of the subject as self-presence. To put it in the terms we have been using here, subject politics (or "identity politics") is a politics of envy or jealousy; that is, of an appropriating movement driven by the inappropriable finitude of the one who says "I" and "I, we." In its dialectical version, the politics of the subject (which may be a class or a gender) theorizes the political *as* appropriation, as the legitimation/delegitimation of appropriated power. Now, the question we are asking is, What other sense of the "political," beyond or outside this dialectics of appropria-tion, becomes thinkable once the deconstructibility of its subject is no longer disavowed, but affirmed?

To suggest at least a direction from which a response to that question might come, let us reconsider one of the best-known watchwords of American feminist political thought in the last decades: "the personal is the political." This categorical statement has, in its most general interpretation, been understood to negate the self-evidence of the division between public and private spheres as concerns women (and therefore men). Implicitly or by extension, it accuses the numerous ways in which that putative self-evidence has been used to justify or overlook everything from violence in the "privacy" of the home to the exclusion of women qua women from the institutions of public life. The act of renaming it performs asserts that there is no "personal" that is not already invested by the "political," that is, by the interests of a power structure that seeks always to perpetuate or legitimate itself even in what are thought to be the most remote or hidden corners of the social fabric. (This thesis is not just that of modern feminism, of course, but one that has characterized revolutionary political thought for at least two centuries.)[22] Now, at the same time as the argument summed up in the watchword has been mobilized in a delegitimizing analysis of patriarchy's division of public domain from private space, it has also been working to legitimate the public or political (in the widest sense) role of women throughout society's institutions. Conversely, and in a consistent application of the "personal-is-political" logic, it has sought political, public recognition and protection of a whole range of concerns formerly relegated to the private domain: child care, family leave, spousal abuse, sexual harassment, and so forth. To a large extent, then, feminist contestation of the social order has undertaken a general *extension* of the public sphere, or rather a recognition and reevaluation of the extension that has effectively been in place for a long time but has been dissimulated beneath the cover of the "personal" or the "private."

There are, nevertheless, significant points at which this contestation takes the opposite form, that is, where it consists in redrawing the limit on this extension of the public domain and in refuting the equation of personal with political against the claims of the state. At those points, the feminist political position stakes out a "personal" space that it would keep free from public purview or regulation. As the increasingly violent confrontation over abortion-on-demand in the United States indicates, however, achieving a *general* consensus to *limit* the extension of the general interest is, as a political aim, a far more divided and divisive matter than achieving a general recognition of women as political subjects. This may suggest that, wherever feminism understands its political task in terms of the public, general subject or in terms of the appropriation of that subjectivity by women, then it will advance that aim fundamentally in accord, in alliance, or in complicity with the interests of a sociopolitical order to bring every domain within its purview. Needless to say, if such interests go everywhere unchecked, if the "personal" is everywhere and always the "political" without remainder, then one has entered the dream or nightmare of the totalitarian state. This is not at all to say that some contrary, and ultimately contradictory, politics of the "personal" can be elaborated in terms that will enforce an effective limit on the totalization of the public domain.[23] It is precisely this notion of "effective limit" that is in question.

What both the "public" and the "personal" versions of subjectivist politics discount is the very divisibility of the division dividing one from the other, a divisibility that limits the limiting function of that limit by, precisely, dividing and redividing it. Once again, the confrontation over abortion-on-demand poses significantly the condition of this dividing limit between "personal" and "political." The limit in question does not fall in this case at the apparent boundaries of a "personal" body or individual life and therefore within the recognized right to personal liberty, but along the uncertain line of division between one body and another, or between a present life and a future one, or finally between a woman and her body/her life, which is at once both hers and not hers, both present and the bearer of a future, another's future, the future as other. This uncertain limit, by definition highly divisible and unstable, cannot therefore reliably set off the political from the personal; it cannot fix the point at which the freedom of individual choice and the right to be free from political constraint is posed unconditionally. It is rather as the inappropriable space of the *other in the one* that this divisible limit becomes the terrain of a struggle for appropriation between the public instance of a plural "we" and the private, singular instance of an "I."

This struggle for appropriation, which has for so long defined the stakes of the political for revolutionary movements on the Right and the Left, movements of liberation as well as nationalist movements, is everywhere driven by the condition of a fundamental inappropriability, what we have here attempted to illustrate with the divisibility of the limit between "personal" and "political." Wherever it is drawn, the limit supposed to separate a personal "I" from a political "we" would be little more than a grammatical or legal fiction, one which the law institutes and to which it refers by way of repetition. The "I" is already a repetition, more than one, always one plus the endless possibility of other ones. That is the condition (the law) of saying "I" and therefore the initial constraint on the freedom or the privacy of the one who says it. From the moment the law of repetition or pluralization is also the condition of "personalization," then one must recognize that, indeed, "the personal is the political." With this recognition or repetition, however, the accent or tone marking that assertion will have itself become divided so as to admit another possible inflection. For in addition to a rallying cry for political mobilization, cannot that phrase now be heard to echo also as an infinite *complaint* that whenever I say or think or otherwise signify "I," a crowd assembles and I am mistaken for everybody else, hence for nobody? And with that I am expropriated of "myself," "my life," "my person," "my personal life," all of which remain only the most approximate, conventional designators for a singular experience without appropriate name, an experience, therefore, inappropriated by any subject? And isn't this complaint itself made to disappear when it is formulated anonymously and in terms of the greatest generality (not my life, in its most secret intimacy, a secret preserved finally even from me who cannot know it as my own, but the so-called personal in general is the political, that is, everybody's person, every body, and therefore no body's, neither mine nor yours)? Can one hear, then, the phrase as the residue of a jealous movement in the face of the effacement of the "personal"'s property, its proper appropriation of itself? Yes. Yes? Yes.

Yes, not once but twice because it is a matter here of a double affirmation, an affirmation that repeats and that affirms the repetition. Deconstruction follows the path of this double affirmation; it affirms (itself as) repetition.[24] Yes, it says first of all, to the echo or residue, to the *tone* that speaks of and from the place of a singular articulation with the general law, therefore to the repetition of the unrepeatable. This "yes" says: "I hear, come again, again and again. The trace of your voice, its tone (its *ton*, its 'yours,' that is, that by which it belongs to you in this strange mode of not-belonging) is held in my ear and in our tongue, the one we share between us." To the inaccessible, impossible pure tone, to undivided singularity, this "yes" opens a channel, so to speak, allowing a kind of passage at the limit between I/we, a passage, therefore, into repetition, division, plurality; but that passage at the same time carries over an echo or a trace of an inappropriable difference. The difference is inscribed at the limit; it is the difference, or differance, *of* that limit—its division—that holds I-we apart together and thus opens each to the other. The first yes, therefore, is already a repetition, already more than one, already a second yes. And with that it affirms repetition not as the loss of singular truth, but as the chance, the only chance, given by necessity—which is to say by the other—to impossible singularity. It is the chance of difference, and thereby the possibility of transformation of what we mean when we say "we," what we mean by the plural, the public, the political. And not just what we mean, but the transformation of the relation to the other as wholly other, unrepresentable therefore, and finally without resemblance to any political "subject." If this transformation could have a horizon, it would be the singular justice of a "politics" of singularity. By definition, however, no such horizon can be drawn that would limit the transformation, which must remain open to what comes and is coming from the other.

In the meantime, the personal *is* . . . in other words (and in the words of the other), it opens up, divides, differentiates, pluralizes, transforms, deconstructs . . . the political. But also vice versa. And yes, it is good that that's the way it is.

If, then, we cannot conclude as to what it will mean for feminism to affirm the inappropriability of its subject,[25] it is because any answer to that question will have to come from places that are unheard-of or not yet heard from, which include vast regions of a past that are still before us, that still have a future. At a guess, one might predict that these unheard-of places will not appear, at first, unfamiliar, but will signal themselves with the most common of names, such as jealousy, love, bliss, pain, death, mine, yours, each time different, each time to be repeated . . .

Notes

1. For an overview of the debate, see Juliet Mitchell's introduction to *Feminine Sexuality: Jacques Lacan and the école freudienne*, ed. Mitchell and Jacqueline Rose (New York: Norton, 1982), 13–24.

2. *The Standard Edition*, ed. James Strachey (London: Hogarth, 1953–74), 18:169; quoted in Kofman, *The Enigma of Woman: Woman in Freud's Writings*, trans. Catherine Porter (Ithaca: Cornell University Press, 1985), 177 n. 19.

3. *Standard Edition*, 11:205.

4. *Standard Edition*, 22:125.

5. I have discussed at greater length the (theological) implications of this position "without-jealousy" in another essay on Derrida, "Reading Between the Blinds," which is the introduction to *A Derrida Reader* (New York: Columbia University Press, 1991), see esp. xxxi–xxxv.

6. *Oeuvres et Lettres* (Paris: Pléïade, 1953), 776, 781–82; my translation.

7. Melanie Klein takes over the classical distinction in her differentiation of envy from jealousy when she adapts these terms to her developmental model. As one of her commentators explains: "Melanie Klein, in *Envy and Gratitude*, makes a proper distinction between the emotions of envy and jealousy. She considers envy to be the earlier of the two, and shows that envy is one of the most primitive and fundamental emotions. Early envy has to be differentiated from jealousy and greed. Jealousy is based on love and aims at the possession of the loved object and the removal of the rival. It pertains to a triangular relationship and therefore to a time of life when objects are clearly recognized and differentiated from one another. Envy, on the other hand, is a two-part relation in which the subject envies the object for some possession or quality; no other live object need enter into it"; see Hanna Segal, *Introduction to the Work of Melanie Klein* (London: Hogarth, 1973), 40.

8. *La jalousie amoureuse*, 3d ed. (Paris: PUF, 1985), 371; my translation.

9. For a helpful survey of the distinction envy-jealousy, see Rosemary Lloyd, *Closer and Closer Apart: Jealousy in Literature* (Ithaca: Cornell University Press, 1995), 2–5.

10. "Certain Neurotic Mechanisms in Jealousy, Paranoia and Homosexuality," *Standard Edition*, 18:223; my emphasis.

11. See Kofman, *Enigma of Woman*, 50–65.

12. In her review article of *The Enigma of Woman*, "The Third Woman" (*Diacritics* [Summer 1982]), Elizabeth Berg has argued that just such a displacement is effected by the third woman in Kofman's reading, the woman who is neither hysteric nor narcissistic. "In her refusal to recognize sexual difference—in refusing castration—she has moved beyond the economy of truth to affirm, simultaneously or in turn, both her masculinity and her femininity. . . . Like the fetishist, who posits the possibility of the phallic mother, the affirmative woman affirms her femininity while refusing to be castrated" (19). The question might still be asked whether an affirmation of the "phallic woman" (Berg writes, "The phallic mother—or the phallic woman—is not a fantasm to be dismissed, or simply the product of the child's imagination; she is the reality of woman who is beyond the 'truth' of castration," ibid.) must not also be displaced—actively, strategically—by, for example, the "generalized fetishism" Derrida works out in *Glas* and Kofman takes up again in "Ça cloche" (*Lectures de Derrida* [Paris: Galilée, 1984]).

13. The tendency to collapse historically and conceptually different notions of the "subject" has contributed to a certain confusion about what we are even talking about. In a recent attempt to sort out this confusion, Jean-Luc Nancy has described debates about the "subject" as "most often false debates of opinion rather than serious debates of concepts around the subject: debates of the type 'death of the subject—return of the subject,' in which the subject becomes a kind of strange little clown that can leave and come back; or else debates of the 'ontology versus subjectivity' kind; and of course debates in which, without any precautions, people jumble up together what is meant by the subject in philosophy, what is meant by the subject in psychology, and what is meant by the subject in psychoanalysis. These are debates that, in large measure, owe their existence, and often their foolishness, to the confusion among meanings or to the absence of clear and distinct meanings"; "Un sujet?" in *Homme et sujet* (Paris: Harmattan, 1992), 49–50; my translation.

14. See Judith Butler, *Gender Trouble*, on this exasperated "etc." that so often concludes the list of predicates elaborated by what she calls "theories of feminist identities" ([New York: Routledge, 1989], 143). See as well Butler's fine analysis of the "subject" of feminism. Given the overall direction of this analysis, one might wonder about her retaining the category of identity for a politics even as she forcefully critiques what is called identity politics in general. The reconceptualizing of identity as an "effect," rather than a constitutive ground, cannot rule out that embracing such an effect will entail the very consequences one wishes to avoid. What she describes as the "critical task," which is "to locate strategies of subversive repetition enabled by [the constructions of identity]," coming as it does at the end of the book, may sound an upbeat note in part because it has forgotten the warning issued at the beginning of the same book: "strategies always have meanings that exceed the purposes for which they are intended" (4).

15. In Derrida's idiom, this figure of nonreturn also clearly says nonappropriation. That which "ne revient pas" to someone—does not come back or return to—is out of his or her purview, it does not belong to him or her. The expression also has the sense, as it does in English, of not recurring to memory, as in "it isn't coming back to me," that is, I can't remember it. With this latter sense, there is an opening onto the unconscious as the uncanny site of expropriation within the ego. One of Derrida's most important texts on this figure of nonreturn is "Le facteur de la vérité" in which Lacan's notion of the phallus as transcendental signifier is deconstructed as that to which all signification would return as to its final destination.

16. Samuel Weber has argued persuasively that one should take account of a shift in

Derrida's writing after the early texts of the 1960s and 1970s. He characterizes this shift as one that moves deconstructive thinking from a putative and always finally "fictional" position external to the discourses it examines, to a quasi-narrative position within the limits of the deconstructible. For Weber, the latter position or strategy, which is exemplified by texts like "Envois" and "To Speculate—on 'Freud'" in *The Post Card*, is the more effective or powerful one; see Weber, "Reading and Writing *chez* Derrida", in *Institution and Interpretation* (Minneapolis: University of Minnesota Press, 1987). Without contesting that evaluation, I have chosen to "go back" to an early text so as to isolate a particular theorem that will remain in force in everything Derrida will later write; see note 18.

17. Paris: Presses Universitaires de France, 1967; trans. David B. Allison as *Speech and Phenomena* (Evanston: Northwestern University Press, 1973). Page references will be given in the text to both the French and English editions; the translation will on occasion be modified.

18. In one of his most recent texts, Derrida has reiterated what he there calls this "aporia" of "my death":

> Is my death possible? Can we understand this question? Can I, myself, pose it? Am I allowed to talk about my death? What does the syntagm "my death" mean? . . . "My death" in quotation marks is not necessarily mine; it is an expression that anyone can appropriate; it can circulate from one example to another. . . . If death . . . names the very irreplaceability of absolute singularity (no one can die in my place or in the place of the other), then all the *examples* in the world can precisely illustrate this singularity. Everyone's death, the death of all those who can say "my death" is irreplaceable. . . . Whence comes a first exemplary complication of exemplarity: nothing is more substitutable and yet nothing is less so than the syntagm "my death." (*Aporias: Dying—Waiting (for One Another) at the "Limits of Truth,"* trans. Thomas Dutoit [Stanford: Stanford University Press, 1993], 22–23)

19. "Unsealing ("the old new language")," trans. Peggy Kamuf, in Derrida, *Points . . . Interviews, 1974–1994*, ed. Elisabeth Weber (Stanford: Stanford University Press, 1995), 118.

20. Nor should we confuse this finite, excessive singularity with the concept of the "individual," which, as Jean-Luc Nancy writes, misses singularity through a certain process of formalization:

> However the *singular being*, which is not the individual, is the finite being. What the thematic of individuation lacked, as it passed from a certain Romanticism to Schopenhauer and to Nietzsche, was a consideration of singularity, to which it nonetheless came quite close. Individuation detaches closed off entities from a formless ground. . . . But singularity does not proceed from such a detaching of clear forms or figures (nor from what is linked to this operation: the scene of form and ground, appearing [*l'apparaître*] linked to appearance [*l'apparence*] and the slippage of appearance into the aestheticizing nihilism in which individualism always culminates). Singularity perhaps does not *proceed* from anything. It is not a work resulting from an operation. There is no process of "singularization," and singularity is neither extracted, nor produced, nor derived (*The Inoperative Community*, trans. Peter Connor et al. [Minneapolis: University of Minnesota Press, 1991], 27)

21. This notion, "the invention of the possible," is one that Derrida has analyzed at length in a text that can provide a model of the formalizing strategies of deconstructive thought: "Psyche: Invention of the Other," trans. Catherine Porter and Philip Lewis, in *Reading de Man Reading*, ed. Wlad Godzich and Lindsay Waters (Minneapolis: University of Minnesota Press, 1989). Here Derrida works out the paradoxical logic of invention; that is, a logic that cannot be totally formalized without excluding the possibility of the very thing in question: invention. If, according to "common sense," an invention must transgress everything that

existing institutions envision as possible, then the invention of the merely possible is not an invention; the only possible invention would be the invention of the impossible, which is not possible. And yet the impossible invention is the only invention possible. In the face of this suspension of decidable grammar, the problematic of invention calls for a deconstruction of the figuration of a homogeneous space that cannot accommodate these absolutely contradictory affirmations. As a result, the concept of invention must open up to another movement which is no longer simply that of pure transgression and of its reception or its nonreception. The limit between these two moments or these two places of invention is displaced and, in displacing itself, divides or repeats. Invention begins by repeating itself and that is why it is impossible. But it is on the basis of this impossibility that the nonpresentable, nonrepresentable other would be traced.

22. Thus it would not be altogether anachronistic or simply facetious to say that Marie-Antoinette, for example, was tried and executed on the strength of the argument: the personal is the political; see Chantal Thomas, *La Reine scélérate: Marie-Antoinette dans les pamphlets* (Paris: Editions du Seuil, 1989).

23. Such a politics would always risk resembling liberal anti-regulationist policies that favor the free market and individual enterprise. It would, in other words, maintain an ambiguous alliance with the individualism and liberalism of traditional American ideology that produces the dissimulation of the "political" as the "personal" in the first place.

24. On this structure of the "yes" as an original repetition, see especially Derrida, "A Number of Yes," trans. Brian Holmes, in *Qui Parle* 2, no. 2 (Fall 1988) and "Ulysses Gramophone: Hear say yes in Joyce," trans. Tina Kendall and Shari Benstock, in *James Joyce: The Augmented Ninth*, ed. Bernard Benstock (Syracuse: Syracuse University Press, 1988).

25. The affirmation would concern the *subject* of feminism in another sense, as in what feminism is *about*. We are saying, then, nothing more, nothing less than this: feminism is not *about* the appropriation of power; it is *about* justice.

5

Toward an Ethic of Desire
Derrida, Fiction, and the Law of the Feminine

Peg Birmingham

In her essay, "Cultural Feminism Versus Post-Structuralism," Linda Alcoff reiterates a familiar criticism against Derrida's invocation of the feminine. She writes: "Applied to the concept of woman the post-structuralist's view results in what I shall call nominalism: the idea that the category "woman" is a fiction and that feminist efforts must be directed toward dismantling this fiction."[1] At this point, Alcoff cites Derrida's *Spurs* wherein woman is understood in terms of total difference, as that which cannot be pinned down. She argues that for Derrida the category of woman is undecidable and indicts him as offering nothing but a "negative feminism." Alcoff asks, "What can we demand in the name of women if 'women' do not exist and demands in their name simply reinforce the myth that they do? How can we speak out against sexism as detrimental to the interests of women if the category is a fiction?"[2] Margaret Whitford makes the same charge, arguing that Derrida's understanding of the feminine as the site of multiplicity leaves us with nothing more than a fiction, a "disembodied nominalism."[3] Susan Bordo makes a similar criticism, arguing that Derridean deconstruction with its emphasis on multiplicity, difference, and polyvalent linguistic fictions merely replaces the "view from nowhere" with the "view from everywhere," ultimately a nominalist view that remains disembodied.[4] Finally, it would seem that Irigaray also levels this charge of a disembodied nominalism against Derrida. As early as *Speculum of the Other Woman,* Irigaray suggests that Derridean deconstruction offers us the latest and most sophisticated version of the masculine subject's attempt to reconstruct a "spectacular rebus" that paralyzes the body's system of gestures within a graphic or representational order, an order that refuses to take into account either embodiment or the feminine.[5]

It is the category of a "nominalist fiction" that I wish to address, arguing that while Derrida does suggest that the category woman is a fiction, it is far from apparent what the status of this "fiction" is.[6] Indeed, it is my argument that it is precisely Derrida's understanding of "fiction," beginning as early as his *Edmund Husserl's Origin of Geometry,*[7] that allows one to grasp why it is that he will argue in his later writings that the literary and the law must be thought together, and, moreover, that the site of the literary and the law is the site of the "play of the feminine." Finally, this reflection on the literary, the law, and the feminine allows one to see that Derrida offers something more than merely a "negative feminism." Indeed, I shall argue that Derrida offers a way to think an "ethics of desire."

Fiction, History, Responsibility

The discussion of fiction emerges early in Derrida's reading of Husserl's *Origin of Geometry.* It emerges in the discussion of origins. The discussion of origins is a discussion of history; Derrida is interested in a notion of history understood in a more primordial sense as *original* repetition: "Provided the notion of history is conceived in a new sense, the question posed must be understood in its most historic sense. It is a question of repeating an origin" (OG 34). In turn, the reflection on origins and history is a reflection on responsibility: "To meditate on or investigate the sense (*besinnen*) of origins is at the same time to: make oneself responsible (*verantworten*) for the sense (*Sinn*) of science and philosophy, bring this sense to the clarity of its 'fulfil[ment],' and put oneself in a position of responsibility for this sense starting from the total sense of our existence" (OG 31). To think the status of "fiction" in Derrida's thinking demands, therefore, that one think the question of origins, responsibility, and history. In other words, to say that woman is a fiction is to invoke a reflection on origins, responsibility, and history.

Derrida begins his reflection on "origins" by discussing a key difference between Husserl and Kant. For Kant there is an "indifference to the factual origin," while for Husserl "both the necessity to proceed from the fact of constituted science and the regression towards the nonempirical origins are at the same time conditions of possibility" (OG 38). Derrida argues that this indifference to the factual origin is more legitimate in Kant than in Husserl because for Kant "the inaugural mutation which interests Kant *hands over* geometry rather than creates it; it sets free a possibility, which is nothing less than historical, in order to hand it to us" (OG 39). On the other hand for Husserl the productive act is *constitutive and creative:* "The objects or objectivities that it intends did *not* exist *before* it; and this *"before"* of the ideal objectivity marks more than the chronological eve of a fact: it marks a transcendental prehistory" (OG 40). The difference between Kant and Husserl is the difference between the "ready-made" and the "constitutive creative" work of reflection. For Husserl, reflection is precisely the activity of instituting. It is productive and creative, whereas for Kant it is "already done." It is the status of this "productive act" that occupies Derrida throughout his thinking.

It is in this context that Derrida first raises the specter of fiction. Indeed, he distinguishes between hallucination and fiction on the basis of the latter's link to a particular kind of history: "Hallucination, then, is truth's accomplice only in a static world of constituted significations. To proceed to the ground and primordial constitution of truth, we must return, starting from the real world, to a *creative experience*" (OG 46; my emphasis). The true contrary of hallucination is fiction understood precisely in terms of a "creative experience," that is, as *constitutive* of reality. Hence, its distinction from hallucination. In order to think the status of this fiction, Derrida insists that we think history, an *original* history in the sense that it is linked to the reawakening of origins.

Paradoxically, Derrida argues that this "original history," as the invariance of the instituting fact, can never be repeated as such. The instituting fact marks a singular historical origin that is irreplaceable and invariable (OG 46). The invariance of this instituting fact must be distinguished from the Husserlian eidetic invariance. In other words, to think the invariance of the fact is to move from eidetic invariance to an institutive history; it is to move from the eidetic to the historical reduction. This historical reduction is one that reactivates the sense of the first time as a unique fact. It takes account of the sense of fact, not the factuality of the fact. The sense of fact is precisely the creative experience of an original history. In other words, the sense of fact is a *fiction.* This for Derrida is the *aperion:* the fact in its pure factuality, or, the fact in its fiction: "Also, when Husserl affirms that a sense-production must have first presented itself as evident in the personal consciousness of the inventor, and when he asks the question of its *subsequent* (in a factual chronological order) objectification, he elicits a kind of *fiction* destined to show the characteristics of ideal Objectivity problematic and to show that they are not a matter of course" (OG 64; my emphasis on fiction).

This *aperion* of the inseparability of fact and sense, or, in other words, the inseparability of fact and fiction, is not unresolvable: "Is this to say that this inseparability of fact and sense in the oneness of an instituting act precludes access for phenomenology to all history and to the pure *eidos* of a forever submerged origin? Not at all" (OG 47). Passage through the *aperion* is achieved through the historical reduction that takes us to the singularity of origins:

> The historical reduction, which also operates by variation, will be *reactivating* and noetic. Instead of repeating the constituted sense of an ideal object, one will have to reawaken the dependence of sense with respect to an inaugural and institutive act concealed under secondary passivities and infinite sedimentations—a primordial act which created the object whose *eidos* is determined by the iterative reduction. (OG 47–48)

This notion of an "iterative reduction" allows us to understand the singularity of the instituting act as *original repetition.* The iterative or historical reduction gives the origin of repetition, a *creative* origin that is marked by the possibility of an absence of the repeated. This must be the case because if the sense of the instituting act to be repeated were totally present, if it were not characterized by lack of plenitude, no repetition could occur.[8] In other words, the sense of the instituting act is given only in the repetition of an origin with which it cannot coincide, since it is of the very essence of the origin to be pure anteriority. If it were not, it would be fully and always present and no activity of repetition would be necessary. The present contains the alterity of an absolute origin. Indeed, Derrida's celebrated notion of "differance" must be understood in terms of this anteriority at the very origin of the historical; that is, at the very heart of Being. Thus, the singular, creative event is marked by the lack of self-presence. Furthermore, this original repetition is the condition for re-production, re-citation, representation. (This will be extremely important in thinking the relation between recitation and law in the next section.) As Gasché points out in *Tain of the Mirror*, "original repetition gives the possibility of citation and must be inscribed in any entity, sign or act of speech in order for an entity or speech act to be possible in its singularity in the first place" (215).

The significance of this is that original repetition gives the sense of an *open* history. Derrida clarifies what he means by such "openness." History is understood here as the infinite totality of possible experiences. There is a unity but it is a unity of a tradition, "infinitely open to all its own revolutions." This is not, however, an abstract history; rather, it is a concrete and specific history that arises in an instituting, temporal, creative act. Derrida argues that the essence of history, history as such, is a primordial concrete essence that makes a generalizing operation possible. Here again he is pointing to an understanding of the historical as *creative adventure*: "A system that has been originally produced only once—that remains de facto and de jure *irreversible*. These then are the *interconnections* of what is, in the fullest sense of the word, *history itself*" (OG 65). These interconnections are nothing but the possibilities of the appearance of history as such, outside of which is nothing. History itself, therefore, establishes the possibility of its own appearing, and this possibility of appearing is through *language*. The creative appearance of the historical adventure is always a *linguistic* appearance.

Here Derrida argues we have the broadest notion of literature or fiction. This is the case insofar as literature, fiction in the broadest sense, is inhabited by a certain distance. This absence or distance that characterizes the origin is, however, "not identical with any of its empirical, phonetic, or graphic materializations" (OG 67). In literary language this distance or absence is *made word:* "Art sets off in quest of a language that can recapture this absence itself and represent the endless movement of comprehension" (OG 51). This "making word" defines the singularity of a narrative that characterizes a historical *adventure.* It is this event of singularity, the singularity of a narrative, that marks the junction of history, fiction, and language. Language, the act of fiction in its broadest sense, inaugurates the appearance of history.

At this point, Derrida begins to explain the relation between history and fiction. The instituting act is a kind of fiction. I start with ideal objectivity, the constituted object, and work my way back to the instituting act. Thus, the primordial sense of the intentional act is given in its final sense. The historical reduction depends on both a teleology and an account of origin. However, this origin has the status of a "fiction." Derrida argues that it is not the case that the narration, the condition of history, is such that it falls into a static, structural, and normative schema. Nor does it give us a merely factual content of development. This historical account of the instituting act, this primordial singularity, is not an account of what really happened. We are not being told a story (OG 65). Recalling the sense of "origins" described above, there is something that is not present, that did not take place. Hence the fiction.

To further understand the status of "fiction," it is important to understand that for Derrida language is not natural. Indeed, it is that which resists the phenomenological reduction. The resistance means that the transcendental discourse remains "obliterated by a certain ambiguous worldliness" (OG 69). Thus, every ideal objectivity is bound to the factual and worldly and is constituted in a historically determined territory. In other words, these "bound idealities" are linguistically fleshed. This historical incarnation is what Derrida also calls "bound ideality" or "spiritual corporeality." Two senses of flesh or embodiment emerge. There is a constituted sensible body (*Körper*) as well as a constituting body (*Leib*). Literature, language in the broadest sense, is both a factual event (*Körper*) and the upsurge of sense (*Leib*). This means that language is no longer representational as though signs follow bodies as their mirrors; instead, language is constitutive, one might even argue, performative—hence its status as a fiction. The constitutive act of fiction, therefore, produces the body (*Leib*) that it then claims to find prior to any and all constitution or signification (*Körper*). Thus, just as there is no natural language, so too there is no natural body. Every body is linguistically and historically fleshed.

While finitude is the essential we can never radically go beyond, nevertheless there is a *rift* in the finite. This marks the irruption of the infinite in the finite: "the always-already-there of a future which keeps the indetermination of its infinite openness intact." Here Derrida is beginning to think the status of the "always already" as a future that is always yet to come; it keeps its "infinite openness intact." At the same time, this historical, linguistic incarnation *sets free* the transcendental, rather than binding it. At this point, Derrida quotes Fink, "In sensible embodiment occurs the "localization" and the "temporalization" (*Temporalisation*) of what is by its being-sense, unlocated and untemporal" (OG 89).

It is this infinite openness that saves the *Leiblichkeit* from corporeal disaster inasmuch as the irruption of the infinite allows for a *revolution* within empirical culture. It is what allows for the "passage to the limit." Derrida argues, "Naturally this passage to the limit is only the going beyond every sensible and factual limit. It concerns the ideal limit of an infinite transgression, not the factual limit of the transgressed finitude" (OG 127). In other words, there is for Derrida no transgressing finitude itself; rather, there is always at the heart of history an infinite transgression. Indeed, I shall argue later, this "infinite transgression" that characterizes the *in-finite* marks the site of sexual difference and the law of the feminine.

Again, the in-finite must be understood in terms of the instituting, fictive act. This means that within the instituting act there is the possibility of an infinite number of births, "in which, each time, another birth is announced, while still being concealed" (OG 131). The institutive in-finitization that characterizes the work of fiction is not access to some possibility that is itself ahistoric yet discovered within a history. Rather, the openness of the in-finite is "the openness of history *itself*, in the utmost depths and purity of its essence" (OG 132). The rift in the finite, this instituting infinitization, characterizes a radical freedom at the heart of history:

> Far from being the access to some possibility that is itself ahistoric yet discovered within a history (which would in turn be transfigured by it), the openness of the infinite is only, on the contrary,

the openness of history *itself*, in the utmost depths and purity of its essence. Without this rift in the finite, historical humanity, or rather historical civilizations, would only claim an empirical type of socio-anthropological unity. (OG 132)

At the same time, the "always already" denotes a fundamental *delay* at the very heart of Being. This is due to the absence at the very origin of the historical. As seen above, the very origin of the historical is the origin of Being. Being is history precisely because of this delay, this absence, that marks "original history":

> And if Being did not have to be History through and through, the delay or lateness of Discourse after the showing of Being would be but a simple misfortune of thought as phenomenology. That this cannot be so, because historicity is prescribed for Being; that delay is the destiny of Thought itself as Discourse—only a phenomenology can say this and make philosophy equal to it. (OG 152)

Delay, then, is the philosophical absolute in the sense that delay marks that historical origin that is ab-solved of all relation, that which marks the limit of all discourse:

> The Absolute is present only in being deferred-delayed without respite, this impotence and this impossible are given in a primordial and pure consciousness of Difference. . . . The primordial Difference of the absolute Origin. (OG 153)

This primordial difference that marks the absolute origin can only be *anticipated.* Hence, it is a delay that is teleological, but a teleology without end. Thus, the "always already" marks a very different sense of temporality; it is a temporality that forever disrupts and challenges the *linear* temporality of a narrative.

Therefore, the openness of the historic present as well as its absolute and inescapable delay is such that the historic present always appears as a *project.* Indeed, at the very outset of the essay on Husserl, Derrida claims that the reflection on origins and history is an act of responsibility: "To meditate on or investigate the sense (*besinnen*) of origins is at the same time to: make oneself responsible (*verantworten*) for the sense

(*Sinn*) of science and philosophy, bring this sense to the clarity of its "fulfil[ment]," and put oneself in a position of *responsibility* for this sense starting from the total sense of our existence" (OG 31). For Derrida the effaced/disclosed trace of the origin (not a past present), and the anticipated differed/deferred end (not a future present) inscribe what must be *performed* as our present. A performing, fictive act *makes* a present. At the same time, responsibility for this historical narrative must be taken up in its present tense. This responsibility requires a persistent effortfulness that makes a "present." This means that the manifold of history is plural, shifting, and can be disrupted and displaced.

Hence, Derrida is not offering an unfleshed nominalism. As seen above, "bound idealities" are always linguistically fleshed. In other words, they are always historically incarnated. Connecting the sense of original history to "linguistic flesh" is to connect the sense of history to embodiment and to the social/historical effects of that embodiment. Alcott, therefore, is simply wrong to suggest that Derrida's understanding of the feminine is not connected to embodiment. Similarly misguided is Bordo's criticism that the deconstructive imagery of a body whose unity has been shattered by the choreography of multiplicity is a body that is everywhere. Again, Derrida analysis of embodiment insists that these reconfigurations are *materially located*. The dancer cannot be everywhere. At the same time, she can perform differently and in multiple ways.

Moreover, while it would be impossible to take up an extended discussion of the relation of Derrida and Irigaray, briefly it can be seen in this analysis of Husserl's *Origin of Geometry* that not only does Derrida refuse to paralyze the body's gestures in a spectacular postmodern rebus, he actually provides a way to think further Irigaray's attempt to think the "sensible-transcendental" or what she also refers to as the "infinite-in-the-finite." The proximity is also marked by the emphasis both place on the ethical responsibility that occurs through this irruption of the infinite in the finite.[9]

To think the subject of a new story, therefore, is to think the notion of an agent of pluralization, alteration. This releases "woman" from a fixed referent, allowing the possibility for new configurations of the term. Moreover, Derrida's notion of history and origins demands that one think a subject *for* history, not a subject of history. This is a subject that is situated but not determined. This is a subject whose temporality violates a historical narrative that understands itself as linear—time as sequence—in which the feminine is written. Thus, in terms of the narrativization of woman, a new story is possible, and a subject for a new story. It makes visible all the open and plural areas of history. This is what is learned through Derrida's reading of Husserl's *Origins of Geometry:* the sense of history as multiple. And it is this plurality that is suppressed when the only representation is Man as subject. Thus, Derrida argues that phenomenology is both a self-understanding (*Selbstbesinnung*) and a responsibility (*Verantwortung*):

> The free resolution to "take up one's own sense" . . . in order to make oneself accountable, through speech, for an imperiled pathway. This speech is historical, because it is always already a *response:* Responsibility here means shouldering a word one hears spoken, as well as taking on one oneself the transfer of sense, in order to look after its advance. (OG 149)

To take responsibility for the feminine is to take upon oneself historical discourses concerning the feminine in order to transform its sense, that is, to write a new fiction.

Fiction, the Feminine and the Law

In his later work, Derrida continues to think the status of fiction by explicitly linking fiction to the feminine and the law. Indeed, it is my suggestion that this continued thinking of fiction not only allows one to understand the status of the feminine, but also why the feminine is linked to the law in Derrida's thinking: the law is precisely the site of the erotic, the site of sexual difference. In other words, Derrida's later thinking on the feminine, the erotic, the law, and sexual difference can only be understood in light of his earlier work on fiction and difference outlined above.

In his essay *Before the Law,* Derrida asks, "what if the law, without being itself transfixed by literature, shared the conditions of its possibility with the literary object?"[10] In his reading of Kafka's story, *Before the Law,* Derrida points out that the law and the story itself appear together, summoned before the other in a "certain kind of relation." Yet, it is a relation where nothing appears: "It seems that the law as such should never give rise to any story. To be invested with its categorical authority, the law must be without history, genesis or any possible derivation. That would be the law of the law" ("BL" 191). Derrida compares the relation of the story and the law with Freud's narration of the murder of the father:

> Freud appears to cling to the reality of an event, but this event is a sort of non-event, an event of nothing or a quasi-event which both calls for and annuls a narrative account. For this "deed" or "misdeed" to be effective it must be somehow spun from fiction. Everything happens *as if.* ("BL" 198)

Referring to Kant's understanding of the categorical imperative, Derrida argues that the "as if" introduces fiction into the very heart of the law ("BL" 190). Here Derrida continues his reflections on history and fiction began in the *Origins of Geometry:* "This 'as if' enables us to reconcile practical reason with an historical teleology and the possibility of unlimited progress" ("BL" 190). Yet this "as if" (*als ob*) must be thought as a kind of negative teleology; it does not offer any determinate, real content. It is *not the condition* for justice. This is precisely because nothing appears in the event. This is why Derrida claims that the force of the law is tied to its fictive quality. He goes on to explain this "fiction":

> The law, intolerant of its own history, intervenes as an absolutely emergent order, absolute and detached from any origin. It appears as something that does not appear as such in the course of a history. At all events, it cannot be constituted by some history that might give rise to any story. If there were any history, it would be neither presentable nor relatable: the history of that which never took place. ("BL" 194)

That the law is "absolutely emergent" means that the law never *has* a place. Thus, there is no taking a position before the law. Lacking position or place, the history of the law is the history of an "impossible narration." It is a story that cannot be told; it is a story that has no place or time. Thus, there is no knowing who or what the law is. Indeed, Derrida argues that the law retreats before the narrative "I." The history of the law, therefore, is the history of an "impossible narration."

If Derrida's discussion of the law was simply a discussion of the difference between the law as an "impossible narration" and the law in its positive form, there would not be much that distinguishes Derrida's understanding of the law from much of the Western tradition from Plato to Cicero to Hegel. Certainly, this tradition has always understood the distinction between something like a transcendent or eternal law and the positive, temporal law. But it seems to me that something else is going on in Derrida's thinking than simply the traditional distinction between positive law, and that which transcends it: the "counter-law" or what Derrida oftentimes calls "justice." This "something else" is precisely Derrida's understanding of the law in terms of what he calls the "feminine silhouette." The law is neither a man nor a woman, but a "feminine silhouette comes as companion to the quasi-narrator of a forbidden or impossible narration (that is the whole story of this non-story)" ("BL" 206). How does one think this "feminine silhouette"? Derrida explicitly suggests that the "silhouette" must be thought of as that which does not appear. Thus the law is the *silhouette* of the feminine insofar as it does not appear.[11]

But why call it a silhouette of the *feminine*? The second question seems to be answered by the understanding of the law as an *emergent erotic* order: "What is difficult to think is that the law is an affirmation, has the structure of an affirmation. It is not something which limits desire or forbids transgression. As soon as you affirm a desire, you perform something which is the law." The law, understood as the emerging erotic, must be thought as the *imperative* of desire; it is a law that says yes. And, Derrida, following Blanchot, points out that it is "usually" the feminine that says yes ("LG" 245). Here Derrida gives another sense of the fictive quality the law. For Derrida, the imperative of desire is *generative*. The law, therefore, is fictive, that is, generative. Derrida continues to think the notion of fiction as constitutive. In his later writings, however, he understands this constituting as generative and erotic.

Here it seems to me that Derrida is thinking further Heidegger's reflections on "causality" as *aitia:* that which *occasions* and is *responsible* for bringing something forth.[12] What is striking in Heidegger's reading of the Greek understanding of *aitia* (and, I argue, this is precisely what Derrida takes up in his thinking of the "lawful origin" as erotic), is that he is thinking against an understanding of causality as *productive*. The "occasioning" brings something forth, lets it appear, but in no sense does the "occasioning" act as a means for some end. The "occasioning" *entwines with* that which is brought forth; it is the continual activity of *becoming.* In other words, this lawful origin, this imperative of desire, is precisely that which disallows anything like a teleology that would result merely in a product or end. Moreover, the "occasioning" is not only that which is responsible for bringing something forth (hence its erotic aspect); it is also that to which we are indebted and responsible: there is a debt, a thanks owed to that which is responsible for bringing forth. In other words, Derrida, taking Heidegger seriously, argues there is a debt to the erotic. As we will see, this debt and responsibility lies at the basis of his rethinking an ethics of desire.

Furthermore, Derrida is thinking an imperative or law that is in no sense prohibitive or negative in its command or effects. The law is not that which *pro-hibits,* but instead, is that which *pro-creates.* This procreative site of the law is prior to any and all prohibition, and, indeed, forces a rethinking of the law as interdiction:

> The gate is not shut, it is "open" as "usual" (says the text), but the law remains inaccessible; and if this forbids or bars the gate to genealogical history, it also fuels desire for the origin and genealogical drive, which wear themselves out as much before the process of the law's engenderment as before parental generation. Historical research leads the *relation* toward an impossible exhibition of a site and an event, of a taking-place where law originates as prohibition. ("BL" 197)

While the above passage says that the law does originate as prohibition, it is my suggestion that one must be extremely careful how one reads this "taking-place" of the law. As seen above, the law is without "place" if by that is meant a position or locality. The law is not thetic. (Which means that the relation to the law is never one of thesis or position. Again, this will be important for thinking an ethics of desire.) The law must be understood in its activity, as a "taking-place" that is always an activity of *becoming.*

The "taking-place" of the law is a procreative place; further, it is this that stands at the "origin" of all prohibitions. Thus, the very notion of "prohibition" must be rethought:

> The law prohibits by interfering with and deferring the "ference" ["feranceé"], the reference, the rapport, the relation. What *must not* and cannot be approached is the origin of differance: it must

> not be presented or represented and above all not penetrated. That is the law of the law, the process of a law of whose subject we can never say, "there it is," it is here or there. It is neither natural nor institutional; one can never reach it, and it never reaches the depths of its original and proper taking-place. ("BL" 205)

The law is prohibitive *only* in the sense that it prohibits any relation *to itself.* This does not mean that it remains in a position of alterity either; rather, as seen above in the reading of Heidegger's *aitia,* it is that which entwines with that which it brings forth. Therefore it is not prohibitive but *in-habitive* in the sense that it in-habits that which it occasions or brings forth. At the same time, there is something excessive about the law. And it is precisely a relation to this excess that is prohibited. This is the case insofar as the very sense of "relation" denotes limit. Excess, that which exceeds limit, is by definition that to which a relation is prohibited. In other words, the excessive is that which stands at the origin of relation but is absolved from all relation. But as the origin of relation, the law is primarily not that which forbids. Here Derrida is very close to Montesquieu for whom the law is also that which *relates* rather than forbids; it is what gives rise to empowering relations rather than forbidding such power. (Montesquieu understands power as that which is *generated* by its *relation* to other spheres of power. Derrida takes over this understanding of power as relational.) This is why Derrida insists that the law is a silhouette that *plays.* The "play" is always creative, engendering, and furthermore, empowering.

Derrida describes this erotic, generative order of the law as a silhouette of the *feminine* because, he argues, it is usually the feminine that says yes. The law is *in* the feminine, *inhabits* the feminine, because it is the feminine that usually is affirmative because "it is 'usually' women who say *yes, yes.* To life, to death. This 'usually' avoids treating the feminine as a general and generic force; it makes an opening for the event, the performance, the uncertain contingencies, the encounter" ("LG" 244).

It is important to note that when Derrida speaks of this imperative of desire, this categorical "yes" that characterizes the law, he is saying something quite different than that the law is *of* the feminine gender. He explicitly states that the law is *in* the feminine as its shadow. The law is the *silhouette* of the feminine; it is the shadow, the outline that accompanies the feminine. Indeed, Derrida makes a distinction between the "female element" and a "female person." The shadow, the impossible narration, is without representation. Thus, the law cannot represent the feminine person; rather, the silhouette is female only in its element of affirmation. It is "usually women" who say yes. Again, the "usually" prevents the universalization of the law into a particular genre. This is why Derrida refuses to identify the law with a universal or essentialist notion of the feminine.

Moreover, the silhouette of the law cannot be said to be the feminine gender because it is that which *engenders*. Furthermore, it is a *double* engendering: "yes, yes." Referring to *The Madness of the Day*, Derrida writes:

> Now the mightiest and most divided trait of *La folie du jour* or of "A *récit?*" is the one relating the birth of the law, its genealogy, engenderment, generation, or genre, the very genre of the law to the process of the double affirmation. The excessiveness of *yes, yes* is no stranger to the genesis of the law. ("LG" 247)

Now at this point Derrida reveals that when he speaks of this opening, shadow or the silhouette, he is not thinking the feminine as such; rather, he is thinking sexual difference. The excessiveness of "yes, yes," the excessiveness of the law, is the "madness of sexual difference" ("LG" 245). Thus, the affirmative law, the law that says yes, the law that *engenders*, is precisely sexual difference. This is the case in so far as it is an engendering that is always double, "yes, yes." Thus the law is always double. Sexual difference, as the law that engenders, is the counter-law "that constitutes this very law, renders it possible, conditions it and thereby makes itself—for reasons of edges on which we shall run aground in just a moment—impossible to edge through, to edge away from to hedge around. The law and the counter-law serve each other citations summoning each other to appear, and each re-cites the other in these proceedings" ("LG" 226).

Thinking the proximity of sexual difference and fiction, Derrida continues to think the proximity of original repetition and *récit*. *The Madness of the Day* begins with the demand that the blind man *recite* his story. Yet, this recitation has numerous beginnings, marking a repetition that resists narration. The very repetition of its beginnings disrupts narration:

> The inaugural decision to answer the demand and to "begin" the
> *récit* does not belong to the *récit*, any more than does the "No,
> no *récit*, never again" at the end of the book, an inverse resolution
> which seems not to cite anything either. "I began" and "No, no
> *récit*, never again" could therefore resemble quasi-transcendental
> commitments on the part of the *recit*. ("LG" 239)

Derrida argues that the first is a kind of performative, while the second
is enunciative but also performative: "to take some kind of responsibility
in answer to the demand for a *récit*, which would tear the canvas of a
narrative text even as it tends to envelop itself indefinitely within itself"
("LG" 239). As already seen in the discussion of Derrida's reading of
Husserl's *Origin of Geometry*, original repetition engenders or makes
possible re-citation, a re-citation without narration. This means that
there is no coherent story, a story that could be told once and for all.
The numerous beginnings that characterize the engendering of sexual
difference demand a plurality of re-citations, each singular in its response
to the demand. Moreover, the above passage suggests that the repetition
or re-citation of "yes, yes" is a response to an impossibility: "No, no
récit, never again."

The above passage also suggests that Derrida's "nominalism" must be
rethought as performative and enunciative. Earlier I pointed out that in
the introduction to Husserl's *Origin of Geometry* Derrida critiques the
representational status of language, which claims that significations
mimic bodies; he argues instead for a conception of language as performative or constitutive. Here, Derrida goes even further, showing that this
performance carries with it an ethical demand. Repetition understood as
re-citation carries with it the demand that some kind of responsibility is
taken in answer to this demand for a recitation. It is that to which we
are indebted. Here one can begin to understand Derrida's claim that the
law shares its conditions of possibility with the literary object. The
affirmative law understood as sexual difference is that which engenders.
This is the engendering of an impossible origin that we have seen is
thought by Derrida in the *Origin of Geometry* as a fiction. Again, Derrida
understands "fiction" as that which engenders—without, however,
pointing back to some origin that can be known. To think the affirmative
law that says yes, to think sexual difference, is to think the impossible
origin, that which occasions or makes possible.

Moreover, as in his reading of Husserl's *Origin of Geometry*, Derrida is thinking the temporality of this procreative origin as delay. "It is all a question of time, *and it is the time of the story;* however, time itself does not appear until this adjournment of the representation, until the law of delay or the advance of the law, according to the anachrony of the relation" (202; my emphasis). The time of the story, that is, the time of the law, is the time of delay. The time of the story is the time that resists repetition, universalization; it is not the time of narrative. Thus, the temporality of delay is *a-topic*, without narration, representation, or place:

> But this singular topos places within and without the work, along its boundary, an inclusion and exclusion with regard to genre in general, as to an identifiable class in general. It gathers together the corpus and, at the same time, *in the same blinking of an eye*, keeps it from closing, from identifying itself with itself. This axiom of non-closure or non-fulfillment enfolds within itself the condition for the possibility and the impossibility of taxonomy. This inclusion and this exclusion do not remain exterior to one another; they do not exclude each other. But neither are they immanent or identical to each other. They are neither one nor two. They form what I shall call the genre-clause, a clause stating at once the juridical utterance, the designation that makes precedent and law-text, but also the closure, the closing that excludes itself from what it includes. ("LG" 231; my emphasis)

Importantly, Derrida suggests in the above passage that the temporality of delay is the temporality of the blinking of an eye that is, the *Augenblick.* Here again, Heidegger, in his analysis of the *Augenblick,* is helpful for illuminating this temporality of the law. Briefly, Heidegger argues that the temporality of the *Augenblick* is the "untimely." This notion of the "untimely" is precisely what Derrida understands by "achronology."[13] The "untimely," however, is not the eternal. Instead, the *Augenblick* is the untimely in time. The untimely in time cannot be understood as the *nunc stans,* the eternal in time; instead, it is the *moment* understood as the cut or gap between the past and the future. The time of the *Augenblick,* therefore, is the time of crisis. The crisis is precisely the cut or rupture with any linear understanding of time. Hence, its untimeliness. In addition, the rupture of the "untimely" means that the a-chronology is a-topos, without a place or position.

Thus, it cannot be *topic:* it cannot give rise to a representation or narrative of itself. Moreover, Heidegger argues that the "untimely" demands a *critical* response that cannot be based on any classical mimetic or representational model; instead, the reply must be to the specific and unique. (As we shall see below, this is why Derrida will argue that the law is always a law of the singular.)

The engendering of the law, therefore, cannot be understood as a production or reproduction; rather, the doubleness of the "yes" indicates a repetition: "I want it to begin again." Not producing anything, the repetition of the "yes" must be thought as a happening, an event: it happens again, it does not reproduce. In other words, *the procreative is not the reproductive.*

Paradoxically, therefore, this double repetition of the "yes" is precisely the "yes" to singularity, to the singular event or encounter: "the law, in its female element, is a silhouette that plays. At what? At being born, at being born like anybody or nobody" ("LG" 249). To be born like "anybody or nobody" is the birth of the unique or singular. The affirmative law gives birth to nobody that was here before. The silhouette of the feminine, therefore, is the silhouette of the singular. Lacking representation, not engaged in production or re-production, the radical alterity that marks the engendering of sexual difference is such that there is no possibility of substitutions. The affirmative law of sexual difference is the shadow of the singular; it is that which gives rise to the singular. This is the ethical dimension of sexual difference: no one can be substituted for an other without violating this affirmative law. Indebted to this occasioning, one has responsibility to respond to this erotic occasioning of the singular. It is this responsibility that marks the ethical dimension of the erotic. Or, to say it differently, it is this responsibility that one has to sexual difference.

Thinking the erotic occasioning of the *singular,* it seems to me that this is why the later Derrida moves from the language that invokes the "other" to a language that invokes the "singular." While it is the case that Derrida often uses the language of "the other" in his later thinking, nevertheless upon closer examination Derrida is actually thinking the law of the singular and what I have referred to above as the "event" of the singular. His work suggests that we must not think the "of" here in terms of a possessive genitive, but rather in terms of an active "engendering." "To engender" is the singularizing event. The "of" of singularity enunciates the singularizing event of the law. Thus, as argued above, to ask of the status of the law is to ask of the status of the singular. To be before the law is to before the singular in its singularity. Thus, the imperative of desire is not the call of the Other still positioned at the margin, but rather the imperative to respond to the *upsurge* of the singular.

In conclusion, then, from his earliest thinking on Husserl's *Origin of Geometry* to his later thinking on the law and the feminine, Derrida has been grappling with the status of "fiction." It is a thinking that has moved from an understanding of "fiction" as a constituting act of sense to an understanding of "fiction" as the engendering activity of sexual difference. What I have shown is how this thinking of "fiction" allows one to understand the shadow of the "feminine" in Derrida's work as precisely sexual difference, that is, erotic generation. To think together fiction, the law, and the shadow of the feminine in Derrida's work is to think the occasioning of sexual difference, the excessiveness of the erotic. This is the "other" law that does not prohibit but is the site of pro-creation (something quite different from reproduction). And, moreover, it is this excessive pro-creating that marks the ethical moment: there is a responsibility to erotic excess, the "yes" of sexual difference, that occasions the singular and the unique.

Notes

1. Linda Alcoff, "Cultural Feminism Versus Post-Structuralism: The Identity Crisis in Feminist Theory," *Signs* 13, no. 3 (Spring 1988): 405–36.

2. Ibid.

3. Margaret Whitford, *Luce Irigaray: Philosophy in the Feminine* (New York: Routledge, 1991), 82–83.

4. Susan Bordo, *Unbearable Weight* (Berkeley and Los Angeles: University of California Press, 1993).

5. Luce Irigaray, *Speculum of the Other Woman*, trans. Gillian C. Gill (Ithaca: Cornell University Press), 1985. See especially "Any Theory of the 'Subject' Has Always Been Appropriated by the 'Masculine,' " 133–46.

6. For a related discussion of Derrida and the status of fiction, see my article on Drucilla Cornell's reading of Derrida, "Feminist Fictions: Discourse, Desire and the Law," in *Philosophy and Social Criticism* (Spring 1996).

7. Jacques Derrida, *Edmund Husserl's Origin of Geometry: An Introduction*, trans. John P. Leavey (Stony Brook: Nicolas Hays, 1978); hereafter referred to in the text as OG.

8. Rodolphe Gasche, *The Tain of the Mirror* (Cambridge: Harvard University Press, 1986), 215.

9. In particular, see Luce Irigaray, "An Ethics of Sexual Difference," in *An Ethics of*

Sexual Difference, trans. Carolyn Burke and Gillian C. Gill (Ithaca: Cornell University Press, 1993).

10. Jacques Derrida, "Before the Law," in *Acts of Literature* (New York: Routledge, 1992), 191; hereafter referred to in the text as "BL."

11. Jacques Derrida, "The Law of Genre," in *Acts of Literature,* 251; hereafter referred to in the text as "LG."

12. Martin Heidegger, "The Question Concerning Technology," in *The Question Concerning Technology* (New York: Harper and Row, 1977), 8–10.

13. See Martin Heidegger, *Nietzsche, Eternal Recurrence of the Same,* trans. D. F. Krell (New York: Harper and Row, 1984), 57. Heidegger argues that the temporality of the *Augenblick* is a decisive (*entscheidend*) temporality. He points out that the root of *entscheidung* is *scheidung,* to cut or rupture. Etymologically, he argues that *scheidung* comes from the word *Krinen.* Thus, the temporality of the *Augenblick* is a critical temporality, one that cuts or ruptures any linear narration or mimic representation.

Editor's Note

The following two chapters were part of a symposium on an essay by Derrida entitled "The Force of Law: The 'Mystical Foundation of Authority'" (published in *Cardozo Law Review* 11 [1990]: 919–1045). In the first part of this essay, Derrida raises several conundrums about the law: the necessity of violence or force within the legal system that is signaled by the English verb "to enforce"; the fact that, at the moment of its founding, a legal system exists only by force, never by law, because it exists outside both the old law it would supplant and the new law it has not yet created; and the fact that justice itself is always extralegal in that it exceeds what the law dictates or demands because it refers to particular cases, while the law always refers to the general case. The second part of Derrida's essay is devoted to a discussion of Walter Benjamin's "Critique of Violence," in which Derrida suggests, as Nancy Fraser points out, that a deconstructive reading of the law is preferable to the kind of critique in which Benjamin engages. This is because Benjamin's enterprise is (necessarily?) embedded in a philosophy of "*droit, Recht,* right or law" (981) that relies on a series of oppositions and distinctions, such as that between the founding violence of the law and the conserving violence necessary to sustain it, that Derrida finds highly problematic, if not self-deconstructing.

6

Civil Disobedience and Deconstruction

Drucilla Cornell

I want to read Derrida against the current.* I am going to address deconstruction as deconstruction has made feminine difference and, more generally, the question of sexual difference, central to philosophy. But I am going to do so with the following specific question in mind: Do women have what John Rawls has called a "natural duty" to obey the law[1] if they lose such fundamental rights as abortion? I hope Derrida will forgive me for not engaging solely with his recent text on the mystical foundation of authority;[2] instead I want to offer a more comprehensive interpretation of what deconstruction has to offer us as legal theorists.

But I must begin with a brief excursion into the work of Jacques Lacan.[3] As I shall show, Derrida's specific intervention into Lacanianism is crucial to the legal question I have posed. Lacan teaches us the very simple lesson that the entire order of patriarchal culture divides us into two sexes, male and female, in the form of a hierarchy that privileges the masculine. It does so through linguistic structures that are so deep that the Law of the Father not only breaks up the mother/child dyad, but does so to the degree that any relationship to the mother is repressed in the unconscious as the imaginary. The entire concept of identity takes place through this repression of the mother. The patriarchal order that Lacan and writers such as Luce Irigaray analyze—and, in Irigaray's case, from a specifically feminist criticism of Lacan's acceptance of the inevitability of this order[4]—denies the recognition of the mother so that women cannot affirmatively identify with their "sex." This is why Irigaray says that any concept of a subject is always on the side of the masculine.[5]

Can there be such a "thing," then, as a feminine subject of right? Not within the Lacanian schema where all there is is the projection of Woman as an imaginary figure, in which women are the signifiers of men's desires—as mommies, whores, mistresses, and as those who can be erased—and in which our violation and our erasure is not noticed or even commented upon. Under this analysis, the "rights of man" are just that: the rights of *man*, because the subject of right is, by definition, masculine.

In a recent text, Marguerite Duras remarked that, "for seventy, eighty, ninety years no play by a woman had been performed [in Paris] or perhaps in the whole of Europe. I found that out for myself. No one ever told me. And yet it was there for all to see."[6] The erasure that was so painful for Duras was not just the fact that no plays had been produced, but that no one noticed.

Similarly, in the field of law, the lack of notice of women's suffering has prompted the movement now called feminist jurisprudence. Writers like Robin West and Catharine MacKinnon have tried to show us that the erasure of specific harms to women—think, for example, of date rape—was "there" to "see," but was not seen because it was "unnoticed" by the official definitions of the legal system.[7] The lack of notice in the arts and in the law also expresses Jean-François Lyotard's profound understanding of the "différend" as that which cannot be articulated and, therefore, is not "seen."[8] The horror is not just in the facts that MacKinnon constantly reminds us of—for example, that a woman is battered every fifteen seconds in the United States[9]—but that our legal system has no mechanism to take notice of that reality as an overwhelming "public" problem demanding eradication.[10]

As has often been noted, very few women who file sexual harassment suits ever take their case to trial. More specifically, what has only too rarely been discussed is the way in which the plaintiff is turned into the defendant through the use of sexual humiliation. The plaintiff is put in the position of having to defend herself against the "charges" that are made against her. Rather than charging the defendant, she is the one who becomes charged. What is her crime? Her very "sex." Lacan helps us understand how sexual shame can be used at all points to silence those women who try to defend their own positions, whether they are rape victims, battered wives, or people like myself who sued because they were denied tenure. In other words, Lacan explains the basis of sexual shame in women through his analysis of the way in which the gender hierarchy perpetuates inequality.

Arendt has written that the Athenian dream of a participatory democracy is a dream long since gone. It might seem strange to quote Arendt in a feminist context. She continually denied any connection between her own writing and feminism. But I want to suggest a very different interpretation of Arendt's own pessimism over the return to "true" political, participatory democracy. I offer a different perspective that may explain the validity of her pessimism, even if from within a philosophical and psychoanalytic context she would never have accepted. (Although I need to add the caveat that we cannot retrospectively know how Arendt would have responded to the psychoanalytic feminist analysis I offer here, because it was not present for her to incorporate into her discourse.) We, as we all know, are, in the end, the products of our time. Ironically, Arendt's denial of feminism can itself be read as an expression of the devalorization and repudiation of the feminine Lacan describes, which is not to say that there is not in Arendt, in spite of her own comments, a unique feminine voice.

But I want to return to her pessimism about the realization of a participatory democracy of equal citizens in modernity, let alone in what now gets called postmodernity.[11] Lacan can be interpreted to teach us that this dream will remain lost until we recognize the truth of the fact that the subject is masculine, and that the masculine subject mirrors himself through the woman. The woman is mirrored through the man's imaginary as whore, mistress, wife, whatever, but she has no reality in herself. She is certainly not, in the recent language of dialogism, an equal citizen of dialogue. So when we talk about dialogue and dialogism, and civic republicanism, we also have to talk about what the conditions would be for the creation of a true subject of dialogue who could engage equally with women as citizens. If women endorse the dream of a dialogic, participatory democracy, and I do, then Lacan is relevant in helping us think about the conditions of its possibility. He consistently reminds us of how the psychical fantasy of woman blocks men from seeing women as equals.

We can now understand why we have to challenge dialogism if it is conceived as the "conversation of mankind." This challenge also takes us to Derrida's specific intervention into Lacan.[12] Once we understand this intervention, we can see why Seyla Benhabib is wrong to suggest that Derrida envisions the politics of the male warriors with their guns, ready to challenge the rulers.[13] Instead, his is an ethical and political exposure of masculine superiority as a "sham." Derrida continually pokes fun at the machoism of the so-called real man. He knows a "dick" when he sees one and he knows the limit of its meaning. He agrees with Lacan that it is not pre-given libidinal "drive" or anatomy that causes masculine privilege and the corresponding subjection and silencing in women. Instead, patriarchy perpetuates itself through the linguistic structures and cultural conventions that prop up patriarchy and have been repeated until they are melted into the unconscious and, indeed, even are the unconscious. Derrida, however, tells us that Lacan's insight into the relationship between *signifiance* and *jouissance*[14] undermines his own pessimistic political conclusions.[15] Derrida argues that the very slippage of language, which breaks up the coherence of gender identity, makes it possible for us to undermine the rigid gender divide that has made dialogue between men and women impossible and the acceptance of violence toward women not only inevitable, but also not "serious."

Let me now try to connect Derrida, Lacan, and Levinas. Why is Levinas relevant to Derrida's intervention into Lacan? Levinas challenges the idea that justice can ever be identified with any descriptive set of conditions or rights. Justice cannot be reduced to convention, no matter how conceived, and certainly not to the current "conversation of mankind." Levinas's messianic conception of justice demands the recognition of the call of the Other, which always remains as a call and can never be fully answered. Put somewhat differently, and this is exactly the notion of justice as aporia that Derrida emphasizes in his own text,[16] justice is the limit to what is, not its endorsement.

Once we introduce Levinas's messianic concept of justice, we can think more profoundly about Derrida's intervention into Lacan. I would argue that the "conversation of mankind" has been based on a masculine imaginary that erases women, and so, in fact, there is no dialogue whatsoever as long as the erasure of woman is accepted as part of our normal engagement with one another as citizens. Until we challenge the idea that the masculine imaginary projects us as wife, mistress, or whore, and does not allow us to have our own elaboration of ourselves as women, then we cannot speak of women as equal citizens. This objection to dialogism turns me to Derrida's criticism of Fred Dallmayr. Dallmayr is concerned about the emphasis on violence for any possible justice.[17] I interpret Derrida's objection to Dallmayr as emphasizing the danger of increasing violence by erasing the reality of its presence. When there is not peace, we should not pretend there is. Certainly the patriarchal order does not provide a "peaceful" world for women. The very recognition of the violence, then, can be understood as a step toward its mitigation. But we also need to emphasize another dimension, crucial to the intersection of Lacan, Derrida, and Levinas.

Levinas argued for the asymmetry of the *ethical* relationship. But Derrida demonstrates that ethical asymmetry must be based on a *phenomenological* symmetry if it is not to be reduced to another excuse for domination and, thus, for violation of the Other. My addition is that phenomenological symmetry demands the specific recognition of the symmetry of woman as ego, and that this is precisely what the psychical fantasy of woman described by Lacan makes impossible.[18] Without phenomenological symmetry, the asymmetry of the ethical relationship is nothing but violation of woman once again, which is why, on one interpretation, there is an indelible universality upon which Derrida insists, even if it cannot be positively described as a set of properties that define the subject. Such a positive definition, if one accepts that the masculine is defined as the subject, would perpetuate, not undermine, the gender hierarchy. But let me return to the relationship between phenomenological symmetry and ethical asymmetry. I am arguing that Derrida's intervention demands phenomenological symmetry as possible and necessary to the aspiration to the ethical relationship as ethical.

Very simply put, to think the ethical relationship, one has to think the question of sexual difference as it has been constituted through the gender hierarchy.

We have spoken now about a world in which whenever we talk about the natural duty to obey the law we have assumed that women have equal rights. When we speak about natural duty to obey the law, some degree of equality is assumed. Derrida has shown us that the relationship between phenomenological symmetry and the ethical asymmetry values the Other as different, indeed as difference. But I am now taking this intervention into what, at first glance, seems to be a very foreign context, the context of equality. The recognition of phenomenological symmetry can be understood as the very basis for any theory of equality. Yet, if Lacan is right, and I believe he is, the only way Woman exists in the gender hierarchy is not as a phenomenological ego, but as an imaginary projection. Our duty to obey the law demands that we be equal, in the sense that we not be denied phenomenological symmetry.

Thus, for me, equal citizenship turns on the phenomenological symmetry that demands the end of violation of women. Derrida's contribution to legal and political philosophy and, more specifically, his interventions into Lacan and Levinas show us that unless we challenge the reduction of woman to an imaginary fantasy, to the *phenomenologically* asymmetrical other, there will be nothing but the perpetuation of violence and violation of women. The loss of our civil rights is not a political coincidence. In a legal system that is systematically taking away the civil rights that so many of us have fought so hard to win, women have no natural duty to obey the law. There is no claim, in my opinion, to validity or legitimacy in a legal system that sweeps away the right of abortion and the right of so much else that we fought in our time to gain. This sweeping away of our rights reflects the denial of the phenomenological symmetry of women. The feminist alliance with deconstruction is precisely Derrida's specific intervention into the work of Lacan and Levinas.

Notes

*This chapter is dedicated to the memory of Mary Jo Frug, whose love and friendship I shall always miss and whose brutal murder is a tragic reminder of how pervasive violence to women is in our society. I also want to thank Rodolphe Gasché, Agnes Heller, and Alan

Wolfe who each in their own way made me rethink the moment of universality in Derrida's deconstructive intervention into Levinas's understanding of the ethical relationship. As always, I must thank A. Collin Biddle and Deborah Garfield for their research assistance, and their constant intellectual enthusiasm and engagement.

1. John Rawls. *A Theory of Justice* (Cambridge: Belknap Press of Harvard University Press, 1971), 114–17.

2. Jacques Derrida, "Force of Law: The 'Mystical Foundation of Authority,' " *Cardozo Law Review* 11 (1990): 919.

3. Jacques Lacan, *Feminine Sexuality: Jacques Lacan and the Ecole Freudienne*, ed. Juliet Mitchell and Jacqueline Rose, trans. Jacqueline Rose (New York: Norton, 1982).

4. Luce Irigaray, *Speculum of the Other Woman*, trans. Gillian C. Gill (Ithaca: Cornell University Press, 1985); and Luce Irigaray, *This Sex Which Is Not One*, trans. Catherine Porter (Ithaca: Cornell University Press, 1985).

5. Irigaray, "Any Theory of the 'Subject' Has Always Been Appropriated by the 'Masculine,' " in Irigaray, *Speculum*, 133–46.

6. Marguérite Duras, *Practicalities: Marguérite Duras Speaks to Jérôme Beaujour*, trans. Barbara Bray (New York: Grove Weidenfeld, 1990), 10–11.

7. See Catharine A. MacKinnon, *Toward a Feminist Theory of the State* (Cambridge: Harvard University Press, 1989); Catharine A. MacKinnon, *Feminism Unmodified: Discourses on Law and Life* (Cambridge: Harvard University Press, 1987); Robin West, "Jurisprudence and Gender," *University of Chicago Law Review* 55 (1988): 1; Robin West, "The Difference in Women's Hedonic Lives: A Phenomenological Critique of Feminist Legal Theory," *Wisconsin Women's Law Journal* 3 (1987): 81.

8. Jean-François Lyotard, *The Différend: Phrases in Dispute*, trans. Georges Van Den Abbeele (Minneapolis: University of Minnesota Press, 1988).

9. Robb, "A Refuge from Abuse," *Boston Globe*, 6 August 1990, p. 31, col. 1.

10. MacKinnon, *Feminism Unmodified*, 169.

11. I have suggested that the modern and the postmodern should be understood allegorically. I have critiqued the conception of a telos as if it were to distinguish the modern and the postmodern as periods of history; see my "Post-Structuralism, the Ethical Relation, and the Law," *Cardozo Law Review* 9 (1988): 1587. I borrow the word "constellation" from Theodor Adorno and from my discussion of what he meant by "constellation" as I described it earlier in "The Ethical Message of Negative Dialectics," *Social Concept* (1987): 3–38.

I write what gets called "postmodernity" to indicate my skepticism about the very idea of the postmodern. The distinction implicitly turns on the acceptance of criteria that can successfully distinguish historical periods from one another. For example, the distinctions between the premodern and the postmodern has often been thought to rest on the teleological development from mythos to logos. It is undoubtedly the case that writers that get grouped as postmodern—writers as diverse as Emmanuel Levinas, Jacques Derrida, and Maurice Blanchot—reject the idea that the movement from *mythos* to *logos* has been or can be completed. Indeed, they have ethically critiqued the out-of-hand rejection of myth as regressive. (I have argued, indeed, that myth is a powerful critical tool in feminist theory.)

Often postmodernity on the part of its critics gets identified with a set of "rejections": the rejection of reason, the rejection of universal ideals of justice, etc. Yet Derrida, in the text presented at this conference, which was the basis for the roundtables, insists that "[n]othing seems . . . less outdated than the *classical* emancipatory ideal"; Derrida, "Force of Law," 971. So the reduction of the postmodern to a set of rejections is clearly a misinterpretation. Several years ago I argued that the relationship between the modern and the postmodern could be understood as a constellation, borrowing the phrase from Adorno. But the transferring of Adorno's, and certainly Walter Benjamin's, metaphor of a constellation has difficulties.

"Constellation" is obviously a term borrowed from astrology. The relevance of its origin is that, as a metaphor, it is meant to indicate the deciphering of what is already "there." A constellation is not constructed or designated by a set of normative ideals or their rejection, the crux of the debate over how one defines historical periods. More specific, in Adorno, the metaphor of the constellation has ethical content. Constellation is associated with the critique of idealism in which the object is smothered by a conceptual apparatus. A constellation is how one, in other words, lets the object speak.

Historical periods are not just deciphered, they are always in part constructed, and as we have seen in the recent debates, normatively constructed. As a result, the metaphor of the constellation is problematic in the context of this debate. But does that mean that there is nothing to it? The answer, I think, is no. I have suggested that the "postmodern" should be understood as an allegory, and, as an allegory, an ethical insistence on the limit to "positive" descriptions of the principles of modernity as the "last word" on truth, justice, rightness, and so forth.

In connection with the allegory are figures and figurations that depict that limit. For example, I have painted Derrida's own ethical positioning through the figure of the *chiffonnier*. The more precise term then, rather than constellation, would be configuration through the allegory of the ethical limit on any "positive" normative description of what constitutes modernity. (Note that I have not used the word "postmodern." I believe that the debate between modernism and postmodernism, because of its historical connection to the aesthetics, should not be confused with the political, ethical debate I have just described.)

12. Derrida, "Force of Law," 995.

13. Seyla Benhabib, "The Call to the Ethical: Deconstruction, Justice, and the Ethical Relationship," *Cardozo Law Review* 13 (1991): 1219.

14. As Jacqueline Rose goes on to explain, "the concept of *jouissance* (what escapes in sexuality) and the concept of *signifiance* (what shifts within language) are inseparable"; in Lacan, *Feminine Sexuality*, 52.

15. Throughout his work, Lacan uses the term *signifiance* to refer to that "movement in language against, or away from, the positions of coherence which language simultaneously constructs"; ibid., 51.

16. Derrida, "Force of Law," 959–73.

17. Fred Dallmayr, "Justice and Violence: A Response to Jacques Derrida," *Cardozo Law Review* 13 (1991): 1237.

18. When I say the "psychical fantasy of woman," I am referring to what Lacan means when he says that what man "relates to is the *objet a*, and that the whole of his realisation in the sexual relation comes down to fantasy"; see "A Love Letter," in Lacan, *Feminine Sexuality*, 149, 157.

7

The Force of Law
Metaphysical or Political?

Nancy Fraser

In part 1 of his essay, "Force of Law: The 'Mystical Foundation of Authority,'"[1] Jacques Derrida distinguishes two different ways of thinking about the relations between force and law, and justice and violence. The first approach, styled "critique," exposes the ideological, superstructural nature of law by showing that it operates in the service of social, economic, and political forces that are posited as external and prior to the law (940–41). The second approach, in contrast, styled "deconstruction," addresses a relation between violence and law that is held to be more "intrinsic," "internal," and "complex," as it uncovers "the origin of authority, the foundation or ground, the position of the law" in a "violence without ground" (943). In Derrida's view, the second, deconstructive approach is the preferred one; it penetrates deeper than the critical approach to the heart of the relation between violence and law (942–45).

That valuation was also presupposed in the title of the symposium that inspired this chapter. Inviting reflection "On the Necessity of Violence for Any Possibility of Justice," this title characterizes the relationship between violence and justice as one of necessity as opposed to contingency. Consequently, it suggests that violence cannot fail to be implicated in any possible legal institution in any possible society, thereby insinuating, at least to my ear, that it would be folly to aspire to eliminate it. Finally, the symposium title implies that the level at which violence is implicated in law is very deep; the suggestion is that violence constitutes the enabling ground or condition for the possibility of justice. Together, these presuppositions entail that the relationship of justice to violence needs to be approached by means of a transcendental inquiry. To be sure, this will be a *negative* or quasi-transcendental inquiry, since it turns out in deconstructive thought that the ground in question is precisely an *Abgrund* (abyss). Nonetheless, the fact remains that quasi-transcendental reflection on violence as a necessary condition for justice will take precedence over critical forms of inquiry. Attempts to understand the relationship of violence and law through, say, critical social theory, political sociology, or cultural studies will be deprivileged as merely empirical and hence, comparatively superficial.

I have argued elsewhere that those versions of deconstruction that privilege the transcendental, even in this qualified form, incur a disability when it comes to thinking politically.[2] My argument is not the usual complaint that deconstruction leads to nihilism, immorality, or amorality. That complaint assumes that a quasi-transcendental deconstructive reflection can delegitimate practices and norms, an assumption I reject. Actually, insofar as quasi-transcendental reflection pertains to the conditions that enable *any* possible practices and norms, it cannot tell us much about *which* of those possible practices and norms are morally indefensible; nor can it tell us what moral attitude we should adopt toward actually existing practices and norms. Thus, the standard objection to deconstruction fails. However, this will provide only limited comfort to those who defend quasi-transcendentalized versions of deconstruction, as the argument cuts two ways. It tells equally against any defense of deconstruction along the following lines: Contrary to those who think deconstruction entails nihilism, precisely the reverse is true. What is really entailed by the radical ungroundedness of judgment is a paradigmatically ethical disposition: a heightened sense of responsibility, an exhortation to vigilance, and a commitment to the future that is all the more ethically intense for its lack of guarantees.[3] This response is entirely on a par with the original objection. It, too, supposes the possibility of deriving a normative conclusion from a quasi-transcendental premise. It, too, therefore, is unsound.

Thus, the argument about whether deconstruction entails nihilism or an ethics of responsibility ends in a stalemate. So long as the discussion remains on this plane, it cannot be resolved. More generally, so long as deconstruction remains committed to privileging even negative transcendental reflection, so long as it continues to concentrate its efforts on disclosing the prior, enabling *Abgrund* behind every merely critical normative judgment about every merely ontic state of affairs, it will never get to ethics or politics. For, as Aristotle understood, politics is a matter of just those contingent but warrantable normative judgments about just those historically and culturally variable practices and institutions that negative transcendental reflection seeks to get behind.[4] To assume, therefore, as Derrida does in his essay, that deconstruction must get beneath critique to a deeper mode of negative transcendental reflection, is to disable or impede the possibility of *political* thought about the relation between violence and law.

I illustrate this claim by contrasting two ways of understanding "the force of law." In Derrida's terms, these two ways are "deconstruction" and "critique." However, in my view, the crucial issue that divides them is: What is the nature of "the force of law"? Is that "force" metaphysical or political?

In Derrida's deconstructive account, "the force of law" inheres most elementally in the ungroundedness of the judge's judgment (960–69). Legal judgment, in his view, is necessarily underdetermined at the moment of decision, however persuasively it may be justified ex post facto. Judging, therefore, can never be "calculation" but always involves a "leap" (960–63). It is here, in the "madness" or "mystique" of a radical freedom,[5] that the "violence" of legal judgment resides. "The force of law," then, is inscribed in the deep structure of judgment. It is not a matter of contingent institutions or social relations that could in principle be altered.

There are three things worth noting about this account of "the force of law." The first is the unnecessarily paradoxical character of the discussion of judgment. Derrida goes too quickly from the uncontroversial claim that judgment is not calculation to the hyperbolic and, I think, indefensible claim that it is "madness," "mystique," and "violence." There is no discussion of intermediate positions, such as those derived from the Aristotelian conception of *phronesis*, which understand judgment as neither the application of an algorithmic decision procedure nor the exercise of an irrational will. Because he fails to consider alternatives like these, which give *nonaporetic* accounts of noncalculative judgment, Derrida fails to justify his claim that judgment is shot through with aporias (960–69). On substantive grounds, then, his account is flawed.

This substantive flaw in Derrida's account of judgment finds expression in a second problem at the level of his rhetoric. Why stylize as "force" or "violence" the fact that judging escapes calculation? This choice of word is troubling, regardless of whether we prefer to think of judging as *phronesis* or as "madness." It ups the rhetorical ante too quickly and risks the loss of important normative political distinctions by conflating a view about the (presumably inescapable) interplay of freedom and constraint in interpretation with (contingent, alterable) modes of individual and institutional coercion.

This brings me to my third and most serious objection to Derrida's account of "the force of law." His account directs our attention to a level of so-called violence in law that is constitutive and inescapable (942–43). This is a "violence" that can in no meaningful sense be called "political," as it is independent of any specific institutional or social arrangements and as it is not subject, even in principle, to change. Thus, "the force of law" in Derrida's account is essentially metaphysical.

Let me contrast that view to an alternative approach that would understand "the force of law" as political. This would be an approach that would locate law's force in contingent social relations and institutionalizations of power. It would foreswear quasi-transcendental reflection on the "violence" that must inhere in *any* possible legal institution in favor of analysis and (mere) critique of the forms of masked, structural violence that enter into social processes of judging in, for example, *our* legal system. I specify the object of critique as "forms of *masked, structural* violence" because these—as opposed to the overt, punctual violence of criminals, armies, and police—are the most difficult and most important to understand. Included here are a range of deadly systemic social processes, responsibility for which cannot easily be attributed to identifiable individual agents, but which culminate in massive harms such as malnutrition, medical neglect, and environmental toxicity.

A political critique of the "force of law" would seek to identify the various levels at which masked, structural violence enters into our institutionalized practices of legal judgment. Let me suggest three such levels that merit critical scrutiny. The first is the level of the basic constitutional principles that constrain legal interpretation. In many cases, these constitutional principles are uncontroversial and unproblematical, at least as abstractions, but in some cases, they are not. The most problematical case seems to me to be the entrenched centrality of the principle of property right in our constitution. I am not talking about the right to personal property, but rather about what we used to call in the old days "private property in the means of production." To be sure, that discourse has lost its cultural legitimacy, but the problem it names has not gone away. It is still possible in our legal system for small numbers of people to make decisions with impunity that imperil the health and livelihood of many others, while degrading the quality of life of everyone. Thus, one task for a political critique of "the force of law" would be to show how an apparatus of legal judgment can be a vehicle for the operation of masked, structural violence when it is constrained by constitutional principle to protect private property in the means of production.

A second level for critique is the deep grammar of our legal reasoning. One salient feature of this deep grammar is evident in the fact that in our legal system it is exceedingly difficult, indeed often impossible, to press claims for harms one has suffered by virtue of belonging to a social group. In contrast, it is comparatively easy to press claims in cases where the parties are identifiable individuals and the alleged harm is the result of a breach of contract or other definite assignable obligation. Thus, the deep grammar of our legal reasoning is individualistic. Problems arise, however, insofar as the legal grammar of individualism is seriously out of phase with the nature of our social system. In our social system, a great deal of harm does not take the form of individuals ripping off individuals but is rather a result of more impersonal systemic processes and of structural relations among differentially advantaged social groups. This sort of harm, however, is not usually legally admissible. In fact, the deep grammar of individualist justice presents obstacles to anyone who seeks judicial standing to claim that a systemic injustice has occurred. Thus, even before legal judging officially begins, there has already been an operation of prejudgment that has severely restricted the scope of the judge-able. This prejudgment, which embodies the individualist, deep grammar of our legal reasoning, is itself a form of masked, structural violence in the law. A political critique of "the force of law" would theorize and name it as such.[6]

Finally, there remains a third level at which a political critique could unmask the "force of law." This is the level of cultural background. When people make judgments, when they weigh the evidence and decide which principle applies and which precedent is applicable, they do so against a background of cultural assumptions. Whether we are talking about professional judges or ordinary citizens serving on juries, there are necessarily many such assumptions in play. Background assumptions—for example, about human nature, the causes of poverty, what counts as work, and proper gender roles—constitute the inescapable horizon of any judgment. Yet, in a society that is stratified by gender, color, and class, many of the most culturally authoritative and widely held assumptions about such things work to the disadvantage of subordinated social groups. They are themselves, therefore, aspects of the sociocultural structure of injustice. When they serve as elements of the tacit backdrop against which foreground legal judgments are made, they, too, become part of "the force of law."[7]

A good example of this is the congeries of androcentric assumptions that has led many judges and juries to reject self-defense as a legal defense in cases where women are accused of attacking or killing men who have battered them over a period of many years. It has been assumed that any legitimate act of "self-defense" must occur in the heat of an assault and cannot involve use of a deadly weapon against an assailant who has used "only" his fists. Yet surely those assumptions are premised on a model of male aggression that is seriously askew of many women's socialization and experience with violence.[8] To the degree that such androcentric assumptions about self-defense permeate the horizon of judgment in cases involving battered women, the "force of law" will come down with a thud on the side of patriarchy.

Let me conclude by summarizing this portion of my argument and connecting it to what went before. I have outlined three aspects of a political critique of "the force of law." In every case, the task of critique is to render visible forms of masked, structural violence that permeate, and infect, legal judgment. But the legal judgment that is the object of this critique is not any possible legal judgment whatsoever. Rather, it is a specific, institutionalized regime of justice reasoning situated in a specific, structured, sociocultural context. The point of a *political* critique of "the force of law," then, is not to identify forms of "violence" that are "necessary for any possible justice"; it is to identify forms of violence that are precisely *not* necessary.

The value of identifying unnecessary, "surplus" violence that is rooted in unjust and potentially remediable social arrangements is, I hope, obvious. This, after all, is the sort of violence we might aspire to eliminate or reduce. And that aim in the end is what dictates my own sense of priorities. To put the matter bluntly: it seems to me to have matters precisely backward to claim priority for a quasi-transcendental deconstruction of "the force of law" over a "merely" political critique.

Notes

1. Jacques Derrida, "Force of Law: The 'Mystical Foundation of Authority,' " *Cardozo Law Review* 11 (1990): 919.

2. Nancy Fraser, "The French Derrideans: Politicizing Deconstruction or Deconstructing the Political?" in her *Unruly Practices: Power, Discourse, and Gender in Contemporary Social Theory* (Minneapolis: University of Minnesota Press, 1989), 69.

3. Derrida's essay contains one version of this defense. See Derrida, "Force of Law," 960–69. For another version, see Drucilla Cornell, "Time, Deconstruction, and the Challenge to Legal Positivism: The Call to Judicial Responsibility," *Yale Journal of Law and Humanities* 2 (1990): 267.

4. Aristotle, *Politics: Book 1*, in *The Politics of Aristotle*, trans. Ernest Barker (London: Oxford University Press, 1946).

5. P. 967. ("The instant of decision is a madness, says Kierkegaard.")

6. For a book that I consider a model of this sort of critique, see generally Patricia J. Williams, *The Alchemy of Race and Rights* (Cambridge: Harvard University Press, 1991). Interestingly, Williams uses deconstructive techniques in the service of critical, as opposed to quasi-transcendental, reflection.

7. Again, the outstanding exemplar is Williams, *Alchemy*.

8. See Elizabeth Schneider, "The Dialectic of Rights and Politics: Perspectives from the Women's Movement," *New York University Law Review* 61 (1986): 589, 642–48, for an account of the difficulties in assuring legal protection for battered women.

8

Sentiment Recuperated

The Performative in Women's AIDS-Related Testimonies

Kate Mehuron

In our highly ideological times, even nostalgia has its politics. The conservatives of the sentiments believe that recovering their own forgotten history is an antidote to shallowness. The ideologues of the future see attachment to the past as that most awful of monsters, the agent of reaction. It is to be extracted from the human soul with no quarter or self-pity, for it obstructs the inevitable march of events into the next Utopia.

—Eve Hoffman, *Lost in Translation*

Eve Hoffman's story of her immigration to America, the loss of her familiar sentiments and their recuperation by her assimilation to an American way of life, graphically embodies dilemmas similar to those faced by women who write contemporary AIDS-related testimonies. Hoffman's comment in the above epigraph expresses the double-bind experienced by those who testify to a crisis that cannot be confined to any total or unitary representation. There is no imminent Utopia, nor can a nostalgically reconstructed past provide an antidote to the social upheavals that accompany this contemporary plague. Individual testimonies face the inadequacy of their singular representations to encompass the ethicopolitical significance of the AIDS pandemic, for the pandemic far surpasses the personal and the naturalized categories of everyday life.

The AIDS epidemic in the United States has exerted an exilic force upon some, defamiliarizing ordinary sentiment and requiring the work of counterdiscourses that seek to contain and to reinscribe in a different key the plague's devastations.

In this essay, I elaborate certain dilemmas faced by testimonial utterance. I defend the usefulness of Derrida's understanding of performative utterance and elegiac writing for my view of the testimonial force and significance of certain AIDS-related life writings by women, produced in the first decade of this epidemic. Additionally, my account of testimony draws on critical perspectives that are crucial to my evaluation of the significance of AIDS-related testimony. Each perspective supplements Derrida's account of performative utterance by including explicit references to the social and political context of AIDS-related testimony. This sort of explicit, sociopolitical contextualization is lacking in Derrida's texts. Hence I locate my appropriation of Derrida in relation to Michel Foucault's analytic of the games of truth within institutionalized power formations. I also draw on Gayatri Spivak's feminist postcolonialist criticisms of Derrida's idealist effacement of systemic, international socioeconomic inequalities, and his preservation of conventional gender categories. Finally, my analysis indicates the possibility offered by Derrida's own elegiac discourse for deconstructing the phallogocentric homosociality that obtains between men's writerly encomia to other men. This possibility is significant for this essay, insofar as it can recuperate a space of reading that is appreciative of denaturalized, nonheterosexist forms of homosociality and homoerotic sentiment.[1] But in order to do so, I supplement Derrida's literary and indirect gestures with the explicit interventions of recent queer theorists.

Many diverse forms of homosocial and homoerotic nurture and sustenance have emerged as gay men have fought the devastating effects of the plague. These materialist interventions of different exchange relations continue to emerge as lesbians, other women, and people of color adopt and invent coalitional relationalities that contribute to new, nonheterosexist forms of social relationships, health care discourses, and political coalitions in the epidemic. Derrida's own oversimplified, reductive references to phallogocentric "virile homosexuality" needs critique from the perspective of emergent queer theories that urge coalitional discourses and social relationships as grounds from which a politicized force can brought to bear against capitalist compulsory heterosexuality and its systematic devaluation of women and gay men, and its punitive policies against those who are HIV-positive or suffering the onset of AIDS.[2] Derrida's own self-critical, homoerotic elegies to his lost friendship with Paul de Man, and his theatrical exposure of the masculinist exclusions of women within literary-theoretical discourses of the gift, indicates his own concern about masculinist complicities in the devaluation of women within covertly homoerotic, overtly heterosexist literary sentiment. I highlight these self-resisting aspects of Derrida's critical gestures toward his own complicity in masculinist heteronormativity.[3] I find that such a reading can help us comprehend similar dilemmas of complicity announced by women's AIDS-related testimonies.

Testimonial Dilemmas and Their Elegiac Contexts

Testimony cannot hope to escape larger battles over ideology; testimony addresses sociopolitical situations and participates in canonic, disciplinary regimes of truth-telling that proscribe philosophical constraints on representation: truth as adequation of thought to its object, language as the transparent medium of reflection. Although all testimony hopes to "tell the truth," some testimonies also resist the institutional protocols of legitimation by which the truth is acknowledged as such. Not all testimonies presume to know the "truths" their resistance may produce. They recommend some truths and they also contest conventional expressions of feeling by foregrounding the new contingencies and necessities of the epidemic; these are fortuities that have destabilized the sense of previously held expressive tropes. Readers encounter moments of choice in their engagement of such texts. The testimonial challenge to institutionalized power formations appeals to the reader to participate in politicized moments that seize, cut, or overturn the present in deliberative activities that are exterior to academic reflection.

Women's AIDS-related writings are vital contributions to the cultural countermemories produced by literary criticism devoted to personalizing and honoring deceased people with AIDS (PWAs). The works that I discuss are Fran Peavey, *A Shallow Pool of Time: An HIV+ Woman Grapples with the AIDS Epidemic*, and Elizabeth Cox, *Thanksgiving: An AIDS Journal*.[4] The simplicity of style and the popular appeal of these texts may make them appear to be unlikely partners within the arena of critical readings of canonic philosophical texts offered by Jacques Derrida. However, the political or ethical urgency of testimonial enunciation often disrupts academically legitimized distinctions between high and low literatures, canonic literary authorship and popular authorship, or disciplinary boundaries between the philosophical, the literary, and the social. Additionally, the elegiac impetus of some of Derrida's most important work can also comprehend and endorse the inclusion of these AIDS-related literary productions in academic discourses.[5] Likewise, Spivak's insistence on the decolonizing gesture that ought to be undertaken by academic, literary-theoretical readings of its "other" in popular, indigenous literatures, can also be taken to affirm the value of academic encounters with literatures that are indigenous to the AIDS epidemic in the United States.[6]

Cox's journal is discussed in Timothy Murphy's "Testimony" in the anthology *Writing AIDS: Gay Literature, Language, and Analysis*.[7] I view this collection and others like it to be elegiac productions that are generated by survivors who continue to fight the disease as people living with AIDS (PWAs), as caregivers to PWAs, or as intellectuals who are coalitionally identified with the struggle of PWAs. Although Murphy and others write in a critical vein about the memoirs, diaries, chronicles, and autobiographies issuing from survivors, neither they nor myself are attempting to categorize these works generically. Within our shared elegiac context, to name a work "testimonial" is to identify a work's performance that could also be generically categorized as philosophical, autobiographical, or literary-theoretical.

The testimonial gesture is the sign of ethical and political exigencies that stem from this pandemic. One such exigency lies in the need to dignify the character of the deceased as well as the character of those who care for them, in opposition to the brutal indifference of demographic quantifications. Other ethicopolitical exigencies call for personal encomnia to offset socially sanctioned homophobic, racist, and misogynist denials of the range and ravage of the pandemic. The impetus of aestheticized commemorative works is to create solidarities among marginalized communities and to directly resist the outright governmental assaults, in the early and mid-1980s, on such projects associated with AIDS.[8]

The urgency of AIDS-related testimony also derives from a growing theoretical and community consensus that the AIDS pandemic is genocidal in its systemic and functional trajectory.[9] Bearing witness in an elegiac context has multiple survival values. Testimony can counter and create a surviving public record of the experience and complexity of the epidemic. Such oppositional knowledge-production also contributes to the theoretical resources that can fuel coalitional practices that resist statist genocidal deployments of the AIDS pandemic.

Representations of the genocidal aspect of the AIDS pandemic are controversial within the activist community. Many AIDS activists prefer to bracket such representations insofar as they are feared to be totalizing "conspiracy theories" that might function to discourage local political strategies. On the other hand, AIDS activism in the 1980s and 1990s exemplified by ACT UP/New York (AIDS Coalition to Unleash Power), has adapted the iconography of the pink triangle to serve as their political emblem of resistance. Despite many objections within the activist community to this tacit reliance on the analogy between National Socialist genocidal policies against homosexuals in the Third Reich and today's governmental administration of the epidemic, the pink triangle continues to serve the AIDS activist community as a mobilizing symbol of active resistance rather than as an icon that encourages the sense of victimization.[10]

Additionally, there is a growing dialogue in the African-American community about the racist, genocidal implications of the United States government's inadequate public policy decisions on behalf of socioeconomically disadvantaged minority groups, and this dialogue is tacitly premised on analogies drawn with the federal government's history of biomedical and militarist experimentation on minority groups, most notably the well-documented Tuskegee syphilis experiments.[11]

Finally, critical literature on the international genocidal aspects of the pandemic is burgeoning. This literature examines the possibility of U.S. governmental militarist, corporatist, and imperialist deployments of chemical-biological experimentation on "Third World" countries, as well as the racist and misogynist character of international scientific research protocols and public policy discourses about AIDS.[12] In the future, activists will draw on these debates to theorize the specific connections between racism, homophobia, class, and imperialism that are mobilized in the genocidal situation facing them in their local contexts.

The AIDS-related testimonies that I discuss in this essay are a local part of a much broader historical and political situation, one that so far defies circumscription by any reductive set of representations. The opacity of testimony to this sort of circumscription can be theorized by reference to Derrida's account of performative utterance.

Testimony's Performative Effect

In her chronicle *A Shallow Pool of Time: An HIV + Woman Grapples with the AIDS Epidemic (SPT)*, Peavey writes about her motivations for keeping a journal on the AIDS epidemic, a project begun in 1984 before she was diagnosed as HIV-positive:

> As a consultant on social change and a political comedian, I have tried to understand the social effects of the impending terrors of our time: ecological degradation, the possibility of economic collapse, and nuclear holocaust. . . . I began to wish I could read the diary of a woman who lived in the time of the Plague. I've often thought, "If we are living in a time of rapid unpredictable change and seeming social breakdown, what can we learn from those who have been through this in the past?" What clues could ordinary people—not kings, scientists, or statesmen—give us about what to watch for as the epidemic begins to affect our community, family relationships? . . . So I decided to start a journal, a personal chronicle of the AIDS epidemic, as it affected my society, as it affected me. (*SPT* ix)

Peavey's statements are straightforward. She intends to keep a chronicle that commends her affective, relational, and social truths to posterity's judgment. Offering a "nonextraordinary" account, she is neither king, statesman, nor scientist; not a power-broker in the production of truth. But she is engaged in truth-telling, and her chronicle is a project that confronts and challenges the local effects on her own body and her communities of what Foucault has described as the "power/knowledge" brokerage of truth in the 1980s AIDS crisis.[13] These effects, felt at their most intimate level of her bodily self-knowledge, have not yet acquired the naturalized status of fact. Although Peavey was diagnosed in 1988 as HIV-positive, she has since received the opposite diagnosis. At the time of this essay, she does not know whether she is dying or not.[14]

This predicament of radical uncertainty with respect to one's own bodily status is shared by many in this epidemic. The confusion has its roots in federal and pharmaceutical battles over research priorities and protocols far removed from the personal scene. Media representations of the HIV virus as the single cause of AIDS has dominated the national consciousness for over a decade, and yet there is compelling evidence that this dominant "truth" is a dissimulation of the actual power-brokerages that harbor corporate interests in maintaining it.[15] The impulse of Peavey's chronicle and others like it is to politicize the contingency and the sense of threat associated with her own bodily experience within biomedical institutionalized codes of the "truth" of AIDS. She writes,

> Today I woke from my nap with two clear thoughts. One was that if they ask all HIV + people to register and tell their previous partners, everyone who is negative should go *en masse* to the registration office and register. I have heard the story of King Christian of Denmark in World War II. The German army invaded and decreed that all Jews were to wear a yellow star of David. In the morning, so the story goes, the king came out on his horse for a ride through town wearing a yellow star; by afternoon the citizenry had followed suit. Now it was impossible to tell the Jews from everyone else, so the order lost its punch.
>
> If hundreds or even thousands of people went to register, it would make the Gann Initiative impossible to enforce. Maybe they should name Governor Deukmajian or Ronald Reagan as their sexual partners. (*SPT* 71)

What Peavey documents is the coerced identity of "HIV + " imposed upon herself, a social activist whose key strategy is coalitional thinking across personal identities, and the unnerving individualizing process by which she becomes a medical "case," increasingly vulnerable to state and federal administrative policy decisions. Peavey's truth-telling occurs within an uncertain epistemic zone; one that is liminal to biomedical "truths" as well as to the calculable political outcomes of her writing and organizing. These specific forms of indeterminacy, and her defiant challenge to resist the dominant order of naturalized "facts" are characteristic of testimonial writing.

The epistemic liminality of testimonial locution and its ethicopolitical value can be clarified by drawing on Derrida's account of performative utterance in his essay "Signature Event Context" ("SEC").[16] Derrida suggests that performative utterance, closely aligned with the momentary event, is itself liminal to other discourses that explicitly function as historical documentation, theoretical analysis, or genealogy in Foucault's sense of that term.[17] Derrida develops this theme by problematizing J. L. Austin's distinction between the performative and the constative operations of speech acts, arguing that the "graphematic system of predicates" is presupposed in the structure of locution itself ("SEC" 14). Derrida's primary agenda in this essay is to illuminate the transient temporal character of speech acts and to dissuade readers from Austin's privileging of teleological and idealist presumptions by which he anchors the "sense" of utterances.

Derrida's essay foregrounds these primary concerns through an exacting critique of J. L. Austin (and Austin's apologist, philosopher John Searle). Austin's distinction relies on the assumption that the sense of the constative locution is fixed by the adequacy (or inadequacy) of its intention to the truth values that putatively adhere to the speech act's delivery. I read the whole of Derrida's book in which this essay is located, *Limited, Inc.*, to be concerned and agitated about the failures of respectful intersubjective address between men who are engaged in the masculinist competition for phallic, self-authorizing authority in academia. Although I recommend this interpretation to those who return to the book, here I only wish to indicate that Derrida's critique of Austin buttresses his broader project of displacing the disciplinary laws of genre and discursive masculinist codes of gender, hegemonically present in American philosophical contexts.[18]

To this end, Derrida disjoins Austin's presumption of the constative's ideal, transparent adherence between intention and truth (or falsity) in the present, by introducing and defending his view of the iterable quality of all speech acts. The iterability of speech acts reside in their dependency on historically antecedent codes of language usage; a dependency evidenced in the ways that utterances partially replicate preexisting forms of expression. The iterability of speech acts resides in their partial, rather than total replication of these antecedent codes. Particularly in the linguistic sphere of writing, the essential predicate of utterance is absence. Derrida argues:

> A writing that is not structurally readable—iterable—beyond the death of the addressee would not be writing. . . . Imagine a

writing whose code would be so idiomatic as to be established and known, as secret cipher, by only two "subjects." Could we maintain that, following the death of a receiver, or even of both partners, the mark left by one of them is still writing? Yes, to the extent that, organized by a code, even an unknown and nonlinguistic one, it is constituted in its identity as mark by its iterability, in the absence of such and such a person, and hence ultimately of every empirically determined "subject." This implies that there is no such thing as a code—organon of iterability— which could be structurally secret. ("SEC" 7–8)

Absence, in this discussion, connotes a series of temporal and epistemic gaps that Derrida argues to be essential to writing. These are gaps between future addressees who receive the textural utterance and the death (absence) of the original addressee of the writing. They effect the postponements of the full sense of the text as it is appropriated in various ways by future readers. The full appropriation of the sense of a text is an indefinitely extended task stretching into the future; the task of formulating the criteria that decides whether a text has been fully appropriated is credited to the future judgments and decisions by this perpetually expanding readership. Derrida describes the illocutionary utterance as a "productive machine" whose effects and trajectory are aleatory. By this he means to emphasize the unpredictability of the sense and the indeterminate ethicopolitical implications of textual address, especially insofar as it is directed to a future (currently absent) readership.

Finally, Derrida takes issue with Austin's assumption that the intelligibility of constative utterances are anchored in ideal states of consciousness unified by teleologically oriented intentionalities ("SEC" 14). To Austin, the performative aspect of the idealistically secured sense of utterances is residual to the constative. As residue, the performative is an accidental manifestation: the mere social or empirical effects of the utterance in the world.

Here, Derrida's gesture is similar to his earlier critique of the rhetorical vehicles chosen by Saussure to discuss the distinction between the graphic and the phonemic. As with Saussure, Derrida locates Austin's moralistic contempt toward the worldly effects of performative utterance, exposing Austin's choice of metaphors such as "residue" to be the vehicle by which to convey the weight and significance of the constative/ performative distinction.[19] Derrida indicts Austin with the philosophical prejudice he has also discerned in certain figureheads of the idealist Continental tradition; a tradition partially coextensive with Plato, Husserl, and Saussure.[20] This is the logocentric prejudice against the "body" of speech, by which Derrida typically means the emotive, figurative, spontaneous, inexact, temporally dispersed, and unpredictable effect of locutions on an era's codes of conventional expression and on empirical collectivities of readers/interpreters.

Associating the performative utterance with these qualities that he also attributes to "events" and to the stigmatized "feminine" that is constructed by masculinist representational discourses, Derrida suggests that the constative dimension of speech is subject to the vicissitudes of chance. Further, he indicates that the judicative impulse of constative utterance—an impulse that attempts the closure of sense within the homogeneous space of collective consensus and communication—can in principle be disrupted by its implicit performative dimension.

Testimonial locutions, on this account, are performative insofar as they are situationally productive of unpredictable ethicopolitical judgments. What distinguishes testimonies from constative utterance is the accreditation for the responsibility of ethicopolitical judgment that they pass on to future others. Neither applauding nor lamenting this risk, Derrida inscribes an autobiographical moment that recurs in his writings: this recurs as a self-reflective gesture that points to the risk taken by his own pronouncements about others' works. Unlike Austin's essentialist predication of the judicative function to the constative speech act itself, Derrida consigns the judicative impulse to the empirical and ethicopolitical effects achieved by the risk taken by testimonies. Their truth-telling significance runs the risk of the phallogocentric inferiorization that Derrida shows to be characteristically garnered by the performative whenever it is appropriated into those conventional regimes of masculinist representational discourses that dominate public consensus. The force of Derrida's argument lies in the unconventional linkages he creates between responsible agency, speech acts, and their indeterminacy of sense. These linkages are unconventional insofar as they are critical of the standards of phallogocentric norms of legitimacy; norms that typically require a stronger degree of determinacy to hold between the present sense of speech acts and the accountability of agents who utter them.

Women's testimonies in the 1980s and early 1990s to the devastations and "sense" of the AIDS epidemic are familiar with the vulnerability of

such locutions to reappropriations by historical revisionism, sentimentality, and undreamed-of deployments of power/knowledge. The vulnerability of testimony to undesirable political appropriations is also broached
by Derrida in other contexts such as the Third Reich's ideological
appropriation of Nietzsche's texts within its totalitarian heteronormative
regime of power.[21]

Literary theorists, intent on describing the generic traits of testimony,
argue that some testimonies insist on political change; testimonial
urgency demands that the theoretical serve the revolutionary.[22] Derrida's
account of the performative encourages the view that testimony destabi-
lizes the academic and disciplinary laws of genre and implicitly destabi-
lizes discursive maculinist codes of gender as well. This defiance of some
testimonies to the totalizing recuperations of conventional discourse
often occurs as a choice to focus optimistically on present ethicopolitical
demands and their indeterminacy. The brunt of testimonial accreditation is felt in the transformed sentiments of others. Peavey writes,

> Maybe we people who carry the AIDS virus are the canaries in
> the mine. Maybe we can whistle such a true and sweet song that
> our species will see that we must get out of the mine; we must
> change our addiction to consumption, pollution and mind-
> lessness.
>
> I, and thousands like me with viruses in our bodies, are
> waiting. This is not a passive waiting: we are not resigned to
> death. In many ways we are busy doing whatever we can to
> increase our chances of "beating this thing" as Dennis put it. But
> there is a lot of waiting, too. (*SPT* 147)

Earlier in this essay, I described the context of this essay as elegiac,
rather than primarily philosophical or literary-theoretical. Deconstructive thinkers such as Shoshana Felman have elucidated elegiac locution-
ary situations that keep wake with the useless suffering endured by those
on behalf of whom some of us speak or act. Felman, Derrida, Paul de
Man, and other deconstructive thinkers are indebted to the post-
Holocaust meditations of Maurice Blanchot on wakefulness and Emmanuel Levinas's thoughts on useless suffering for the value which they place
on elegy.[23] The elegiac situation entails that one keep wake with an
other's useless, unjustifiable suffering within a cognitive twilight that
avoids the resolution of that experience by subsumption to the witness's

frames of reference. When I occupy the twilight subject-positionality of the witness, I encounter the other's bodily suffering or sentiments as exteriorities that limit the constative trajectory of my thought. In this situation, I risk ethically violating the testimony of the other by subsuming her body or her sentiment to the reductive frames of my apologetic, rational, or apocalyptic discourse. Blanchot, in *Writing and the Disaster*, has sketched the relevant paradox: an "authentic" witness, within the post-Holocaust and post-Enlightenment elegiac situation, is necessarily a "false" witness.

The difficulty faced by the witness in such elegiac contexts resides in the contradiction that obtains between the effort to honor and commemorate the other, even as one's own complicities in the conditions that perpetuate the suffering are exposed. This predicament is illustrated in Derrida's homoerotic elegiac work, *Memoires for Paul de Man*. Derrida's preface announces the elegiac, and loving context of his lectures on de Man's essays on autobiography and on Hegel's theory of memory. In his preface, Derrida comments that he has "never known how to tell a story."[24] This enigmatic phrase points to the disjunction between Derrida's intention to extend a fidelity of memory on behalf of his deceased friend; a fidelity that occasions an "impossible mourning" whose success is signified by the failure to introject the deceased's memory. Derrida describes storytelling, an activity crucial to the shared art of commemoration, as an alibi "to remain awhile longer near my friend, to keep watch over, take in, slow down, or annul the separation."[25]

Those who grieve know the tenuous place of words and memorabilia, the power that they possess to preserve as well as to efface the living reservoir of the other within the self. Derrida's appropriation of de Man's essay "Sign and Symbol in Hegel's *Aesthetics*" philosophically reiterates what is practically known: that storytelling, insofar as it is a signifying way of marking memory, disrupts the work of interiorizing recollection. Derrida's reflection appears to reinscribe de Man's proper name and text within the context of a meditation on bereavement that wants to work through the impossible emotional situation presented to him by the loss of his friend. Derrida writes,

> We can only live this experience in the form of an aporia: the aporia of mourning and of prosopopeia, where the possible remains impossible. Where *success fails*. And where faithful

interiorization bears the other and constitutes him in me (in us) at once living and dead. It makes the other a *part* of us, between us—and then the other no longer quite seems to be the other, because we grieve for him and bear him *in us*, like an unborn child, like a future. And inversely, the *failure succeeds:* an aborted interiorization is at the same time a respect for the other as other, a sort of tender rejection, a movement of renunciation which leaves the other alone, outside, over there, in his death, outside us.

Can we accept this schema? I do not think so, even though it is *in part* a hard and undeniable necessity, the very one that makes *true mourning* impossible.[26]

Derrida's intellectual appropriation of de Man is politically sententious, insofar as he textualizes de Man's anti-Semitic, youthful journalistic publications, elucidating their specific complicities with National Socialism. His elegy is also self-critical, insofar as he demonstrates his resistance to the typically masculinist urge to master, in writing and theory, the ineliminable emotional residues of memory in the wake of grieving.

Derrida's resistance to, yet complicity with masculinist tropes of male friendship is evident in the way that he attempts to aestheticize his overtly homoerotic pathos by feminine tropes of tenderness and perpetual pregnancy. From a queer-theoretical reading stance, I view Derrida to use these tropes to invert the standard masculinist denigration of "effeminacy." By assuming an effeminate tropology, his elegiac works displace the aggressively phallogocentric tropes of exclusionary homosocial address that so often orchestrate men's encomia to men. If read in this way, Derrida's elegies can be interpreted to donate an honorable discursive effeminacy to the future of philosophical, meditative discourse itself.

The coupling of criticism and feminized grieving is achieved by Derrida's incisive discussion of his friend's complicities in National Socialism. He thus foregrounds ways in which male friendship can honorably, and perhaps effeminately avoid the misogynist exclusion of women, grieve the other and take responsibility by speaking. In doing so, this sort of self-resistant writing also accredits the responsibility of ethicopolitical judgment to one's future readers and witnesses. Enacted in the elegiac context, Derrida's critique of de Man's complicities is simultaneously a challenge to those most tender sentiments associated with the work of the interiorization of the other: the yearning to take time with the other, to continue to speak with him.

Conceiving the encomia in this way illustrates why the most coura-geous and ennobling testimonies are those that most expressively love, yet enact the most profound disjunctive relation with the memory of the other. Such ruptures are wrought by the witness's obedience to the ethicopolitical mandates of the writing. In this context of useless suffering, where a virus's effects are profoundly denaturalized by the racist, homophobic, and misogynist public policy decisions of our gov-ernmental institutions and corporate bodies, activism in writing and in the world is a vital alternative to the ethical paradoxes of sententious mourning. The activist impulse of testimony aestheticizes the other's suffering body and grants it with political agency within the realm of public visibility. At its best, testimony can also explore the complicities of political agency with the oppressive regimes that have politically constructed the necessity of testimony from the outset.

Peavey's testimony shows that engaging the body's field of sensibilities for its agonistic potential can and ought to be done on behalf of identities that may be experienced as radically "other" to one's own. This perspective is increasingly important in AIDS activism, where for example, gay men and lesbians have initiated needle-exchange programs in socioeconomically disadvantaged urban areas: AIDS-aware or HIV-positive faculty and students affiliate with feminist projects to diversify the academic curriculum in the interests of inscribing race, class, gender, and sexual difference in the "canon." Aesthetic and political body performatives enacted as witness to the useless suffering of the other offer an alternative to the idealist games of narcissism that an apologetic, confessional, or ratiocinative consciousness can endlessly play with itself. Cultural critic Douglas Crimp describes his requisite activist resistance to the exclusivist norms of identity politics:

> It's not that "queer" doesn't any longer encompass their sexual practices; it does, but also entails a *relation* between those prac-tices and other circumstances that make very different people vulnerable both to HIV infection and to the stigma, discrimina-tion, and neglect that have characterized the societal and govern-mental response to the constituencies most affected by the AIDS epidemic.[27]

The 1980s debate concerning "identity politics" has met its empirical challenge and theoretical limit in the AIDS crisis. Concrete coalitions are demonstratively based on politically personifying the plight shared by identities not one's own, the plight occasioned by stigmatized and useless suffering. The survival value of linking codes of compulsory heterosexuality, the AIDS epidemic, and the social and political devaluation of sexual and racial minority populations is becoming clear. The capacity to distinguish phallogocentric homosocial and heterosexist forms of intellectual and literary complicity in these interlocked oppressions is a responsibility explicitly delineated by queer and feminist theorists and chroniclers of the epidemic. It is also a critical activity to which the self-resisting gestures of academic deconstructive discourses can contribute.

Counterfeit Sentiment

The transgendered home space is a ubiquitous theme throughout the testimonial literature written by people with AIDS or their carepartners. Many of these accounts are written by gay men in the 1980s and early 1990s who, in working through their own bereavement and perhaps their impending AIDS-related deaths, document the traumatization and reduction of their domestic space to a caregiving situation laden with only terminal and anguished outcomes.[28] Queer-theoretical appropriations of these testimonies emphasize the political gestures of these documents of grief; documents that demonstrate a sententious resistance to the stigmas imposed by compulsory heterosexuality, and to the nostalgic neoconservative deployments of "family values" that have reactively burgeoned in the political epicenter of the AIDS crisis in the United States.

The heteronormative home space has also been the theme of recent feminist critiques that focus on the domestic economy as a site of gender oppression that requires theoretical interventions and practical strategies that can reconfigure the power relations constituting masculinist home space in late capitalist societies. Feminist criticism is characterized by a variety of methodologies, each privileging specific materialist factors that are relevant to home spaces in late capitalism. Feminist critiques of the patriarchal domestic cannot be reductively characterized; they range from Marxist, socialist, and dual-systems approaches, to more recent analyses that focus on the racialization and postcolonialist stratification of the domestic. Such critiques also include feminist-Foucauldian analyses that call for genealogical accounts of the types of gender oppression that continue to be endemic at late capitalist home sites.[29]

Little critical attention has been given the testimony by Elizabeth Cox, *Thanksgiving: An AIDS Journal (TAJ)*, although her book continues to be well stocked at local feminist, lesbian, and gay bookstores in this country. This lack of critical discussion about Cox's journal can be partially attributed to the book's narrative limits. It is written by an upper-middle-class heterosexually identified woman, whose discovery of the secret of her husband's past homosexual encounters occasions a resentment that constitutes a dominant strand of her efforts to work through her bereavement. The class and heterosexual privilege assumed in Cox's narrative may render it less interesting to queer-theoretical or feminist analyses that are more likely to discuss testimonies that feature subject-positionalities marginal to the dominant white heterosexual culture in the United States.

However, Cox does portray the gender-specific dilemmas and forms of resistance that haunt and mobilize middle-class women affected by the AIDS epidemic. Reading her testimony provides the occasion to think through the problem of counterfeit sentiment presented to many avowedly heterosexual women who find themselves in a domestic care partnership with men who have contracted HIV through nonheterosexual modes of transmission.[30] Read from a deconstructive point of view, Cox's journal can help readers to comprehend the stakes in Gayatri C. Spivak's materialist-deconstructive departure from the concept of value and gift-giving that animates Derrida's analysis of the counterfeit.

Elizabeth Cox bears witness to the grief and resentment associated with her husband's betrayal by his homosexual affair that occurred early in their marriage. As Keith's wife and care partner, Cox chronicles the month-by-month decline of her husband's health and the circuitries of her resentment and sadness. Her writing documents her emotional movement from the isolated, nuclear family perspective that takes her situation as a "personal" problem, to the politicized stance formed by her involvement in the coalitional settings of gay-affirmative, homosocial support groups and her involvement in the alternative health care institutions of the Gay Men's Health Crisis in New York City. Cox describes her marriage to Keith as an escape from her upper-middle-class status and future. She writes,

> He was an escape from the world of Ivy League colleges, stories of my ancestors' accomplishments, and remarks tinged with suspicion about anything that had to do with self-expression or, God forbid, vanity. An escape from a world where the emphasis was on external achievement void of any hint of introspection. I felt Keith had saved me from the world of unspoken emotions, a world where you could cry and tear your hair out all afternoon alone in your room and no one would take notice as long as you showed up for dinner. (*TAJ* 33)

The marriage is portrayed as Cox's escape from the counterfeit sentiment generated by middle-class normative expectations about her social role; her escape is her entry into the world of authentic sentiment in what appears to be its expressive immediacy.

Cox envisions her home with Keith as a sort of "home" under erasure; Keith's different class background functions as a different and pleasurably unfamiliar template upon which to base her emotional and professional priorities. The life of creative expression that she imagines to be possible with him occurs in a relationship offering a free space within which both could pursue musical careers. It is a "home" that privileges artistic excellence and intellectual autonomy over predictability or financial security. The painfully ironic repetition of traditional gender roles induced by Keith's illness, occasions a depth of resentment that is worsened by a class-related ethos: "And, since the WASP ethos is built on getting your just deserts, I keep thinking: What did I do to deserve this? Did I do something wrong?" (*TAJ* 112).

Cox puts into question her own representations of the value of her care partnership and chronicles the process as a significant way to reconstitute a self that is separate from the traditional gender roles of a woman who gives her time as the primary caregiver in a family unit. In her recuperative process, she questions the binaries of giving or taking, the counterfeit or the real, the gift or restitution: binaries that also dominate Derrida's analysis of the gift and Spivak's call for critical attention to materialist assessments of value in late capitalist domestic space. Derrida's critical readings of the domestic or private economies in canonic philosophical texts have ranged from Aristotle's discourse on the distinction between household and private economies found in his *Politics*, to Heidegger's discourse on the dwelling place of poetic language, and the metaphoric values of proximity, propriety, and sheltering associated with his poetic, a/humanist use of language.[31] On the level of theoretical analysis, Derrida shows the metaphorical and metaphysical underpinnings of naturalized heterosexual sentiment. On the level of practical meditations, Cox unfolds the same and confirms Derrida's suspicions about the binaries that supplement and reinforce the attachment of subjects to gender-oppressive positionalities.

In the initial essays in *Given Time: I. Counterfeit Money*, Derrida conducts his interrogation of these binaries by showing the aporetic structure that is common to the traditional opinions about time and the gift that are presumptively retained in many canonic works of literature, criticism, and philosophy.[32] Interrogating these themes in the work of Heidegger, Marcel Mauss, and Emile Benveniste, Derrida locates the concept of economic exchange that is implicit to these texts' locutions of "giving" and "taking" time. As usual, Derrida concentrates on the metaphorical vehicle chosen by these writers in order to infer their evaluative stance about the subject of their discourse.

Especially in his reading of Mauss, Derrida elucidates the aporia posed by Mauss's semantics of the gift: the gift's intelligibility relies on its antonymic contrast to all the semantic values associated with economic exchange.[33] Derrida shows that in Mauss's discourse, the comprehensibility and value of the gift presupposes its absolute autonomy from economic rationality and its associated conditional rhetoric of reciprocity, debt, restitution, credit, and payment. Derrida concludes that the sense of the gift remains privative in such discourses. That is, the gift in Mauss's discourse is absolutely exterior to the cycle of exchange; it is interruptive of exchange and annuls exchange by its presence. But the gift can only be understood privatively as a disruption, and its entry as such is analyzed by Derrida in an argument that is homologous to his discussion of Saussure's cognitive aporia: an aporia occasioned by the temporal alterity of the linguistic event in relation to conventional codes of language.

The aporetic structure of the gift is located in the fact that its phenomenal manifestation remains economic, yet its value as "good" remains associated with the rhetoric of *pure* generosity, authenticity, and gratitude. Its ethical value is thus located within the realm of a regulative ideal that is essentially barred from concrete actuality. Derrida implies that insofar as the gift is understood by reference to such an absolute standard, its complicitous involvement in masculinist domestic and public spheres of exchange remains idealized, thus concealed from ordinary view. Further, its actual value within ordinary modes of exchange is trivialized by the hegemony of the absolute standard; a standard consistently betrayed by the gift's compromises of its purity by its participation in phenomenal, discursively "feminine" forms of exchange.

Thus Derrida locates the traditional metaphysical and phallogocentric prejudice which in this case inferiorizes the qualities associated in Mauss's texts with the gift: its transience, its opacity to mastery and absolute possession within gift-giving economies, and its quotidian contamination by degrees of indebtedness, resentment, or inauthentic displays of sentiment. Derrida's reading implicitly alludes to the emotional dilemma that Cox explicitly acknowledges: the dilemma of possible counterfeit sentiment that is occasioned by the necessary gift-giving within the heteronormative domestic exchange depicted by these testimonies. Gender difference and gender inequity in the masculinist domestic site complicates the issue of counterfeit or authentic sentiment for both writers as well. The first mystification to be dispensed with, for many heterosexually identified women who testify to such AIDS-related care partnerships, is the masculinist regulatory ideal of "pure" and "feminine" generosity. Cox's own concrete process of affirmatively choosing to engage in such a partnership is fostered by disrupting the iron-clad laws of gender through the rejection of these metaphysically laden, systemic mystifications of gender roles.

Derrida continues to probe and displace the linkages between the laws of gender and the laws of genre in his reading of Baudelaire's story "Counterfeit Money." In his writing, Derrida falls short of either feminizing his own text or performing a transgendered subject-positionality. But he does forefront the sexual politics of textual authorization and canonicity, taking Baudelaire's tale of the monetary donation as his starting point. Here Derrida relies on certain theatric aspects of his commentary that provoke questions regarding the sexual politics of reading, especially questions regarding the reader's sexed and gendered "interests" that are engaged by his writing. In this work, Derrida highlights the issue of accreditation, specifically addressing the mysterious accreditation process that establish the worth of a text by masculinist literary institutions.[34] The multivalent "secrets" of the text, a text self-consciously and complicitously legitimated by masculinist institutional authorization, are donated to readers for commentary and reinscription.

Derrida reiterates Baudelaire's story as a scene of masculinist, homosocial friendship. In such a scene, the phallogocentric symbolic structure mediating the friendship requires the notable absence of women. As notable exclusions, women thus are present as possible addressees of the story. Women are the witnesses, present in the mode of notable absences, to the narrative staging of the rivalrous games of interest that circulate between men around the questionable authenticity of the coin donated to a beggar. The beggar's subjectivity is also excluded from the masculinist games of self-authorization that are taking place. Yet the beggar's face remains as a memory: a haunting memory that, when narrativized, invokes his mute, needy demand. Derrida's reiteration thus recasts Baudelaire's scene as a double exclusion of two figures traditionally scorned by the phallocentric philosophical canon: women, and the immediacy and pathos of need, especially need as it is embodied by disenfranchised minority populations. Derrida's reading insists upon raising the issue of the exclusion of women from the accrediting agency of literary and philosophical institutionality, isomorphically aligning their absent presence with the mute and needy demand of the beggar. I suggest that this tropological gesture at once forefronts the bourgeois concerns of some women, and yet occludes materialist issues associated with socioeconomic disenfranchisement.

As performance, Derrida's essay solicits the reader's gendered and interested investment in the decideability of the coin's (text's) value. He intensifies the games of interest he plays with his reader by framing his commentary with citations from Baudelaire's own oeuvre that poetically invoke the figure of the prostitute; a figure that in Baudelaire's text didactically portrays the indiscriminate tastes of literary critics. Derrida's second citation is also from Baudelaire: a poetic fragment depicting the fall of Icarus in his defeat by his credulous embrace of the sublimity of beauty.[35] The citational, poetic frame chosen by Derrida appears to highlight and reiterate the enigma of Derrida's authorial intention and sentiment. The autobiographical "secrets" of Derrida's text remain undisclosed, as does the mysterious identity of the woman or women who are excluded. The reader is placed in the discursive "feminized" subject-positionality of the witness who is invited to take the challenge of responding to the masculinist scene of effacement provoked by Derrida's text. This is what I have undertaken to do in this essay.

In my view, Derrida has thus donated a puzzle to his readers to articulate what sentiments are closeted by the norms of compulsory heterosexuality, whose exclusions continue to be enforced by masculinist privilege in the academic institution, and what downfalls are poetically presaged by Icarus's voyage to the absolute phallogocentric realm of the sublime. Derrida, who "cannot tell a story," tells others' stories and performatively enacts his own. He opens his book with the signature of Madame Maintenon, who loves within the "time of the king." This is time structured by a phallogocentric transcendental illusion, a time unfolding in the privatized space of heterosexual love where confusion reigns about who is taking and who is giving time. The normative masculinist expectation of woman's pure generosity elides her calculations of her own gains and losses in the household.

As if doubling, on the level of quotidian struggle, the issues raised by Derrida's discursive games, Elizabeth Cox's chronicle presents readers with a woman's concrete effort to work through these perilous phallogocentric shoals. She depicts the naturalized proprieties of domestic space, in which her generously given time is a presumed natural derivative of the ever-nourishing natural world. Within this utopian metaphysical shelter, her household is presumed to bar the voracious profit motives proper to the economic vertigo of public exchange.[36] The household love that is "natural" to women is normatively required in the AIDS crisis; this is heterosexual sentiment, metaphysically hence nostalgically described. It is the normative expectations of her role that Cox resists by the production and publication of her journal. Derrida and Cox pose the possibility of counterfeit sentiment, the sexual politics of love that mystify the conditions of the gift exchange within the phallogocentric domestic economy of privatized love. The interventions of both texts incite readers' oppositional interest that might forestall the reinscription of gender hierarchies in the literary productions occasioned by this epidemic. Derrida leaves it to readers to remark on the overt masculinist homosocial scenes he depicts, and on the regulative ideals that bind the compulsory heterosexual backdrop of these literary scenes. On the other hand, Cox leaves it to readers to philosophize about the transgendered transvaluation that she undertakes; a transvaluation necessary so as to be able to embrace the care partnership and to reconstruct her self in bereavement.

Spivak's materialist deconstructive thesis would imply that neither writer adequately interrogates the question of the materialist exchanges that subtend value, although the aporetic dimensions of value provokes the writing of their texts. Spivak argues that the form of counterfeit sentiment most in need of interrogation by Derrida, is the sentimental indulgence of the ideological status quo that literary critics import to their critical practices. In at least two essays, Spivak indicts Derrida for the same failing, claiming that Derrida ought to "literalize" his interests by moving away from his idealist engagement with canonic metaphors of value and by clarifying his ongoing conceptual conflation between commercialized exchange value and usury.[37] She calls on Derrida to bring his analytic focus to bear on the effects of the proliferation of commercial value in globalized, imperialist economies. His method could thus contribute to the feminist project of identifying global systemic stratifications and differentiations of different classes of exploitable populations under postindustrial capitalist societies.

On Spivak's terms, a critical reading of *Thanksgiving* requires academic readers who would simultaneously disrupt the literary and philosophical canon by taking testimony seriously, yet resist theoretically domesticating such books. Such domestication occurs when readers implicitly analogize the relations highlighted by Cox's narrative. Spivak writes,

> But in order to see in those similarities the structural essence of the formations thus analogized, it is necessary to exclude the fields of force that make them heterogeneous, indeed discontinuous. . . . It is to exclude those relationships between the ego/phallus and money that are attributive and supportive and not analogical. Inheritance in the male line by way of patronymic legitimacy, indirectly sustaining the complex lines of class-formation, is, for example, an area where the case of the money-form, and that of the ego-form in the dialectic of the phallus, support each other and lend the subject the attributes of class- and gender-identity.[38]

Spivak's critique suggests that certain representations of value, if accepted without question, reinforce dissimulative forms of sentimentality that are threatening to heterosexual women who are positioned as care partners in the epidemic. On my interpretation, those representations of value that also enervate women's gift-giving are the tropes and prescriptions of compulsory heterosexuality that enforce the attributive and supportive relations between heterosexuality, naturalized gender roles, and middle-class identities.

By my synthesis, I suggest that the bourgeois games of interest that dictate both the field of liberal feminist academic criticism and Derrida's playing field of masculinist literary accreditation and heterosexual privilege, serve to obscure the actual, material predicates of the "subject" of the AIDS pandemic. Cox enacts a partial and brave resistance to her own WASP ethos and its self-defeating sentimental and normative codes by her participation in a gay-affirmative, counterinstitutional health care context and in nonmasculinist homosocial support groups. Spivak would philosophically intervene by interrogating capitalist and colonizing fields of force that disrupt as well as prescribe the prevailing consensus that, in turn, legitimates masculinist and heterosexist sentimentality in the pandemic. What is recuperated by Spivak's materialist-deconstructive questioning are forms of denaturalized sentiment that could supplant hegemonic sexual and class identities. I suggest that from an activist perspective, such denaturalized sentiments can emotionally fuel coalitional relationalities. These in turn can begin to fracture the normalized, masculinist gender hierarchies that truncate and distort the exchanges necessary for nurture and survival in the epidemic.

An example of such a political hope is given by Patricia Williams in her essay "On Being the Object of Property." She extrapolates the supportive and attributive relation between bourgeois sentiments of motherhood, racist devaluations of nonwhite babies commodified for adoption in the U.S. marketplace, and the international devaluation of HIV-infected babies demographically contained in "Third World" regions.[39] The strategy of her writing consists in questioning the specific material predication of the "subject" of AIDS discourses, and parallels Spivak's interrogation of the exchange value of wet nursing in Mahasweta Devi's story "The Breast Giver." Both partially expose the other scene of the sentimentality of bourgeois images of motherhood by examining the commodification of that sentimentality, the exchange value of which is predicated on the devaluation of other, materially specific subjects of the pandemic.

The activist counterpart to the deconstructive exposure of complicity in AIDS-related literatures is the political critique of AIDS-related death and public policy decisions. If our academic recuperation of AIDS-related testimonies only involves the exposure of our own complicities, then a "confessional effect" is propagated that Foucault argues to to be inherently conservative insofar as it is deployed by regimes of biopower to subjugate individuals by normalization.[40] Collaborative testimonies that use hybrid forms of writing to strategize opposition to racist, heterosexist, and misogynist stigmatizations of HIV-infected women resist this confessional effect and tell the stories of practices that displace the binarisms of counterfeit/real sentiment.[41] Such practices enact different exchange relationships that counter capitalist and heterosexist representations of value and sentiment. Williams describes her experience of a community that uses bartering as an oppositional exchange relationship: "Cradled in this community whose currency was a relational ethic, my stock in myself soared. My value depended on the glorious intangibility, the eloquent invisibility, of my just being a part of the collective—and in direct response I grew spacious and happy and gentle."[42] The bartering of safe-sex stories, oppositional maternal practices, transgendered care partner arrangements, clean needle exchanges, HIV-infected women's activism in prisons and urban housing projects—these practices and many others perform the promise of resistant communities that Wiliams's words invoke. These are the "home" stories that middle-class white Americans have not yet learned to tell, but to which they ought to testify.

Notes

1. The distinction between heterosexist and masculinist forms of homosociality, and forms of homoerotic sentiment and homosociality that display resistance to misogynist, heterosexist hegemonic frameworks has been incisively established. For helpful accounts, see Eve Kosofsky Sedgwick, "Introduction: Axiomatic," in *Epistemology of the Closet* (Berkeley and Los Angeles: University of California Press, 1990), 1–63; Jane Gallop, *Thinking Through the Body* (New York: Columbia University Press, 1988).

2. For references to, and brief discussions of Derrida's phrase, see the Introduction to this volume. For a full elaboration of the concept of compulsory heterosexuality, see Adrienne Rich, "Compulsory Heterosexuality and Lesbian Existence," in *The Lesbian and Gay Studies Reader*, ed. Henry Abelove, Michele Aina Barale, and David M. Halperin (New York: Routledge, 1993), 227–54.

3. For her description of deconstructive self-resistance, see Barbara Johnson, "Deconstruction, Feminism, and Pedagogy," in *A World of Difference* (Baltimore: Johns Hopkins University Press, 1987), 42–46.

4. Fran Peavey, *A Shallow Pool of Time: An HIV + Woman Grapples with the AIDS Epidemic* (Philadelphia: New Society, 1990); hereafter *SPT*. Elizabeth Cox, *Thanksgiving: An AIDS Journal* (New York: Harper and Row, 1990); hereafter *TAJ*.

5. Jacques Derrida, *Memoires for Paul de Man*, trans. Cecile Lindsay, Jonathan Culler, Eduardo Cadava, and Peggy Kamuf (New York: Columbia University Press, 1989); Eve Sedgwick, *Tendencies* (Durham: Duke University Press, 1993), 252–66.

6. For example, see Gayatri Spivak's readings of the popular short stories "Draupadi" and

"Breast-Giver" by Mahaweta Devi in her *In Other Worlds: Essays in Cultural Politics* (New York: Methuen, 1987), 179–268.

7. Timothy F. Murphy, "Testimony," in *Writing AIDS: Gay Literature, Language, and Analysis*, ed. Timothy F. Murphy and Suzanne Poirier (New York: Columbia University Press, 1993), 306–19. For annotations on all of the testimonies I discuss, see the "Annotated Bibliography," in *Confronting AIDS Through Literature: The Responsibilities of Representation*, ed. Judith Laurence Pastore (Urbana: University of Illinois, 1993).

8. For an account of the Reagan-Bush Administrations' assaults on the aesthetic productions of PWAs and their advocates through the imposition of the Helms Amendment's judicial restraints on the National Endowment for the Arts, see Steven C. Dubin, "AIDS: Bearing Witness," in *Arresting Images: Impolitic Art and Uncivil Actions* (New York: Routledge, 1992), and C. Carr, *On Edge: Performance at the End of the Twentieth Century* (Hanover: Wesleyan University Press, 1994).

9. For a feminist account of this genocidal situation, see Gena Corea, *The Invisible Epidemic: The Story of Women and AIDS* (New York: HarperCollins, 1992). For an account that emphasizes the organizational failure to address the epidemic adequately, see Charles Perrow and Mauro F. Guillen, *The AIDS Disaster: The Failure of Organizations in New York and the Nation* (New Haven: Yale University Press, 1990). For arguments that defend a homophobic conspiracy by the U.S. military, see Robert Lederer, "Origin and Spread of AIDS: Is the West Responsible?" *CovertAction* 28–29 (Summer 1987–Winter 1988): 43–54, 52–65.

10. For a critique of ACT UP's use of the pink triangle iconography, see Stuart Marshall, "The Continued Political Use of Gay History: The Third Reich," in *How Do I Look? Queer Film and Video*, ed. Bad Object Choices (Seattle: Bay Press, 1991). For further response, see Les Wright, "Gay Genocide as a Literary Trope," in *AIDS: The Literary Response*, ed. Emmanuel S. Nelson (New York: Twayne, 1992), 50–68.

11. The well-documented study to which all AIDS conspiratologists refer is James H. Jones, *Bad Blood: The Tuskegee Syphilis Experiment* (New York: Free Press, 1981).

12. Renee Sabatier, *Blaming Others: Prejudice, Race and Worldwide AIDS*. The Panos Institute (Philadelphia: New Society, 1988); Renee Sabatier, *AIDS and the Third World*. The Panos Institute (Philadelphia: New Society, 1989); Richard Chirimuuta and Rosalind Chirimuuta, *AIDS, Africa and Racism* (London: Free Association Books, 1989); Paula Treichler, "AIDS and HIV Infection in the Third World: A First World Chronicle," *Remaking History: Discussions in Contemporary Culture*, ed. Barbara Kruger and Phil Mariana, DIA Art Foundation Discussions in Contemporary Culture (Seattle: Bay Press, 1989), 31–86; Cindy Patton, "From Nation to Family: Containing African AIDS," in *Nationalisms and Sexualities*, ed. Andrew Parker, Mary Russo, Doris Sommer, and Patricia Yaeger (New York: Routledge, 1992), 218–34; Paul Farmer, *AIDS and Accusation: Haiti and the Geography of Blame* (Berkeley and Los Angeles: University of California Press, 1992).

13. For Foucault's understanding of the intellectual's activist engagement of theory as a particular practice that is local and regional, and for his view of certain knowledges as systematically disqualified by the politically legitimized systems of cognition and scientificity, see Michel Foucault, "Intellectuals and Power," and "Two Lectures," in *Power/Knowledge: Selected Interviews and Other Writings, 1972–1977*, ed. Colin Gordon, trans. Colin Gordon, Leo Marshall, John Mepham, and Kate Soper (New York: Pantheon Books, 1980).

14. I heard Peavey announce the news of her false-positive status at her recent presentation at Common Language Bookstore in Ann Arbor, Michigan, May 1993. Her chronicle of this experience is forthcoming in her book *By Life's Grace* (Philadelphia: New Society, 1994).

15. For discussions of the pharmaceutical and corporatist investments in the HIV dogma, see Bruce Nussbaum, *Good Intentions: How Big Business and the Media Establishment are Corrupting the Fight Against AIDS* (New York: Viking, 1991); John Lauristsen, *The AIDS War:*

Propaganda, Profiteering and Genocide from the Medical-Industrial Complex (New York: Asklepios, 1993); John Lauristen, *Poison by Prescription: The AZT Story* (New York: Asklepios, 1992).

16. Jacques Derrida, "Signature Event Context," *Limited Inc.*, trans. Samuel Weber (Evanston: Northwestern University Press, 1988).

17. Foucault's understanding of genealogy as the historicizing and activist displacement of dominant knowledge systems by the retrieval of subjugated historical memories, can be found in Michel Foucault, "Nietzsche, Genealogy, History," in *Language, Counter-Memory, Practice,* ed. Donald F. Bouchard, trans. Donald F. Bouchard and Sherry Simon (Ithaca: Cornell University Press, 1977).

18. Jacques Derrida, "The Law of Genre," in *On Narrative,* ed. W. J. T. Mitchell (Chicago: University of Chicago Press, 1981), 51–77. For a challenging appropriation of Derrida's essay in the context of thinking through the transsexual and transgendered predicament in the twentieth century, see Sandy Stone, "The *Empire* Strikes Back: A Posttranssexual Manifesto," *Camera Obscura: A Journal of Feminism and Film Theory* 29 (1992): 150–76.

19. Derrida parodies the moralism he discerns in Saussure's choice of vehicle. He emphasizes Saussure's choices, showing that for Saussure writing is a "garment of perversion," a "debauchery," a "festival mask" concealing the original fallenness of language from its intuitive stronghold in an originary act of consciousness. See Jacques Derrida, *Of Grammatology,* trans. Gayatri Chakravorty Spivak (Baltimore: Johns Hopkins University Press, 1976), 35.

20. For his argument showing the equivocality of the philosophical value of writing for Plato, see Jacques Derrida, "Plato's Pharmacy," *Dissemination,* trans. Barbara Johnson (Chicago: University of Chicago Press, 1981). Derrida identifies the logocentric, and later, what he calls the phallogocentric bias against temporal flux and its innate, "feminine" passivity, which Husserl illustrates in his transcendental phenomenology of internal time consciousness. See Jacques Derrida, *Of Grammatology,* 66; *Speech and Phenomena,* trans. David B. Allison (Evanston: Northwestern University Press, 1973), 70–87.

21. Jacques Derrida, "Otobiographies: The Teaching of Nietzsche and the Politics of the Proper Name," in *The Ear of the Other,* ed. Christie McDonald, trans. Peggy Kamuf (New York: Schocken Books, 1988), 23–32.

22. Doris Sommer, " 'Not Just a Personal Story': Women's *Testimonios* and the Plural Self," in *Life/Lines: Theorizing Women's Autobiography,* ed. Bella Brodzki and Celeste Schenck (Ithaca: Cornell University Press, 1988), 107–30; John Beverly, "The Margin at the Center: On *Testimonio,*" in *De/Colonizing the Subject,* ed. Sidonie Smith and Julia Watson (Minneapolis: University of Minnesota Press, 1992), 91–114.

23. Shoshana Felman, "After the Apocalypse: Paul de Man and the Fall to Silence," in *Testimony: Crises of Witnessing in Literature, Psychoanalysis, and History,* ed. Shoshana Felman and Dori Laub, M.D. (New York: Routledge, 1992); Emmanuel Levinas, "Useless Suffering," in *Emmanuel Levinas: Collected Philosophical Papers,* ed. Alphonso Lingis (Norwell, Mass.: Kluwer Academic Press, 1987), 156–67; Maurice Blanchot, *The Writing of the Disaster,* trans. Ann Smock (Lincoln: University of Nebraska Press, 1986), 27–29.

24. Jacques Derrida, "Mnemosyne," in *Memoires for Paul de Man,* trans. Cecile Lindsay, Jonathan Culler, Eduardo Cadava, and Peggy Kamuf (New York: Columbia University Press, 1989), 3.

25. Derrida, "The Art of Memoires," *Memoires,* 48.

26. Derrida, "Mnemosyne," *Memoires,* 35.

27. Douglas Crimp, "Right On, Girlfriend!" *Social Text* 33 (1992): 16.

28. Neil Bartlett, *Ready to Catch Him Should He Fall* (New York: Dutton, 1992); Michael Cunningham, *A Home at the End of the World* (New York: Farrar, Strauss and Giroux, 1990); Paul Monnette, *Borrowed Time: An AIDS Memoir* (New York: Avon Books, 1988); Bo Huston, *Remember Me* (New York: Amethyst, 1991); Herve Guibert, *To the Friend Who Did Not Save My Life,* trans. Linda Coverdale (New York: Macmillan, 1990).

29. Biddy Martin and Chandra Talpade Mohanty, "What's Home Got To Do With It?" in *Feminist Studies/Critical Studies*, ed. Teresa de Lauretis (Bloomington: Indiana University Press, 1986); Lee Quinby, "Resistance on the Homefront: Re(con)figuring Home Space as a Practice of Freedom," in *Anti-Apocalypse: Exercises in Genealogical Criticism* (Minneapolis: University of Minnesota Press, 1994); Leslie Kanes Weisman, *Discrimination by Design: A Feminist Critique of the Man-Made Environment* (Chicago: University of Chicago Press, 1992).

30. For other similar books see Carol Lynn Pearson, *Good-Bye, I Love You* (New York: Random House, 1986) and Barbara Peabody, *The Screaming Room* (New York: Avon Books, 1986).

31. Jacques Derrida, "Ousia and Gramme: Note on a Note from *Being and Time*," and "The Ends of Man," in *Margins of Philosophy*, trans. Alan Bass (Chicago: University of Chicago Press, 1982), 29–67, 109–36.

32. Jacques Derrida, *Given Time: I. Counterfeit Money*, trans. Peggy Kamuf (Chicago: University of Chicago Press, 1992).

33. Derrida, "The Madness of Economic Reason: A Gift Without Present," *Given Time*, 34–70.

34. Derrida, " 'Counterfeit Money' II: Gift and Countergift, Excuse and Forgiveness," *Given Time*, 108–71.

35. The first citation is from Balzac's chapter titled "What Prostitutes Are," in his *Splendeurs et misères des courtisanes*. See Derrida, " 'Counterfeit Money' II: Gift and Countergift," *Given Time*, 71; the second citation is from Baudelaire's poem "The Complaints of Icarus," in his *Oeuvre complètes*, 1. See Derrida, " 'Counterfeit Money' II: Gift and Countergift," *Given Time*, 171–72.

36. Derrida, *Given Time*, 158.

37. Gayatri Chakravorty Spivak, "Scattered Speculations on the Question of Value," in *In Other Worlds*, 156; "Limits and Openings of Marx in Derrida," in *Outside in the Teaching Machine* (New York: Routledge, 1993), 94–119.

38. Spivak, "Scattered Speculations," 156.

39. Patricia Williams, "On Being the Object of Property," in *The Alchemy of Race and Rights: Diary of a Law Professor* (Cambridge: Harvard University Press, 1991), 216–36.

40. Michel Foucault, "Scientia Sexualis," in *The History of Sexuality*, 1:51–73.

41. The ACT UP/New York Women and AIDS Book Group, *Women, AIDS and Activism* (Boston: South End, 1990); *Positive Women: Voices of Women Living with AIDS*, ed. Andrea Rudd and Darien Taylor (Toronto: Second Story, 1992); *AIDS: The Women*, ed. Ines Rieder and Patricia Ruppelt (San Francisco: Cleis, 1988); Katie King, "Local and Global: AIDS Activism and Feminist Theory," *Camera Obscura* 28 (January 1992): 79–98; Caren Kaplan, "Resisting Autobiography: Out-Law Genres and Transnational Feminist Subjects," in *De/Colonizing the Subject*, ed. Smith and Watson, 115–38.

42. Williams, *Alchemy*, 230.

9

Crossing the Boundaries Between Deconstruction, Feminism, and Religion

Ellen T. Armour

Why Derrida? Why Religion? Questions and Contexts

Any survey of feminist theory/philosophy over the past decade makes it clear that the status of Derrida's relationship to feminism is hardly unambiguous or uncontested. Many feminist theorists acknowledge a general debt to Derrida's work but find his own engagements with gender issues problematic (to varying degrees).[1] Feminist theorists willingly credit Derrida with acute exposure of the partiality of Western metaphysics' claim to universality. Similarly, they credit him with developing strategies to undercut its master "text," strategies they want to appropriate for feminist projects. However, they argue that Derrida's own explicit considerations of feminist issues simply perpetuate (though perhaps in more dangerous guise) business-as-usual among men. His discussions of the place of feminism and its strategies on the contemporary political scene are dismissed as antifeminist.[2] His attempts to think or write from the place of woman are rejected as yet another instance of a man's appropriation of women's voices.[3]

The issue of religious motifs in Derrida's work has elicited even stronger defensive reactions from contemporary theologians—feminist and otherwise. In 1982, the volume *Deconstruction and Theology* appeared, which proclaimed in its opening pages that deconstruction was "in the final analysis *the death of God put into writing.*"[4] That apocalyptic announcement served as a rallying cry around which theologians denounced Derrida as the latest version of nihilism against which religion must be defended. Some theologians defended religion against Derrida by separating religion from what they understood Derrida to be questioning, philosophy or metaphysics narrowly understood.[5] Some argued that Derrida was simply telling religiously minded people what Martin Luther had been saying all along: believers know God "by faith alone."[6] All the philosophical systems in the world cannot establish that faith on firm ground. Thus in their view, Derrida's challenge disturbs philosophy (and theology insofar as it has relied upon philosophy as its ground) but religion per se escapes unscathed.

Other than certain similarities in tone and strategy, it would seem that these evaluations of Derrida's usefulness have little in common. After all, what do feminism and religion have in common? Certainly, from the perspective of many feminist philosophers, feminism is of a piece with postmodernism while religion is hardly *au courant*, and at least potentially a throwback to the premodern. From many theologians' perspectives, feminism constitutes a critical perspective that promotes constructive thinking and brings new life to religious discourse; deconstruction, on the other hand, seems aimed toward silencing religious discourse once and for all.

Both attempts to keep deconstruction at bay (from feminism on the one hand, and from religion on the other) misconstrue deconstruction's value for these enterprises. Theologians are right to recognize Derrida's work as a challenge to business-as-usual within theology's discourse about God. However, this challenge opens up other possibilities for religious discourse. Similarly, feminists also rightly recognize Derrida as posing certain challenges to their work. Deconstruction calls critical attention to some of feminism's assumptions, but alternative possibilities that can further feminist goals emerge from that disruption. Rather than sounding the death knell of religion or of feminism, I would argue that Derrida holds out the possibility of helping both feminism and religion follow certain courses that each deems important. Moreover, Derrida's work with religious discourse also calls into question any facile dismissal of religion by feminists. I shall argue that the debts to Derrida that feminists acknowledge are integrally bound up with the place of religion in his thought. As this essay will show, connections between God and gender figure prominently in deconstruction's exposure of the limits of the text of Western metaphysics' claims to absolute truth and to universality. Thus, Derrida's work makes it clear that feminist theory/philosophy needs to be engaged with religion; indeed, his work suggests that it already is.

Two French thinkers who have come to be important for current feminist thought, Julia Kristeva and Luce Irigaray, have recognized feminism's stake in religion. Both Kristeva and Irigaray are trained psychoanalysts, but their writings cover a broad range of scholarship. Both are attempting to address the absence of attention to "woman" by psychoanalysis and by Western culture in general. This interest leads both thinkers to religion as one site of the West's primordial forgetting of woman and thus of her potential recovery. Both Kristeva and Irigaray write with Jacques Lacan's re-reading of Freud in the background. Irigaray uses that background to interrogate the tradition of Continental philosophy. Her interrogation of psychoanalysis and, through it, the West's philosophical tradition, reveal that both are governed by an economy of sameness whose standard is masculine. In this economy, woman simply serves as mirror and resource for man; she has no existence in and of herself. Thus, though the economy of sameness purports to be heterosexual, it is actually monosexual: it is geared toward men's pleasure (*jouissance*) in every sphere (including economics and sexuality) but it allows no place for women's pleasure (*jouissance*).[7] Irigaray's interrogation of the West's sexual economy also seeks to recover woman's place as forgotten resource *and* to enable women to come into their own.

Irigaray's work with religion is particularly relevant to this essay because of strong connections between her work and that of Derrida. Both her connections with deconstruction and her revival of religious discourse have given some feminists pause. Feminists familiar with her work acknowledge its strategic similarities to Derrida's work. On the grounds of this proximity, some feminists reject Irigaray (along with

Derrida) as ultimately antithetical to feminist projects. This rejection views deconstruction as a powerful but relentless critique offering no place from which to make the kind of ethical distinctions and political claims that feminism requires. Other feminist theorists locate Irigaray on the other side of the dividing line they see as separating Derrida from feminism.[8] At precisely those points where they dismiss Derrida as antifeminist and not to be trusted, they embrace Irigaray as unambiguously pro-feminist, often on the grounds that she moves beyond deconstruction of a masculine system to constructive activity on women's behalf.

This scenario suggests that some feminists are willing to allow deconstruction a (suspect) place alongside feminism as long as it keeps its hands in places considered "male-identified" (like philosophy). When deconstruction threatens to challenge feminism itself, fences spring up to protect feminist terrain. Consequently, Derrida is labelled "antifeminist" and Irigaray's attempt to rethink "woman" is defined as something other than "deconstruction." As this essay will show, these views misread the proximity between Irigaray and Derrida, misconstrue deconstruction, and fail to see its value for feminism.

Any strong demarcation between Irigaray as pro-feminist and Derrida as antifeminist overlooks criticisms of feminism articulated by Irigaray that are all but identical to Derrida's.[9] In "Choreographies" and "Women in the Beehive," Derrida warns feminism that it cannot take its transgressive status for granted. It is as vulnerable to the text of metaphysics as any other aspect of Western culture. It can fall into the trap of becoming a discipline (with exclusionary boundaries, orthodox positionings, and so on) like any other in the academy. In its drive toward liberation, feminist politics can find itself captive to schemas that hinder its pursuits. As early as *This Sex Which Is Not One*, as well as in more recent essays and interviews, Irigaray also warns feminism against the traps inherent in its political options.[10] Demanding equality risks adopting a male pattern as the standard. A separatist retreat conceived of as permanent risks establishing another hegemonic structure built on sameness, though with "woman" (rather than "man") as its standard.

The warnings offered by both Irigaray and Derrida speak directly to problems that feminists acknowledge as besetting their work. Certainly debates within the feminist movement throughout its history over whether to ground feminist political action in claims that women are "just as ———" as men or in claims that women are different from men illustrate the dilemmas both Derrida and Irigaray discuss. Feminism's history of excluding women of color from both its politics and its scholarship provides another multilayered example of feminism's suscep- tibility to the problems Irigaray and Derrida describe. White feminists have acknowledged that this exclusionary history is grounded in their tendency to assume that what it means to be a woman is the same across other socioeconomic divisions like race and class. In Irigaray's terms, this scene is symptomatic of feminism's inscription by the West's economy of sameness. In response, white feminists have attempted to root out any residual assumptions that all women share certain "essential" features. Ironically, the tone and substance of debates over essentialism within feminist theory are also symptomatic of feminism's susceptibility to becoming a discipline with exclusionary orthodoxies. Several feminist scholars have noted recently that what began as an attempt to counter exclusionary tendencies has become a strategy for creating new ones.[11] Anti-essentialism has become the mark of orthodoxy among white feminists. According to some, white feminists have spent more time attacking each other in the name of essentialism than in developing sustained accounts of the difference race makes for gender.

Irigaray and Derrida offer more than acute criticisms of feminism's shortfalls; they also offer important resources for helping feminism move beyond these impasses. This potential constitutes the ultimate value of deconstruction for feminism in my view. The problems that beset feminism have their roots in Derrida's text of Western metaphysics (what Irigaray calls the West's "cultural grammar"). Derrida and Irigaray offer strategies for excavating this text/grammar and intervening in its governance. The strategies they offer are not relentless critiques, as some feminists would have it, but something much more complex. Both Irigaray and Derrida practice a double reading and a double writing; that is, both thinkers read through the Western tradition with an eye for the ways it masters its others (for example, "literature" or "myth" as "other" to philosophy; "woman" as "other" to "man"). At the same time, they also reveal the gaps that undercut the Western tradition's ability to maintain this position of mastery ("philosophy" finds itself unable to maintain its distance from "literature"; "woman" eludes capture as man's "other"). Thus, both writers engage in a "deconstruction" of the system that gives rise to these repressions and resistances. Their proximity is more than strategic, however. They take on the Western tradition through many of the same texts (from Plato to Nietzsche to Heidegger to Lacan). Like Irigaray, Derrida investigates issues of gender in these texts; like Derrida, Irigaray is concerned with the play of language and meaning in these texts. Both Derrida and Irigaray also understand their strategies of reading and writing doubly as guarding against easy recapitulation by the systems they question. These strategies achieve this aim by disrupting any one-sided reading *and*, through that disruption, making possible the writing/reading of what has been repressed or what has yet to be written.

Given the clear proximity between the two thinkers as I have developed it to this point, it might still seem that Irigaray's work is sufficient on its own (and perhaps even best suited) for feminism. I find, however, that feminism needs *both* thinkers' work. In my view, feminism can benefit most by reading Derrida and Irigaray as *suppléments*. This way of describing a relationship, as developed by Derrida in *Of Grammatology*, draws on the many connotations of *supplément* and *suppléer* in French (thus, I will use the French words when invoking this relationship).[12] Like "supplement" in English, *suppléments* can add to and reinforce each other. In addition, *suppléments* can also exceed each other. The verb *suppléer* can mean "to supplant" (to replace; to stand in for/substitute for) and "to overcome" as well as "to supplement."[13]

Derrida uses *supplémentation* to describe the relationship between pairings that constitute the text of metaphysics. To cite an example that will be focal for this essay, the text of Western metaphysics identifies writing as derivative of speaking; writing is understood to supplement speech (take speech's place; stand in for it) in the absence of the speaker. Writing is a poor supplement for speaking, however, because it lacks the guarantee provided to speech by the speaker's presence. That presence guarantees that a particular act of speaking successfully carries intended meaning to the recipient, according to the text of metaphysics. However, Derrida's analysis shows that the text cannot maintain its association of speech with plenitude of presence and writing with absence (and therefore speech as origin and writing as supplement). Instead, the conditions of supplementarity (deferred presence, substitution for an assumed plenitude) attend speaking as well as writing. A failed plenitude gives rise to speech's supplantation by writing but, insofar as a failed plenitude attends speech as well as writing, speech's origins lie in writing. One cannot be marked off from the other as origin to supplement; each exceeds the other.[14]

Reasons for using *supplémentation* as a strategy for reading Irigaray's proximity to Derrida already appear in the scenario enacted between "feminism" and "deconstruction" in some feminists' evaluations of Derrida and Irigaray that I described above. *Supplémentation* is already at work in feminists' construal of the proximity between and relative value of the two thinkers. Some feminists posit Irigaray as replacement/substitute for Derrida because he fails to offer feminism the full scope of what it needs. In other words, Derrida (and deconstruction) fail to fulfill feminism's desire for plentitude leading feminists to seek a replacement elsewhere. Certainly Derrida's work is not sufficient on its own for feminism; there are places beyond which Derrida cannot go. I have argued elsewhere that the limits of his work emerge most clearly when read with Irigaray as *supplément*.[15] However, Irigaray is not sufficient on her own, either. I shall argue in this essay that feminism will continue to need Derrida's work as *supplément—especially* if it wants to work out of the resources Irigaray has to offer. Thus, neither thinker alone can stand in for the other; neither alone offers a plenitude of resources to feminist thinking. *Supplémentation* is already at work in their proximity.

Rather than siding with one or the other and attempting to stop *supplémentation* in its tracks, I shall follow the strands that overlap in their thinking through *supplémentation.* This reading will allow each to stand in for the other on occasion and show that each exceeds the other on those occasions. Rather than positing one as origin and the other as derivative, one as paving the way for the other to come along and surpass the other, reading them as *suppléments* keeps them circulating around one another. As I shall demonstrate, reading their proximity in this fashion enables multiple feminist interventions in the text/grammar whose workings Irigaray and Derrida uncover and the vast terrain that text/grammar inscribes—including feminism itself.

I follow this strategy of reading Derrida and Irigaray as *suppléments* through their discussions of religion for two reasons. First, both thinkers help us gain new insight on religion's significance for feminism. Second, certain tensions in Irigaray's work that I find troubling appear with particular clarity around her use of religious discourse. In my view, the strongest single contribution Irigaray brings to feminism is her attempt to rethink what it means to be a woman. Her claim that the West has yet to allow women genuine alterity is compelling. Furthermore, her own vision of that alterity as based in difference (rather than identity and sameness) offers the promise of thinking and practicing "woman/women" so that differences between women (as well as within each woman) really matter. However, Irigaray's invocations of religious motifs constitute sites in her work where her attempts to think sexual difference seem to lose the radicality of that promise. In those places, Irigaray risks sliding into the very traps both she and Derrida identify as dangers for feminism when it succumbs to an economy of sameness. Reading her with Derrida as *supplément* ameliorates that tendency.

Of necessity, this essay will be a very limited foray into the significance of religion in both thinkers' work. I shall focus primarily on both figures' solicitation of the dominant metaphor for the divine in Western religion, God-the-Father. I am adopting the locution "God-the-Father" in this essay in order to avoid conflation of this figure with other invocations of the sacred in either thinker's work (or elsewhere, for that matter). It will be clear that God-the-Father is inextricably tied to the text of metaphysics. However, I think both Irigaray and Derrida leave open the possibility of notions of the sacred that exceed this text's mastery (though I shall not be able to do justice to those possibilities here). I shall also have to leave aside consideration of other topics that both thinkers' invocation of religious motifs raise (the issue of belief, the referent of talk about the divine, the future of religion, and so forth)— issues that raise enormously thorny problems for discussion.

This investigation is textually limited as well. I am going to focus primarily on both thinkers' readings of Plato. However, questions of religion and gender are pertinent to both thinkers' readings of Heidegger, Hegel, and Nietzsche as well as the texts in question here. An adequate account of the place of religion would also need to follow both thinkers' work with theological texts (Meister Eckhart and Dionysius the Aereopagite, in Derrida's case; women mystics as well as Eckhart and Ludwig Feuerbach, in Irigaray's case). Despite these limitations, I offer here some important first steps.

Derrida and Religion: Is God Dead? Should Women Care?

One of Derrida's early books, *Dissemination,* takes up themes for which Derrida is most famous in American circles: questioning the division between writing and speaking, textuality and reality, books and their interpretations, authors and readers, philosophy and literature.[16] Readers of *Dissemination* come to see that these divisions have their roots in a central feature of the text of Western metaphysics: the hierarchical opposition of presence and absence. Derrida explores these themes through reading various philosophical texts in tandem with texts not usually deemed "philosophical" (such as Mallarmé's poetry).

"Plato's Pharmacy," the middle section of *Dissemination,* focuses on the value of writing in Western thinking through an exploration of its status in the Platonic corpus and the history of its interpretation. Traditionally, the discussion of writing in the *Phaedrus* (and elsewhere in Plato's corpus) has been read as writing's condemnation. Derrida argues for a more complex interpretation. His reading reveals, on the one hand, the attempt by the *Phaedrus* and other texts to master writing, understood as other to philosophy, by inscribing it in a certain economy of truth. "Economy" of truth is a deliberate and apt metaphor. The question of the truth of writing is bound up with questions of "proper"/ propriety/property. Socrates and Phaedrus discuss issues of propriety (whether it is good to write) and of property (what are the qualities of writing that determine its capacity for truth?).

The answers to these questions are governed by a logic of oppositionality. A collusion of opposites—inside/outside, life/death, essence/appearance, presence/absence—separates philosophy from myth, reality from textuality, speaking from writing. However, writing resists this attempt at mastery and thereby exposes the limits of the logic of oppositionality. In this instance, Derrida's double reading exposes both the assertion of oppositions and resistance to their mastery. When Phaedrus asks Socrates about the truth of writing, Socrates responds by reciting the myth of its origin. Writing's truth, he says, is only available to us through a recitation of its history. This is particularly interesting because, at the beginning of the dialogue, Socrates dismissed myth from the scene both to allow it its own space and because it has nothing to do with the task of philosophy—the pursuit of truth/knowledge—especially self-knowledge. Myth, like writing, is philosophy's other. Now, writing calls him back to myth. Plato's inclusion of this myth is more than a simple borrowing. Derrida's analysis will show that the myth's structural elements coincide with certain features of Plato's thinking. What might seem to be an infection of philosophy by myth is possible because both are inscribed in this larger text. This coincidence, Derrida argues, calls any simple division between philosophy and mythology into question.

The myth goes as follows: Theuth, a minor god in the pantheon, presents the king of the gods with his invention, writing, in order that the king may determine its value. He presents it to him as a *"recipe,"* according to the translation, for memory; a *"remedy"* for forgetfulness. The king, however, exposes Theuth as a deceptor. Rather than a cure for memory, he states, writing is a "poison." The king's diatribe against writing defines it according to clear-cut oppositions: good/evil, inside/outside, true/false, essence/appearance. It produces a bad thing, forgetfulness. It equips students with only a *semblance* of wisdom. However, Derrida's double reading of the Platonic text brings to light interruptions of these oppositions that subvert this attempt to master writing. The two characters in this mythical scene are father (the king/determiner of value) and son (Theuth). Derrida argues that it is no coincidence that writing is presented to this *father* so that he may determine its value, or that *writing* is presented to this father so that he may determine its value. Theuth (or a parallel figure) is found throughout different Near Eastern pantheons. His role is that of displacement, replacement, and difference. He is the god of writing, of linguistic differences, of death, of medicine, of counting. In Egyptian mythology, he is the god of the moon; invited by his father, the sun god, to take his place in the sky in the sun god's absence.

The trope of the father figures prominently in relation to writing and beyond in the Platonic corpus. The relationships of fathers and sons in many instances parallel the relationship of the king and Theuth. Writing is understood to be a derivative form of *logos*—or speech. Socrates images logos in this sense and in its broader sense as that which organizes being as a living organism; a *zōod*. A good speech, Socrates tells Phaedrus, should have an organic unity; it should flow naturally from the beginning, through the middle to the end. Like other living things, logoi have fathers. Socrates frequently refers to speaking subjects as fathers of their speeches. Good speeches are of noble birth. Speech is preferable to writing because its father is there to watch over it; to prevent it from going astray. When logos is committed to writing, this benevolent paternal relation is compromised. Writing inscribes the absence of the father.

On the surface, this could seem like a trivial argument. However, Derrida also shows that patrocentrism plays a much larger role in Plato's logic. The economy of truth turns out to be ruled by fathers and their figures. The Greek word for father, *patēr*, carries a polysemic network of its own. "Father," "capital," "goods" all resonate within *patēr*. The metaphor of fatherhood colors discussions of the Good and of Capital elsewhere in Plato's corpus. In *The Republic*, for example, Socrates declines to speak of the good itself, offering instead to speak of its *offspring*, which are made in its likeness. He describes this as *counting up the interest* on the capital itself. The offspring he goes on to discuss is the visible sun; it illuminates vision like the Good illuminates the intellect. As analog, it stands in for the Good.

As it turns out, Socrates' deferral of this opportunity to speak of the Good is not a temporary avoidance. One can no more speak directly about this Good/Father than one can look directly at the visible sun, Socrates says.[17] A similar movement occurs in the *Phaedo*. Direct contemplation of *ta onta* (beings) is impossible because it is too dangerous to the mind's eye. Socrates turns, therefore, to the realm of "ideas" (Benjamin Jowett's translation of logoi) to seek truth.[18] Logoi in this broader sense protect our metaphorical eyes from the blinding metaphorical sun *(Republic) and* serve as our resource in its absence *(Phaedo)*. These paternal relationships parallel the relationships of Theuth and the king. The locus of origin of logos, of the Good, and of ultimate value is accorded to the paternal position. The sons replace the absent or deferred father.

The play of father/son dynamics around God and "truth" in Plato's texts is striking on its own. Insofar as the dynamics attending the attribution of value to writing and speaking in Plato's texts is emblematic of trends elsewhere, it would seem that the text of metaphysics and its economy of truth is patrocentric as well as logocentric. Gender marking is intrinsic to the metaphysical text; as intrinsic as its notorious hallmark, presence/absence, the questioning of which is most frequently associated with Derrida. In fact, the marks of gender are directly related to presence/absence. Speech is deemed good because its metaphorical father is there to watch over it, to ensure that it says what "he" means. Writing's distance from such a guardian renders it problematic. Its father's presence has been deferred; its words differ from those that came out of the father's mouth. The standard of value against which writing is measured is proximity to the father. Can it be mere coincidence that the father is the determiner of value in this economy of truth and that fathers occupy such high status in Western culture—including the throne of the divine? Moreover, can it be a mere coincidence that women are conspicuously absent from this drama? Further reading in Derrida's work suggests that neither the absence of women from this drama nor the place the drama assigns to the father are coincidental. Patro/logo/theocentrism is hardly limited to classical Greek philosophy. Derrida follows his reading of Plato in *Dissemination* with signs of similar patterns in later aspects of Western culture. Derrida argues that the advent of the medieval encyclopedia (which ideally would systematize all knowledge) arose out of the concept of nature as a "book" through which one can read the acts of God the Creator. When one recalls that this concept rests upon a biblical account of creation in the Book of Genesis, which depict a male God who "fathers" the cosmos through acts of speech, the full constellation of associations familiar now from Derrida's reading of Plato appears.

Derrida's reading of Plato in *Dissemination* takes off from a reference to the *Phaedrus* in *Of Grammatology*, a text that offers further evidence that the association between God, presence, and truth (as guaranteed meaning) continues to govern distinctions between speaking and writing in Western culture after Plato. Movements as diverse as the Cartesian shift to the subject as the locus of knowledge, Hegel's dialectical thinking and the advent of structuralism maintain the priority of speech over writing within a patro/logo/theocentric economy of truth.

Texts other than *Dissemination* also take up the question of woman's place within the West's economy of truth. In *Spurs, Of Grammatology*, and *The Post Card*, Derrida follows an important dimension of woman's (non-)place in this drama. His readings of Nietzsche, Rousseau, and Lacan reveal "woman" as the always elusive object of desire within this economy of truth. Thus, the economy of truth is marked not only by patro/logo/theocentrism but by a sexual trajectory of man's-desire-for-woman. What, then, does feminism stand to gain from Derrida's exposure of the place of God-the-Father and of woman within this economy of truth?

Surely feminism can acknowledge a stake in Derrida's exposure of difference and deferral at the heart of God-the-Father's mastery over the text of Western metaphysics. Feminists might also acknowledge that his exposure of "woman's" place in that economy as the always elusive object of desire is worthy of their attention. However, some feminists might argue that my account simply bolsters their ultimate rejection of Derrida. Insofar as Derrida deconstructs a masculine system, they might argue, feminism can find common cause with him. On the other hand, exposing the holes in a masculine system is not enough; something needs to be done about the absence of women from this system. Doesn't feminism have to go its own way at this point?

I would agree (and have argued elsewhere) that Derrida can only carry feminism so far. However, I view that limit rather differently than others. Whereas some feminists argue that feminism, at a certain point, has to abandon deconstruction, I would argue that feminism will continue to need it. Moreover, this "more than" that feminism seeks should exceed Derrida, not regress to a pre-Derridean mode. In other words, feminism needs to heed Derrida's warnings against the ever-present danger of simply recapitulating the status quo. Assumptions that feminism is unambiguously on the side of the non-"metaphysical" (in Derrida's sense of that term) are unfounded. I noted certain symptoms of feminism's inscription by the text of metaphysics in the problems that continue to attend its activity on women's behalf; let me note a more basic sign of this situation here.

Derrida's analysis of God-the-Father's place in the text of Western metaphysics also challenges any easy association of Derrida with proclamations of the death of God in general and God-the-Father in particular.[19] His excavation of the problematic of writing shows that the effects of God-the-Father reach to the level of basic presuppositions of Western thinking, the distinction between writing and speaking. Insofar as that distinction continues to operate in Western thought and culture, God-the-Father remains "alive" in some sense and feminism remains as vulnerable to his mastery as any other artifact of Western culture. Insofar as feminism assumes it can mean what it says without problem, it continues to invoke the text of Western metaphysics and its Father God, Guarantor of Meaning.[20] Thus, despite assumptions to the contrary, Derrida's analysis suggests that feminism is always already involved with religion through its involvement with the text of metaphysics; the question is, What should feminism do with this situation?

Derrida's exposure of the fissures in God-the-Father's mastery makes possible a number of interventions in the text of metaphysics through the terrain of religion. I would argue that feminism has a stake in these possibilities. Derrida's exposure of difference and deferral at the heart of God-the-Father's governance opens up space for the proliferation of other metaphors for the divine, including female metaphors. As I shall note shortly, an important aspect of Irigaray's work with religion follows that line. However, feminism's stake in the possibilities Derrida opens up for religion range more broadly still.

Western religious traditions have always claimed to be founded on a notion of the radical alterity of the divine, yet they have found it enormously difficult to maintain the thought of alterity; a fact of which

Derrida is well aware. Some scholars in religion have noted an affinity between Derrida's attempts to think the trace, *différance,* the repressed others of Western thought, and religion's attempt to think the divine as radically other.[21] Derrida is wary of such connections. The few places where Derrida takes up this topic are carefully crafted to avoid certain traps and yet to refuse closure.[22] Clearly, Derrida wants to distinguish his thinking of alterity from efforts to think the alterity of God within Western theology that remain in the service of metaphysical religion. However, Derrida's reticence also maintains his distance from antireligious stances.

Investigating the complexities of this scene lies beyond the scope of this essay; however, let me offer the following rationale for feminism's stake in such an investigation. This essay's limited foray into terrain shared by religion and gender suggests that religion and sexual difference have followed similar trajectories in Western thought. More thorough investigation would further substantiate evidence presented here. The West has claimed alterity as fundamental to its thinking about the sacred and to its thinking about gender. However, Irigaray's analysis of what purports to be heterosexuality graphically illustrates the West's failure to sustain the thought of sexual difference. Acquaintance with the history of Christian theology offers compelling evidence that many efforts to think the alterity of the sacred have failed to break the boundaries of the text of metaphysics. Irigaray's work with religion takes off from a similar insight about the career of alterity in religion and in thinking about gender; thus, it would seem that Irigaray is headed in a direction feminism needs to follow. However, where Derrida adopts a guarded stance toward the possibility of a sacrality "beyond" religion-as-usual, Irigaray plunges right ahead, with mixed results. It seems as though she assumes that returning to religion in the name of woman offers sufficient protection against recapitulation by religion-as-usual. However, as I shall show, such an assumption is misguided.

Irigaray on Religion

Accounts of the significance of religion for Irigaray's thinking have dealt primarily with its place in her more recent work. Invocations of God and other religious motifs appear in several essays in *Sexes et Parentés* (translated as *Sexes and Genealogies* [SG]) and *Ethique de la différence sexuelle* (translated as *An Ethics of Sexual Difference*).[23] In several places in these texts, Irigaray argues that women need to imagine God in *their* own image in order to ground their subjectivity. She writes: "If she is to become woman, if she is to accomplish her female subjectivity, woman needs a god who is a figure of the perfection of her subjectivity. . . . Having a God and becoming one's gender go hand in hand. God is the other that we absolutely cannot be without" ("Divine Women," SG 64). It is this aspect of her deployment of religious discourse that seems most disturbing to feminist theorists and philosophers. Elizabeth Grosz, one of the few feminist theorists to deal substantively with this aspect of Irigaray's work, notes that Irigaray's readers tend to view with suspicion her bold-faced deployment of deity imaged as female as part of her project of rethinking "woman."[24] Feminists have good reason for being wary of invocations of God; after all, women have certainly suffered at religion's hands. Some feminists read Irigaray's call to women to image God in female form in order to ground their subjectivity and see the "good old God" (in whose name women were forbidden to speak and relegated to secondary status) in disguise.

Unfortunately, feminists are right to be suspicious of Irigaray. I find a tension in Irigaray's work between a vision of religion that moves beyond religion-as-usual and a failure to recognize sufficiently the scope of religion-as-usual's reach. Reading Irigaray with Derrida as *supplément* exposes and undercuts this tension in favor of the move beyond religion-as-usual. To explore this tension and the effects of Derrida's *supplémentation* upon it, I shall situate Irigaray's recapitulation of religious categories in these more recent texts against the background of her earlier work.[25] Specifically, I shall focus on Irigaray's dealings with the metaphor of God-the-Father and some of its associations.

I noted above that Derrida's investigation of writing's status in Plato's work exposed a patro-logo-theocentric economy that governs how the West accords "truth." Irigaray's early work does something strikingly similar. Her first book, *Speculum of the Other Woman*, consists of double readings of the "masters" of Western thought: Freud and the philosophers.[26] *Speculum* closes with a close reading of the motif of the cave in Plato's thought (and the network of metaphors that accompany it) entitled "Plato's *Hystera.*"[27] Significantly, Irigaray finds herself taking up the theme of God in Plato's texts. Her reading and Derrida's supplement each other nicely in several ways. In Irigaray's reading, as in Derrida's,

God is indelibly marked as male. He serves as the ground of all that is, the guarantor of truth and presence, the linchpin in an economy of sameness built around a male standard. The resonances that sound when "Plato's *Hystera*" is read with Derrida as *supplément* connect the God unearthed by Irigaray with God-the-Father, even though she makes no explicit use of the paternal metaphor in this essay.[28] Irigaray's reading, like Derrida's, intervenes in this God's mastery by showing him to be afflicted by difference and deferral, though she takes a different route toward this end. God is described by Plato as the self-same, as eternal, as One. However, Irigaray's reading of Plato uncovers a set of mirrors upon which God's self-sameness is dependent. One set appears to be located at the heart of God (where God reflects himself to himself); another is located in the created order that also serves to reflect God (although imperfectly) to himself. Thus, this male God is subject to the same specular logic that locates "woman" as man's other, as Irigaray argues elsewhere.

Irigaray's excavation of the place of a male God that resonates so strongly with Derrida's excavation of God-the-Father in Plato's texts acquires fuller significance when situated against Irigaray's rereading of Freud via Lacan.[29] Freud's theories of the Oedipus complex and of penis envy are notorious in American circles and caused at least one generation of American feminism to reject Freud out of hand. Irigaray, however, finds Freud useful in part because his thinking is symptomatic of the West's sexual economy. The emergence of penis envy as the determining factor in his account of femininity reflects the values of the West's "cultural grammar." Similarly, the centrality of the Oedipus complex to the process of becoming a subject in Lacan's rereading of Freud reflects/is reflected in the values of this "cultural grammar" in which the phallus figures as the standard of value. Moreover, the structure of the subject (indelibly marked as "masculine" in the phallocentric economy) and the structure of God the Father, Guarantor of Meaning, overlap. According to Lacan's account, being a subject has everything to do with coming into language (and being able to "mean what one says"; that is, approximate truth). Thus, implicit in the notion of subjectivity is God-the-Father as guarantor.

Irigaray is sensitive to the intersection of subjectivity, God, and "woman." The reason for the invocation of religious categories in her later work emerges most clearly against this background. Much of Irigaray's later work builds on the position articulated by the nineteenth-century theologian and philosopher Ludwig Feuerbach who argued that theology was anthropology. According to Feuerbach, all statements about God are projections of idealized human nature (read "man's" nature) that "man" should internalize and realize. Feuerbach's understanding of religion provides the impetus for Irigaray's critical analyses of connections between God and the subject in the philosophical tradition and her proposals for religion's place in contemporary feminism. In *Ethics*, Irigaray targets God as the ground of male subjectivity. Several of Irigaray's essays in this collection explore the effects of a mutually reflective relationship between a God figured as male and the (male) subject as these effects register in the work of philosophers from Descartes to Levinas. This relationship both founds and funds the epoch of monosexuality, which Irigaray sees as coming to a close. The end of this epoch is signified by the demise of traditional conceptions of divinity and the potential emergence of new manifestations of the sacred in a new epoch of sexual difference.[30]

Irigaray's double reading of the relationship between God as male ground and the subject as male opens up the possibility for writing the divine otherwise in the service of writing what has yet to be written: female subjectivity. Essays in *Sexes and Genealogies* seem to argue that women should take Feuerbach by the horns. If God is "only" a projection of idealized humanity, then women need to seize control of the projector and shine *their* image on its screen. Projecting a female deity will accomplish several things for women. First of all, it will give their subjectivity a ground that it needs. Second, it will make genuine exchange between the sexes possible as well as exchanges between women.[31]

As I noted earlier, a number of Irigaray's feminist readers are wary of such an invocation. I share their hesitation, but for slightly different reasons. Suggesting that women project their own image onto the divine seems to run the risk of setting up an economy of sameness for women that would parallel the current phallocentric economy. I also noted earlier that Irigaray's most significant contribution to feminism is her attempt to rethink woman's subjectivity as founded upon differences between women and within women. That theme is altogether absent from the places where Irigaray advocates projecting a female deity as the ground for female subjectivity. Irigaray seems to forget her own warning that changing the gender of the standard from masculine to feminine can still recapitulate phallocratism if a single standard remains in place.

This lapse on Irigaray's part is surprising and certainly disappointing given that she, perhaps more than any other feminist thinker, has exposed the depth of the workings of an economy of sameness. Taken on its own, I think Irigaray's strategy of projecting a female deity fails to take seriously enough the depth of God-the-Father's inscription of the text of Western metaphysics and, in turn, feminism's ongoing susceptibility to his mastery. As Derrida's analysis reminds us, God-the-Father's gender is more than skin-deep.

Even as I raise these questions about Irigaray's deployment of the divine in the service of rethinking woman, I also have to acknowledge that there are resources within her thinking that counter the dangers I find as well as those that seem to trouble other feminists. Those feminists who fear a reassertion of religion-as-usual can take some consolation in knowing that Irigaray goes beyond invoking God in the traditional sense by distinguishing between God and the divine. In *Sexes and Genealogies,* Irigaray is careful to insist on the immanence of the divine in women in contrast to the unreachable transcendence of traditional Western con-cepts of God.[32] This aspect of her attempt to think "woman" is paralleled by her related invocation of the "sensible transcendental" in many texts, including her reading of Plato. Underneath the male God explicitly invoked by Plato, Irigaray unearths "woman/mother/matter" as forgotten/obscured ground/source of Plato's thought. Irigaray carries forward this same project of rewriting/reading the forgotten matter/nal ground in other readings of the philosophic tradition. Her readings of Heidegger and Nietzsche expose certain elements (air, in Heidegger's case; water, in Nietzsche's) as the forgotten context of their work. These elements are transcendent (in that they serve as ground) but also sensible (in that they are material). Moreover, at particular points in these texts (espe-cially in her reading of Heidegger), Irigaray does make a point of thinking the sensible transcendental (and the relationship between divine and human) through an economy of difference rather than sameness. While the interplay of the variety of Irigaray's other uses of the discourse of divinity provides some amelioration of the dangers in her reversal of Feuerbach, reading Derrida on religion as *supplément* aids immensely in the disruption. Reading Irigaray's call for a "divine woman/woman divinity" against the background of Derrida's exposure of the tenaciousness of God-the-Father, Guarantor of Meaning gives her call the status of a strategic intervention in the text of God-the-Father's dominance (versus an attempt to establish a separate but equal subjectiv-

ity) by reinforcing Irigaray's own exposure of God-the-Father's dominance.

Conclusion: The Fruits of *Supplémentation*

Following this reading of Derrida and Irigaray on religion and gender
through the strategy of *supplémentation* offers a distinctive perspective on
Derrida's value for feminism and on the significance of religion for
feminist thought. First of all, I have shown that religion is an important
terrain for feminist engagement. The analyses of God-the-Father's place
in the text of metaphysics provided by both Derrida and Irigaray suggest
that our culture (and feminism as a cultural artifact) has not moved so
far beyond religion as is sometimes assumed.

Following out both thinkers' work with religion and gender also
allowed us to reconsider Derrida's significance for feminism. As I noted
at the outset, feminists are often wary of deconstruction and of Derrida,
in particular. Irigaray is sometimes put forward as providing feminism
the resources deconstruction has to offer without its problems. However,
our exploration of terrain where Derrida and Irigaray overlap suggests
that reading them as *suppléments* is far more productive for feminism
than abandoning Derrida in favor of Irigaray.

Clearly, the work of excavating the text of Western metaphysics'
inscription of various aspects of Western culture—including religion and
feminism—will continue. Derrida and Irigaray offer resources necessary
for that work. However, their work also calls feminism and religion
toward possibilities that are only beginning to appear within the fissures
in the text of metaphysics. Though I have only been able here to take
preliminary steps in both directions, feminism and religion together have
much to gain from exploring the paths opened up through reading
Derrida and Irigaray.[33]

Notes

1. For examples of the gamut of discussions of Derrida's value for feminism, see Drucilla
Cornell, *Beyond Accommodation: Ethical Feminism, Deconstruction and the Law* (New York:

Routledge, 1991), the work of Gayatri Chakravorty Spivak (e.g., "Feminism and Deconstruction, Again: Negotiating with Unacknowledged Masculinism," in *Between Feminism and Psychoanalysis*, ed. Teresa Brennan (New York: Routledge, 1989; repr., Routledge, 1990); "Displacement and the Discourse of Woman," in *Displacement: Derrida and After*, ed. Mark Krupnick (Bloomington: Indiana University Press, 1983): 169–95, "Feminism and Critical Theory" in *In Other Worlds: Essays in Cultural Politics* [New York: Routledge, 1987]; and Rosi Braidotti, *Patterns of Dissonance* (New York: Routledge, 1991).

2. For these discussions, see "Choreographies: An Interview with Christie McDonald" in this volume (Chapter 1), and "Women in the Beehive: A Seminar with Jacques Derrida" in *Men in Feminism*, ed. Alice Jardine and Paul Smith (New York: Routledge, 1987).

3. See especially *Éperons: Les Styles de Nietzsche/Spurs: Nietzsche's Styles*, trans. Barbara Harlow (Chicago: University of Chicago Press, 1978; French/English version, 1979) and *The Post Card: From Socrates to Freud and Beyond*, trans. Alan Bass (Chicago: University of Chicago Press, 1987).

4. Carl A. Raschke, "The Deconstruction of God," in *Deconstruction and Theology*, ed. Thomas J. J. Altizer, Max A. Myers, et al. (New York: Crossroads, 1982), 3.

5. See, e.g., Robert Magliola, *Derrida on the Mend* (West Lafayette: Purdue University Press, 1984), Joseph O'Leary, *Questioning Back: The Overcoming of Metaphysics in the Christian Tradition* (New York: Winston, 1985). Kevin Hart's *The Trespass of the Sign: Deconstruction, Theology, and Philosophy* (Cambridge: Cambridge University Press, 1989) is the best treatment of deconstruction's relationship to theology that has been published to date. However, Hart, too, thinks religion as it stands holds something beyond the grasp of deconstruction.

6. Magliola and O'Leary both hold this view. Louis Mackey was the first to articulate it in print; see his "Slouching Toward Bethlehem: Deconstructive Strategies in Theology," *Anglican Theological Review* 65 (July 1983): 255–72.

7. I use the term "pleasure" here advisedly to translate Irigaray's term *jouissance*, which has multiple connotations, including possession or use, delight, as well as sexual pleasure (including orgasm). Thus, to offer no place for women's *jouissance* is to fail to allow her (self) possession, sexual pleasure of her own, and so forth.

8. Margaret Whitford makes this demarcation in *Luce Irigaray: Philosophy in the Feminine* (London: Routledge, 1991), 53 and 116ff. Rosi Braidotti also distinguishes them from one another in *Patterns of Dissonance*. Braidotti and Whitford view Derrida as too nihilistic to suit feminism's needs. Toril Moi, on the other hand, faults Irigaray for not being Derridean enough and falling into a recapitulation of metaphysics against her will; see *Sexual/Textual Politics: Feminist Literary Theory* (London: Routledge, 1988).

9. These demarcations also overlook aspects of Derrida's work that exhibit his own sense of his limited place: for example, in "Women in the Beehive," Derrida asks not to "sign off" on this interview. He asks the editors/interviewers to leave all replies to questions anonymous. I have argued elsewhere that Derrida is acknowledging that his position as a man (and therefore "master and author") will leave its effects on what he says about feminism. I read his refusal to be marked as author-ity as an attempt to undercut those effects.

10. See *This Sex Which Is Not One*, trans. Catherine Porter and Carolyn Burke (Ithaca: Cornell University Press, 1985), esp. 27–33, 127–28, and 165–66.

11. See Teresa de Lauretis, "Upping the Anti in Feminist Theory," in *Conflicts in Feminism*, ed. Marianne Hirsch and Evelyn Fox Keller (New York: Routledge, 1990), 255–70. See also Jane Roland Martin, "Methodological Essentialisms, False Differences, and Other Dangerous Traps," *Signs* 19, no. 3 (Spring, 1994): 630–56.

12. See especially "That Dangerous Supplement," in *Of Grammatology*, by Jacques Derrida, trans. Gayatri Chakravorty Spivak (Baltimore: Johns Hopkins University Press, 1974).

13. In Derrida's words, "The supplement adds itself, it is a surplus, a plenitude enriching another plenitude. . . . It cumulates and accumulates presence (as writing supplements

speaking; but speaking in turn supplements thought). It adds only to replace; it intervenes or insinuates itself *in-the-place-of*; if it fills, it is as if one fills a void. If it represents, it is by the anterior default of a presence. Compensatory [*suppléant*] and vicarious, the supplement is an adjunct . . . which *takes-(the)-place* [*tient-lieu*] . . . it produces no relief, its place is assigned in the structure by the mark of an emptiness. . . . Unlike the *complement*, . . . the supplement is an "exterior addition" (Robert's French Dictionary). It compensates for [*sous l'espèce de la suppléance*] what *ought* to lack nothing at all in itself" (*Grammatology* 144–45).

14. The character of this challenge to the West's assumptions about grounds and origins leads some feminists to argue that Derrida fails to provide feminism what it needs for ethical and political action. Developing a full answer to this objection is beyond the scope of this essay, but I can point in the direction of an answer. To be sure, there is an abyssal quality to *supplémentation*, but it is not nihilistic as Derrida deploys it. *Supplémentation* is both productive (in that it is the condition of possibility for thinking the difference between writing and speaking) and disruptive (in that it prevents the fixing of that difference). Moreover, if Derrida's readings of these dynamics is convincing, as I find that it is, it suggests that ethical or political action of any sort needs to rethink what it understands as its grounds. Insofar as *supplémentation* produces thinking, meaning, action, then political and ethical activity has always been (un)grounded there, whether consciously or not.

15. See my "Questions of Proximity: Woman's Place in Derrida and Irigaray," forthcoming in *Hypatia: A Journal of Feminist Philosophy* (Winter 1997), and *Deconstruction, Feminist Theology and the Problem of Difference: Subverting the Race/Gender Divide* (manuscript under review).

16. Jacques Derrida, *Dissemination*, trans. Barbara Johnson (Chicago: University of Chicago Press, 1981).

17. Although time does not permit one to deal with this now, I should note the other appearance of this analogy between the sun and the Good in the famous allegory of the cave later in *The Republic* (book 7) in which Plato describes the process of coming to real knowledge. Irigaray also takes up the questioning of this allegory and its traditional feminine associations in her essay on Plato, which I shall discuss in a moment.

18. See the *Phaedo* in *Dialogues of Plato* (New York: Washington Square Press, 1951) as cited by Barbara Johnson in *Dissemination*, 84. In order to bring the English text in line with Robin's French translation that Derrida is using, Johnson breaks with her usual practice of citing the translations in *The Collected Dialogues of Plato*, ed. Edith Hamilton and Huntington Cairns, Bollingen Series 71 (Princeton: Princeton University Press, 1961); see 66 n. 4 of *Dissemination*. In that collection, Hugh Tredennick translates *logoi* as "theories" (*Phaedo* 100a).

19. Derrida distances himself from that position in "Implications: Interview with Henri Ronse" in *Positions*, trans. Alan Bass (Chicago: University of Chicago Press, 1981), 6: "I try to keep myself at the *limit* of philosophical discourse. I say limit and not death, for I do not at all believe in what today is so easily called the death of philosophy (nor, moreover, in the simple death of whatever—the book, man, or god, especially since as we all know, what is dead wields a very specific power)."

20. I have argued elsewhere for other signs of feminism's inscription by the text of metaphysics in its inability to deal adequately with the difference race makes for gender. See my "Questioning Woman in Feminist/Womanist Theology: Irigaray, Ruether, and Daly" in *Transfigurations: Theology and the French Feminists*, ed. C. W. Maggie Kim, Susan M. St. Ville, and Susan M. Simonaitis (Minneapolis, Minn.: Fortress Press, 1993) and "American/French Intersections: The Play of Race/Class/Politics in Irigaray" in *Reinterpreting the Political: Continental Philosophy and Political Theory*, ed. Stephen Watson and Lenore Langsdorf, Selected Studies in Phenomenology and Existential Philosophy, 20 (forthcoming, SUNY Press).

21. Of those theologians who draw such connections, Kevin Hart offers the most sustained attempt at connecting Derrida with the *via negativa* in Christian theology. On that basis, he posits an affinity between Derrida and Christian mystical theology; see note 5.

22. Two places where Derrida's reticence is most pronounced include the last pages of *Of Spirit: Heidegger and the Question*, trans. Geoffrey Bennington and Rachel Bowlby (Chicago: University of Chicago Press, 1989) and "How to Avoid Speaking: Denials" in *Derrida and Negative Theology*, ed. Harold Coward and Toby Foshay (Albany: State University of New York Press, 1992). As Derrida's inquiry into the thematic of *Geist* in Heidegger's work draws to a close, he stages a dialogue with theologians who claim a stake in what Heidegger is thinking about the withdrawal of being. In "Denials," Derrida takes on the questions he has been avoiding for so long about connections between his thinking and (so-called) negative theology.

23. *Sexes et parentés* (Paris: Editions de Minuit, 1987); translated as *Sexes and Genealogies*, trans. Gillian Gill (New York: Columbia University Press, 1993); *Ethique de la différence sexuelle* (Paris: Editions de Minuit, 1984); translated as *An Ethics of Sexual Difference*, trans. Carolyn Burke and Gillian C. Gill (Ithaca: Cornell University Press, 1993).

24. See especially Grosz's "Irigaray and the Divine," in *Transfigurations*.

25. My reading of Irigaray follows Grosz's trajectory, to some extent. She, too, argues for situating Irigaray's deployment of "God" in the larger context of her work. My reading of Irigaray in light of Derrida's work adds a different dimension that, in some ways, complements Grosz's reading and responds to her critique of Whitford's account of Irigaray's relationship to Derrida's thought. See Whitford's acknowledgement of this exchange in *Irigaray*, 212 n. 5.

26. Luce Irigaray, *Speculum of the Other Woman*, trans. Gillian C. Gill (Ithaca: Cornell University Press, 1985).

27. The associations invoked by this title are almost too numerous to mention, but I want to highlight just a few of them. Traditionally, caves have been associated with wombs and wombs with hysteria. Moreover, to entitle the essay "Plato's *hystera*" is to suggest that perhaps another "dialogue"—a dialogue with/about "woman"—lies underneath Plato's corpus.

28. Irigaray does discuss God-the-Father in other essays, most notably in *Sexes and Genealogies*.

29. See "The Blind Spot in an Old Dream of Symmetry," in *Speculum*; and "Psychoanalytic Theory: Another Look," and "The Power of Discourse," in *This Sex*.

30. The particularly relevant essays for my discussion here are "Sexual Difference," "The Envelope," "An Ethics of Sexual Difference," and "The Love of the Other." In this context, it is interesting to note that Irigaray reads the pronouncements of the death of God made by Nietzsche and Heidegger not as proclamations of the final disappearance of divinity altogether, but as holding out the possibilities of the coming of new deities ("The Love of the Other," 140).

31. Grosz argues that Irigaray's turn to discourse about the divine moves away from concerns about women's subjectivity. It seems clear to me that Irigaray thinks women's ability to enter into genuine exchanges with each other and with men rests upon being subjects in their own right (as defined by Irigaray). See especially "Divine Women" and "Belief Itself," but also "The Universal as Mediation" and "Each Sex Must Have Its Own Rights" in *Sexes and Genealogies*.

32. She also speaks of God as something that "we" (women? women and men together, in some cases?) would create together: for example, "In order to *become*, we need some shadowy perception of achievement; not a fixed objective not a One postulated to be immutable but rather a future, the bridge of a present *that remembers*, that is not sheer oblivion and loss, not a crumbling away of existence, a failure" ("Divine Women," SG 67).

33. I would like to thank Rhodes College for its financial support. A summer Faculty Development Endowment grant made the writing of this essay possible.

10

Kolossos

The Measure of a Man's Cize

Dorothea Olkowski

Jacques Derrida's *Truth in Painting* begins with a hesitation in the text that occurs everywhere *(se passe-partout)*.[1] Derrida attests that someone comes and announces vaguely, without any gesture, "I am interested in the idiom in painting" (1). And oddly enough, there is, writes Derrida, no frame, no determined context for this remark. Nonetheless, Derrida has something on his mind because he quickly attributes the "idiom in painting" to an utterance written by Cézanne to his brother in 1905: "I owe you the truth in painting and I will tell it to you" (2). Since no frame or determined context has been provided by the speaker, Derrida has provided them himself. He has linked the vague remark concerning "the idiom in painting" to the promise given by the painter. Derrida concludes that insofar as this utterance does not refer to something outside of itself, it is no assertion; thus it must belong to the category of utterances called performative speech acts.

Cezanne's utterance is a performative because it *does* something: "It promises another 'performative,' [truth in painting] and the content of the promise is determined, like its form, by the possibility of that other" (3), a possibility that, of course, opens up the promise to infinite supplementarity. Cézanne promises the truth "in painting," leading to Derrida's initial question as to whether or not linguistic speech-act theory operates in the realm of painting. Of course speech-act theory follows certain formal rules:

> One of the conditions for the performance of such an event, for the unchaining of its chain, would according to the classical theorists of speech acts, be that Cézanne should mean to say something and that one should be able to understand it. . . . Let's suppose that I wrote this book in order to find out whether that condition could ever be fulfilled. (3–4)

Given the infinite chain of supplementarity that lurks around the edges of this entire discussion, one suspects already that while Derrida may have written this book in order to find out whether that condition could ever be fulfilled, "told" ("I will tell it to you") in the work of art, it will not be.

Still, Derrida asks: Does semiology frame a painting? Is formalization the outside of the work of art? Do we know if Cézanne means to say something and, if so, can it be understood? Can the truth be *rendered* in painting as Cézanne promises? And it is worth our time to hesitate here insofar as the difficulty that emerges at the beginning of this book is one that also occurs everywhere, in the analysis of the *kolossus* that is the task of this essay. Because he has promised to "tell" the truth "in painting," this characteristic or "trait" of Cézanne's work as art and as painting is linked to "the economy of language," which means, for Derrida, that while it may be framed by the formalizations of classical speech-act theory, those formalizations (or any formal system—Kant's, for example) cannot escape being framed by play and chance, by the infinite chain of supplementary promises, and by undecidability. Thus in the case of Cézanne's characteristic trait—to render truth "in painting"—art is divided at its edges, insofar as Cézanne's performative exceeds and overflows the edges of linguistic formalization that establish the criteria for speech acts.

In rendering his analysis of the undecidability of judgments concerning the application of formal linguistics to art, Derrida is impelled to make a disclaimer immediately. Bide your time *(patienter)*, really, it's active, *exercise* patience, *hesitate* with the text (as Derrida himself has done right here at the beginning), in order to discover that any formalization of the text is replete with the very indecision formalization attempts to reduce. If the reader hesitates: "You would discover that I cannot dominate the situation, or translate it, or describe it. I cannot report what is going on in it, or narrate it, or depict it, or pronounce it, or mimic it, or offer it up to be read or formalized without a remainder" (2). If readers do not hesitate or exercise patience, Derrida cannot be responsible for their inability to see that *he* does not dominate, translate, describe, report, narrate, depict, pronounce, mimic, read, or formalize this situation with any sense of completion. That is, whether the promise of truth "in painting" is a statement, an assertion, or a performative, there remains some level of indecision in every *judgment* or formalization of truth "in painting." In the end, the "connection [*trait*] between the letter, discourse, painting is perhaps all that happens in or all that threads its way through *The Truth in Painting*" (8). It is clear that Derrida is making no promises.

While unable to reduce remainders and indicision, Derrida can still give an account; he tells a "tale," *his* tale, *his* narrative. The tale that Derrida renders here has to do with Kant's *Critique of Judgement*, and with both the "Analytic of the Beautiful" and the "Analytic of the Sublime."[2] (Such tales, Gilles Deleuze has noted, may serve a surprising role, if not that of a foundation, then at least that of a model or a standard that in and of itself is thought to be beyond demonstration.)[3] Derrida's tale is about what happens when a system of art is "parasitized" and thus is opened up to what is outside it. Parasitism, as Derrida defines it, does not allow a system to be opened to just anything that happens to be outside it; it is opened up only to its *own* outside, to what in some sense belongs to the system yet is excluded from it. The tale Derrida tells is about what happens when parasitism allows a system's own outside to enter it in such a way that it divides the system at its edges.

Cézanne's promise to render the truth "in painting" operates precisely in this way. The pure practice of art is immediately opened to the play, chance, and economy of language and so also to the formalizations operating to dominate or describe language systems. This sort of partitioning of the edges of a system occurs everywhere *(se passe-partout)* in Kant's Third Critique, according to Derrida, and it accounts for the indecisive nature of Kant's system of formalization. In French, *le passe-partout* refers to the matting that surrounds a painting, that visible edging that lets the painting appear in the cut-out portion *(Truth in Painting* 12). Derrida's story is also such a *passe-partout.* It lets something else appear even while it remains within the Kantian frame itself, but as its outside, thus never as entirely separate from that frame. Derrida is not proposing a new framework, but simply a partitioned or frayed edge that occurs everywhere in relation to Kant's *Critique of Judgement.*

In this essay I shall examine one aspect of these edges that occur everywhere *(le passe-partout qui se passe-partout)* in the four essays of *Truth in Painting* with an eye to the story Derrida tells about the grafting and contamination, the division and parasitism of each of the edges of the Third Critique within and outside of the others. I shall ask about what Derrida lets appear as well as what does not appear in these edges. Specifically, I am concerned with the limits of representation of the beautiful and the elimination of such limits with regard to the presentation of the sublime. What concerns me here is that the movement of thought from the representation of an object of the beautiful to the sublime presentation of ideas comes, for Derrida, at a price that is paid, not by Derrida himself, nor even by Kant, and certainly not by the geniuses who produce art, but by women, who are left firmly attached to the Kantian representational system they neither control nor endorse. There may also be a heavy price paid by artists like Cézanne, who are not in their lifetimes recognized as geniuses and so whose works of art are subject to linguistic formalization and aesthetic policing—which, in fact, may well amount to the same thing.

Certainly, for Kant, the beautiful is the object of sheer delight devoid of all interest, but this means only that it is without finality, without an end. That is, we are not interested in the beautiful either for the sake of knowledge nor for any moral claims it may permit us to make. Taste is the capacity to judge an object apart from any interests on the part of either sensation (moral interests for Kant) or cognition (interest in knowing an object). This is why all judgments of taste, although they include a demand for universal agreement, are nonetheless singular and refer immediately to feelings of pleasure/displeasure and not to cognition. The state of mind producing feelings of pleasure/displeasure must be one in which no definite concept provides a rule of cognition for the manifold of intuitions gathered by imagination; that is, sensibility is not ordered by any concept that alone would allow it to be known. Although taste must be an "original faculty" (*Critique*, sect. 17), so not determined according to some empirical model, it is a priori. Taste can be trained (even mere charm and emotion are useful for this) (sect. 14), but only men who have got "all they want" (sect. 5) can tell who has taste. Presumably they are the ones with the means to go and look at reputedly beautiful things with their own eyes, and they are the same men who can train the others whose taste is still untrained though not barbaric (sect. 13). Taste cannot be simply learned; it is not cognitive, though not everyone can possibly have the originary faculty that can be trained. So, taste is concerned with objects of delight, yet it simply plays with them without devoting itself to any sincerely (sect. 5). In fact, it puts them on a pedestal so as to receive the strongest possible *sensation* from them "just as if our delight depended on sensation" (sect. 7, 8). Sensation is very important for Kant, because we become conscious of the *universal* (thus objective and true) nature of a judgment through sensation and sensation alone. The harmonious "quickening" of imagination and understanding (sect. 9) amounts to a pure sensation whose uniformity is unbroken by anything foreign—that is to say, anything outside it (sect. 14). This, of course, is a claim that Derrida will contest. According to Derrida, it is precisely the asignifying play of forms and lines that are external but necessary to the representation of the object that produce a pure judgment of taste (*Truth in Painting* 111). The *paregonal* structure of the intuition emerges at the heart of any judgments about it.

For Kant, the beautiful must be the simple mode of sensation, what is most exactly, definitely, and completely intuitable, the pure form of an object, without the charm or emotion provided by brilliant or composite colors or other forms of ornamentation (*parerga*) such as drapery on statues or columns on palaces (*Critique*, sect. 14). However (and this is its limitation), the beautiful must have a relation to a concept that, of course, has definite boundaries (sect. 26). This relation consists of a pretense. It must be as if there were no aim or purpose, no representation of an object; we must never be interested in the object with regard to its actual existence in order to judge it beautiful. The relation of the beautiful to a concept then is that the beautiful presents an indefinite concept of understanding (sect. 23). Thus although the beautiful in a judgment is *parergonal* and operates on the borders of the domain of cognition, detaching itself from the logic of objectivity, it does this, as Derrida says, only in order to attach itself more firmly to the objective standard. "In the case of a given intuition [of the beautiful], this faculty of the imagination is considered as in agreement with the faculty of concepts of understanding or reason" (*Critique*, sect. 15). There is agreement between imagination and concepts, the condition of *logical objectivity*, even though there is no determinate concept. In the language of Derrida's introduction, formalization operates, but not without hesitation; it operates *parergonally* yet, it gives rise to beauty.

It's clear then that it is not the intuition of the beautiful that provides an alternative to cognitive or moral representations; even in the sensible intuition of the beautiful, the imagination is considered to be in agreement with the faculty of concepts of understanding or reason. Such agreement is the condition of objectivity, the condition of logical judgments and discursive reason. Among sensible presentations, only the sublime is not conditioned by the logic of concepts; thus the sublime accounts for no sensible form, and no object of nature that is known according to concepts is sublime. The sublime is "nature in its chaos or in its wildest and most irregular disorder and desolation" (*Critique*, sect. 23). The sublime is the formless and limitless sensation that operates to reveal imagination and understanding's inadequacy to present the absolutely great in a representation and so produces a feeling of pain. It is in this regard that the sublime exceeds the limits of the beautiful. Beauty has "purposivenessness" in its form; that is, in the intuition of the beautiful, we have a presentation of something that we may also have a representation of, thus we may have cognition or interest in it (sect. 23). But the sublime is an idea, not of understanding, but of reason; it presents something that cannot be represented in the categories of understanding as they gather together sensible intuitions; it presents an idea of reason. With the intuition of the sublime, our pain and our pleasure arise from the *excess* of feeling and the *overwhelming* encounter with the powerful, that radical finitude whereby every standard of sensibility is inadequate.

When he sets about rendering the sense of the "sublime," Kant makes use of the German word for presentation, *Darstellung*. Historically, *Darstellung* has referred to representation in the sense of theatrical presentation; as such it stands opposed to *Vorstellung*, a kind of symbolic activity whereby an image substitutes for an absent thing.[4] As *Darstel-*

lung, representation is the tangible, physical presence of a thing that is visually replicated. It is representation in the sense of *Darstellung,* not *Vorstellung* which Kant has recourse to in the *Critique of Judgement,* "Analytic of the Sublime." So, Derrida reminds us that in Kant's text, not only is the representation of the sublime a question of mere presentation, the *"bloβe Darstellung,"* but that it is the presentation, not of an object determined by the formal categories of understanding, but of a concept (*Truth in Painting* 124). For his part, Derrida is primarily interested in examining the theatrical presentation of the sublime. He finds this presentation in Kant when Kant first states that the sublime is a feeling of the inadequacy of imagination for presenting the idea of a whole (sect. 26). Casting about for an example of the mere presentation of a concept, Kant discovers the *colossal.* Derrida writes:

> *Colossal (kolossalisch)* thus qualifies the presentation, the putting on stage or into presence, the catching-sight, rather, of some thing, but of something which is not a thing, since it is a concept. And the presentation of this concept inasmuch as it is not presentable. Nor simple unpresentable: *almost unpresentable.* And by reason of its size: it is "almost too large." This concept is announced and then eludes presentation on the stage. One would say, by reason of its almost excessive size, that it was obscene. (*Truth in Painting* 125)

What seems to interest Derrida, as he tells his tale of the sublime, is the theatrical presentation of what is almost unpresentable, what is, because of its size, obscene. A theatrical presentation of obscenity—in a concept. Perhaps it is for this reason that Derrida fixes on the concept of the colossal. As Kant wrote: "An object is monstrous where by its size it defeats the end that forms its concept. The colossal is the mere presentation of a concept which is almost too great for presentation, i.e., borders on the relatively monstrous" (*Critique,* sect. 26). So Derrida focuses on the existence of the term "colossal" in Kant's text on the sublime; and on the idea that the word colossal is used to *qualify* the presentation of a concept whose *presentation (Darstellung)* is "almost too great."

Derrida cannot resist the temptation of this concept "colossal." He tells us that according to Jean-Pierre Vernant, the Greeks did not understand colossal to imply anything with "a value of size *(taille)."* It did not designate (until later and by accident) "effigies with gigantic dimensions."[5] With regard to the word "size," what colossal only later and accidentally came to imply, to size *(tailler)* is, in French, also suggestive of cutting, the delimitation of contours in wood, fabric, or even in stone. Thus the English translators of *La vérité en peinture* have chosen to translate this word *taille* not as size, but as *cize* as in (the now obsolete) "cizars" (scissors). This serves, they note, the purpose of keeping the double sense of colossal before us.[6] It is simultaneously the "almost too great" presentation and the delimitation of contours. However, even this "almost too great" needs further articulation.

In the pre-Hellenic world *colossos* would have been connected to the root *kol,* which carries the idea of something upright, something erect *(Truth in Painting* 121). The obscene *Darstellung,* the concept, is announced but eludes presentation or almost eludes presentation (it's not clear in the text which) on stage by reason of its excessive cize. That is, the colossal, says Derrida, qualifies an "erection," the standing there upright of an excess of cize that is both the delimitation of a contour, and a presentation that is almost too great, although "without edging or overspill, of the colossal" (125). And it is the *"philosophos kolossos"* (the genius, the philosopher of the colossal) who must calculate the "almost too great" in relation to "his" power of apprehension *(Auffassungsvermögen)* that provides him with the measure of what is "almost too great."[7]

More than one kind of apprehension may be at work here, since at the limits of apprehension, the colossal is almost frightening, bordering raw nature (untamed by concepts) which can present the *Ungeheur,* the actually too great, the monstrous that invites actual seduction or fear, perhaps the fear of seduction *(Truth in Painting* 124). Fear of the annihilation, the reduction to nothing of the presentation of the erection? Of whom is Derrida writing here? Whose tale is he telling? *Pure* aesthetic judgments of the sublime explicitly forbid fear or pleasure even while acknowledging the "relatively monstrous" character of the colossal, which is nonetheless not an object like the monstrous, but a concept *(Critique,* sect. 26). By its size, the monstrous object defeats its concept. The intuition that produces the feeling of the sublime, however, is only almost too large, thereby not overrunning, or overspilling its concept.

It should be clear by now that the experience of the sublime is not easily accomplished, that it demands a delicate balance between imagination's two operations. First, it is absolutely necessary that the apprehension is only almost too large, but not too large. Imagination as apprehension can continue to infinity through the addition of number, but it must not. This is because of imagination's second characteristic. Imagination as comprehension is aesthetic: it is "an absolute measure beyond which no greater is possible subjectively (that is, for the judging Subject)" (*Critique,* sect. 26). As Derrida notes, imagination has two cizes, two edges, two traits or limits. On the one hand, apprehension goes to its limit without difficulty. On the other hand, this is balanced by subjective apprehensiveness, because comprehension cannot follow infinitely, but instead arrives quickly at a maximum that then becomes the fundamental measure of the evaluation of cize (*Truth in Painting* 140). The colossal, as erect, upright, but also as cutting a contour, operates as the passage between these two. It is the passage from the small and measured cize to the beyond measure of the without cize, the immense. The colossal effigy *detailler* divides, enumerates, and liberates the excess of cize in passing from the column (the ornamental or *parerga* that is the outside of the beautiful) to the colossal. And what kind of effigy does Derrida have in mind here? A fantastic representation, an idol that cannot be moved.

> It is a stony, fixed immobility, a monument of impassivity which has been stood up on the earth, after having been a little in it, and sometimes buried. . . . Although philologists or archaeologists don't look in this direction . . . one ought to link here the discourse on the *kol* to the whole Freudian problematic of the Medusa (erection/castration/apotropaic) (121).

Indeed. According to Derrida, the *kol* of the colossus would look rather like a column. Together *kol* and column are described quite strangely. They share semantic and formal affinities (120). As stone they have nothing to see, they see nothing but also they let *nothing be seen.* Contrary to Kant's own claims, they do not frame—not even the column. They stop our sight. We turn away from them rather than risk sight of their stony visages. They show nothing and cause nothing to be seen; they display (on stage?) none of what one thinks. They do not allow the presentation of an object or a concept.

Certainly, one thinks here of the example of the column as a parergon. I have noted above that columns are, for Kant, *parerga* exterior to the building itself. But how, in architecture, asks Derrida, can we distinguish integral from detachable parts? And among the most interesting examples here would be columns that represent a human figure, columns in the form of clothed or unclothed human bodies that are *kol*; that is, "erected" in the space where framed paintings are hung, the space of historical, economic, and political inscriptions (*Truth in Painting* 61). Within this space it is the colossal that serves as the double, that is, as we have seen, as both cutting a contour and as almost too great for the contour it cuts: *kol*, which is the measure of cize and which delimits that which is liberated in this contour (140).

Yet it is only by some "accident" (see above) that the colossal has come to be something other than the erection whereby the body of man becomes or does not become integral to the building. "Accidentally" the *kol*/colossal has stepped away from the building, that space inscribed historically, economically, and politically, and no longer serves as parergon in relation to it. This stepping away follows a double set of restrictions throughout Kant's text on the sublime. Kant's examples are crucial here. Given the limits of imagination, its rule-following constraints guaranteed by understanding, apprehension proceeds by counting numbers or units until it reaches its limit. Comprehension, however, intuits an aesthetic maximum or whole in the evaluation of size. The intuition of the sublime must remain balanced between these two. Whatever provokes the feeling of the sublime must be far enough away for the maximum size to appear to apprehension, while remaining close enough to be seen and be comprehended. The two examples Kant draws on in section 26 accomplish this in the medium of stone. The measure of sublime erection is a question of the body's relation to stone (*Truth in Painting* 141). Kant writes:

> [I]n order to get the full emotional effect of the size of the Pyramids we must avoid coming too near just as much as remaining too far away. For in the latter case the representation of the apprehended parts (the tiers of stones) is but obscure, and produces no effect upon the aesthetic judgment of the Subject. In the former, however, it takes the eye some time to complete the apprehension from the base to the summit; but in this interval the first tiers always in part disappear before the imagination has taken in the last, and so the comprehension is never complete. (*Critique*, sect. 26)

Similarly, upon entering Saint Peter's, the same feeling of the inadequacy of imagination for presenting the whole produces what Kant eventually calls "negative satisfaction." The experience of either of these piles of stones as sublime demands, as Derrida points out, the measure of man's cize: "an average place in the body would provide an aesthetic maximum without getting lost" (141). In what? In the too far, the abyss that the mathematically infinite threatens. In the too near, the dynamically sublime Medusa that castrates pleasure by turning to stone anyone who comes too near her snake-haired head and sees her, preventing the median placement of the body, an ideal and idealizing placement. This image is suggested by Derrida when he says that "someone" should pursue the relation of the sublime to the Medusa and castration. Derrida does not himself wish to be entangled in it here.

Elsewhere, in *Spurs,* Derrida writes, "La femme sera mon sujet," but also "La femme n'aura donc pas été mon sujet." "She will be," but also, "She will not *have been* my subject"—Is there no end to what she is subject to? These words have an ominous sound. Here too, a great deal rests on not getting too close to "la femme." In *Glas* Derrida does finally turn his attention to the link he proposes between the the discourse on the *kol* and the Freudian problematic of the Medusa. Clearly he has it in mind in *Truth in Painting,* where the displacement of the erect column into the *colossus* problematizes the status of "man" as subject. Spivak has characterized this move as follows:

> If a man is obliged to perform by means of a single or singular style (stylus, phallus [that style determined by the *kol,* by what is erect]), he can at least attempt a plural style, always try to fake his orgasms, never speak for himself, be forever on the move away from a place that might be locatable as his own.[8]

As we shall see, this move is not unrelated to Derrida's interest in the colossus. In this context, Derrida attempts to encounter the Medusa, not as the Freudian fetish, the sight of whose head "makes the spectator stiff with terror, turns him into stone," but as an encounter that increases his subjective feeling of power: "For becoming stiff (*das Starr-werden*) means an erection. Thus in the original situation it offers consolation to the spectator: He is still in possession of a penis, and the stiffening reassures him of the fact."[9]

Derrida, following Jean Genet, attempts to reinterpret the parergonal stiffening that turns the subject to stone, but only in order to attach itself more firmly to the objective standard, that is, to the style of the male subject. Here Derrida recommends that that "he" must be Medusa to himself, in fact, that to be oneself is to be Medusa'd. "He" must "give oneself/itself up for lost," no longer assuming the style of the subject, but disseminating his subject position into an agglomeration or concretion that is "[s]elf's dead sure biting (death)" (Derrida, *Glas* 202bi-203bi). The dissemination of one's subject position accords with the style of a male subject so even the addition of the Medusa position to his style still has the effect of producing the reassuring stiffening. As Spivak notes, perhaps this is the most deconstruction can offer.

In Derrida's tale concerning the "colossal," the move away from the column returns to the "sublime body," which, in order to experience pleasure *(Wohlgefallen)* must be far enough away for the maximum size to appear, but not so far as to fall into the abyss. And what about pleasure? The *Wohlgefallen* in the case of the beautiful is, says Derrida, highly subjective, "In truth, I please myself in pleasing myself in what is beautiful, insofar as it does not exist" (*Truth in Painting* 47). "There is" an autoaffection, but it goes outside itself to the beautiful object and then returns itself to its pleasure; thus Derrida takes this pleasure in the beautiful to be also heteroaffection, a pleasing oneself in what is other. In the case of the beautiful, Derrida notes that judgment is the bridge between the beautiful object, though not as an existing object, and the subject who receives the pure pleasure, though not as an existing subject. Derrida writes: "I, me, existing subject never have access to pure pleasure insofar as I exist. Yet 'there is' pleasure, 'it gives' *(Es gibt)*, pleasure is what it gives, to nobody, but some remains and it's the best, the purest" (48). Perhaps then the trace of pleasure that "is given" and given to nobody in particular is the most spiritual. Spiritual pleasure is the *oikonomia* of *mimesis*. The subject, if "he" is a genius is a free imitator, that is, his freedom is analogous to, ana-logos with Divine freedom. "He" may experience pleasure in the beautiful, a beautiful woman, to take one of Kant's examples, but the best, the purest and most spiritual pleasure derives only from total lack of interest in "her" existence as well as in "his" (own?). It is instructive that these rules are "furnished" by nature as imperatives, nature, as Derrida notes, furnishes *logos*:

> Nature furnishes rules to the art of genius. Not concepts, not descriptive laws, but rules precisely, singular norms which are

also orders, imperative statements. When Hegel reproaches the third *Critique* for staying at the level of the "you must" he very well evinces the moral order which sustains the aesthetic order. That order proceeds from one freedom to another . . . and as discourse it does so through a signifying element. Everytime we encounter in this text something that resembles a discursive metaphor (nature says, dictates, prescribes) these are not just any metaphors but analogies of analogy, whose message is that the literal meaning is analogical: nature is properly *logos* towards which one must always return. Analogy is always language. (Derrida, "Economimesis" 13)

In the interest of pure judgments of taste, we admire nature's displays in its beautiful art products, yet their end or purpose does not appear to us (Derrida, "Economimesis" 14). This purposelessness, says Derrida, leads us back inside ourselves. "Cut off from what we seek outside . . . we seek and give within, by giving ourselves orders, categorical imperatives" (14). Such idealizing interiorization guarantees our autonomy, guarantees the analogy with the Divine, our freedom, and the moral law within; most of all it guarantees that we shall not engage our taste in the political or social economy of human society (Derrida, "Economimesis" 12). We shall not have the bad taste to "lick our chops," or to be caught "smacking our lips or whetting our palate" (14). Dis-tasteful and disgusting actions all.

In the case of the sublime, there is a negative pleasure. Sublime *Wohlgefallen* includes something repulsive that provokes disagreement of the faculties, *disorder in the subject,* yet the "system of reason can account for it" (21; my emphasis). The effects of the Medusa are evident; the only question is the role of the subject. By virtue of its *hesitation,* its silence in the face of the too much and too little, the sublime extends the power of the subject so that what is gained greatly exceeds what is lost, and the subject's freedom is preserved. Simple economic calculation on the part of the philosopher—that is, the erection of the body in a median place in relation to pyramid or cathedral—allows the work of mourning as idealization to continue ever more profoundly, and the work of the spirit continues by operation of Divine analogy (22).

But Kant also states that these examples of man's art do not suffice for a pure aesthetic judgment of the sublime. Pure aesthetic judgments can be neither cultural (a human end determines the form) nor natural (like animals whose very concept includes a determinate end). "Suitable" examples of the sublime, if our aesthetic judgment's are to be pure, are found only in "rude nature merely as involving magnitude (and only in this so far as it does not convey any charm or emotion arising from actual danger)" (*Critique*, sect. 26). The colossal *Darstellung* is a theatrical presentation of the concept, a conceptual performance piece, the con-cept of a relatively monstrous object that is only almost too large. *This* is what constitutes its rudeness. It is neither cultural nor natural, says Derrida, but both cultural and natural. A familiar phrase, but what does it say here? It is both with and without a human end or purpose as are found in buildings, statues, or an out-of-work tool lying on an ancient archaeological site. With and without a concept determining a natural end or use as in the case of animals or shapeless mountain masses, pyramids of ice, and the dark tempestuous ocean. The colossal, writes Derrida, is always between the with and the without, between what can be presented and what is unpresentable, it is the edge, the cut, partaking of both.

The pyramids and the cathedral provide examples of human ends in which the body of man is the measure, and the final example in section 26 of Kant's *Critique* provides an example of the body of man in relation to natural ends. A tree judged by the height of man that is then given as the standard for a mountain, which measures the earth's diameter, which measures the known planets, which moves as a measure toward what Derrida calls the "milky dissemen," so that "there is no prospect here of a limit" (*Truth in Painting* 146; *Critique*, sect. 26). Apparently, there is nothing the body of man cannot measure.

Except when there is an "accident." When the body of man cuts the contour too close to the Medusa, or miscalculates so as to place itself too near the abyss, then the *kol* steps away from the building, and "accidentally' the column is transposed into the colossal. Here, Derrida's tale discovers the excess in the system of formalization. In the case of the beautiful, it is taste and distaste that delimit the system of pleasure, the autoaffection predicated upon nonexistence of the beautiful object, the return to self, interiorization, and idealization of affection. Even the ugly, false, and monstrous, can be swallowed, assimilated, or colonized by the system by being represented in works of art called beautiful (Derrida, "Economimesis" 22). Only when consumption is forced, when mourning contradicts itself, when instead of idealizing it produces dis-gust in actual taste, or rather, in the supplement of taste: smell. It's obvious, says Derrida, that even the disgust of "vomit" belongs to the system of the beautiful, as its "other," as "the very quintessence of its bad taste" (25). But confronted with stench, its "nausea," and "internal penetration" from which one cannot simply turn away, freedom and mourning are impaired, without exception. Smell defeats beautiful interiorization, *economimesis*, the logocentric system. Smell defeats even God.

Now if the colossal is always between what can be presented and what is unpresentable, it is, I have noted, the edge, the cut, partaking of both, a performance of rude nature, deriving from neither art nor culture, yet somehow from both; its very inadequation in the face of art and culture serves as the site of its erection. And Derrida is quick to note this:

> Kant calls it subjective, in this we decipher the psychic ideality of what is not in nature, the origin of the *psyche* as *kolossos*, the relation to the double of *ci-devant* (what is formerly something else) who comes to erect himself *"là-devant"* (in front), superelevating himself, beyond height. (*Truth in Painting* 144)

What then is interior nobility, this genius stripped of his title, elevating and erecting (medusaing) himself as colossal "on the excessive movement of its own disappearance, its unpresentable presentation, the obscenity of its abyss" (144–45), that borders both the beautiful parergon and the sublime median? Is this "it" that erects itself the cipher of the unconscious? If so, does not the Medusa whose snake-hair points to other readings of "erection" also share this trait of being unpresentable? If the Medusa can only be represented in terms belonging to the style of a male subject, has she not merely been colonized, a case of sublime auto/heteroaffection? So I might ask again, Who is Derrida writing about here? Where the colossus appears, can Oedipus be far behind? For the unconscious of Derrida's tale, marked by the borders of the colossal, still defines itself only by keeping its distance from "la femme."

Notes

1. Jacques Derrida, *The Truth in Painting*, trans. Geoff Bennington and Ian McLeod (Chicago: University of Chicago Press, 1987); originally published in French as *La vérité en peinture* (Paris: Flammarion, 1978).

2. Immanuel Kant, *The Critique of Judgement*, trans. James Creed Meredith (Oxford: Oxford University Press, 1986).

3. Gilles Deleuze, "Plato and the Simulacrum," in *The Logic of Sense*, trans. Mark Lester with Charles Stivale (New York: Columbia University Press, 1990); originally published in French as *Logique du sens* (Paris: Editions de Minuit, 1969).

4. Craig Owens, "Representation, Appropriation and Power," *Art in America* (May 1982): 9–21, citation on 13.

5. Jeanne-Pierre Vernant, *Greek Myth and Thought* (London: Routledge and Kegan Paul, 1983), 305–20. Quoted in Derrida, *Truth in Painting*, 120.

6. See Derrida, *Truth in Painting*, 120 n. 32.

7. See Jacques Derrida, "Economimesis," *Diacritics* 11 no. 2 (1981): 3–25.

8. Gayatri Chakravorty Spivak, "Displacement and the Discourse of Woman," in *Displacement: Derrida and After*, ed. Mark Krupnick (Bloomington: Indiana University Press, 1983), 179.

9. Jacques Derrida, *Glas*, trans. John P. Leavey Jr. and Richard Rand (Lincoln: University of Nebraska Press, 1986), 44a.

Suggested Further Reading

[Articles published in anthologies are not listed separately here, but references to them appear where originally cited.]

Abelove, Henry, Michele Aina Barale, and David M. Halperin, eds. *The Lesbian and Gay Studies Reader*. New York: Routledge, 1993.

Alcoff, Linda. "Cultural Feminism Versus Post-Structuralism: The Identity Crisis in Feminist Theory." *Signs* 13, no. 3 (Spring 1988).

Allen, Jeffner, and Iris Marion Young, eds. *The Thinking Muse: Feminism and Modern French Philosophy*. Bloomington: Indiana University Press, 1989.

Allison, David B., ed. *The New Nietzsche*. Cambridge: MIT Press, 1985.

Altizer, Thomas J. J., Max A. Myers, Carl A. Raschke, Robert P. Scharlemann, Mark C. Taylor, and Charles E. Winquist. *Deconstruction and Theology*. New York: Crossroads, 1982.

Austin, J. L. *How To Do Things With Words*. Edited by J. O. Urmson and Marina Sbisà. Cambridge: Harvard University Press, 1975.

Benhabib, Seyla. "The Call to the Ethical: Deconstruction, Justice, and the Ethical Relationship." *Cardozo Law Review* 13 (1991).

———. *Situating the Self: Gender, Community and Postmodernism in Contemporary Ethics*. New York: Routledge, 1992.

Benhabib, Seyla, and Drucilla Cornell, eds. *Feminism as Critique: On the Politics of Gender*. Minneapolis: University of Minnesota Press, 1987.

Benhabib, Seyla, Judith Butler, Drucilla Cornell, and Nancy Fraser. *Feminist Contentions: A Philosophical Exchange*. Edited by Linda Nicholson. New York: Routledge, 1995.

Bennington, Geoffrey, and Jacques Derrida. *Jacques Derrida*. Chicago: University of Chicago Press, 1993.

Benstock, Bernard, ed. *James Joyce: The Augmented Ninth*. Syracuse: Syracuse University Press, 1988.

Berg, Elizabeth. "The Third Woman." *Diacritics* 12 (Summer 1982).

Bernasconi, Robert, and Simon Critchley, eds. *Re-Reading Levinas*. Bloomington: Indiana University Press, 1991.

Birmingham, Peg. "Feminist Fictions: Discourse, Desire and the Law." *Philosophy and Social Criticism* (Spring 1996).

Blanchot, Maurice. *The Writing of the Disaster*. Translated by Ann Smock. Lincoln: University of Nebraska Press, 1986.

Bloom, Harold, Paul de Man, Jacques Derrida, Geoffrey Hartman, and J. Hillis Miller. *Deconstruction and Criticism*. New York: Seabury, 1979.

Bordo, Susan. *The Flight to Objectivity: Essays on Cartesianism and Culture*. Albany: State University of New York Press, 1987.

————. *Unbearable Weight: Feminism, Western Culture, and the Body*. Berkeley and Los Angeles: University of California Press, 1993.

Boundas, Constantin V., and Dorothea Olkowski, eds. *Gilles Deleuze and The Theater of Philosophy*. New York: Routledge, 1993.

Bowlby, Rachel. "Flight Reservations." *Oxford Literary Review* 10, nos. 1–2 (1988).

Braidotti, Rosi. *Patterns of Dissonance: A Study of Women in Contemporary Philosophy*. Oxford: Polity, 1991.

Brennan, Teresa, ed. *Between Feminism and Psychoanalysis*. London: Routledge, 1989.

Brodrib, Somer. *Nothing Mat(t)ers: A Feminist Critique of Postmodernism*. Melbourne: Spinifex, 1992.

Brodzki, Bella, and Celeste Schenck, eds. *Life/Lines: Theorizing Women's Autobiography*. Ithaca: Cornell University Press, 1988.

Budick, Sanford, and Wolfgang Iser, eds. *Languages of the Unsayable: The Play of Negativity in Literature and Literary Theory*. New York: Columbia University Press, 1989.

Butler, Judith. *Gender Trouble: Feminism and the Subversion of Identity*. New York: Routledge, 1990.

————. *Bodies That Matter: On the Discursive Limits of "Sex."* New York: Routledge, 1993.

Butler, Judith and Joan W. Scott. *Feminists Theorize the Political*. New York: Routledge, 1992.

Cardozo Law Review 11, nos. 5–6 (July–August 1990).

Chanter, Tina. *Ethics of Eros*. New York: Routledge, 1995.

Christian, Barbara. "The Race for Theory." *Cultural Critique* 6 (Spring 1987).

Cixous, Hélène. *"Coming to Writing" and Other Essays*. Edited by Deborah Jenson. Cambridge: Harvard University Press, 1991.

Code, Lorraine, *Rhetorical Spaces: Essays on Gendered Locations*. New York: Routledge, 1995.

Corea, Genea. *The Invisible Epidemic: The Story of Women and AIDS*. New York: Harper, 1992.

Cornell, Drucilla. *Beyond Accommodation: Ethical Feminism Deconstruction and the Law*. New York: Routledge, 1991.

————. *The Philosophy of the Limit*. New York: Routledge, 1992.

Cornell, Drucilla, Michel Rosenfeld, and David Gray Carlson, eds. *Deconstruction and the Possibility of Justice*. New York: Routledge, 1992.

Coward, Harold, and Toby Foshay, eds. *Derrida and Negative Theology*. Albany: State University of New York Press, 1992.

Cox, Elizabeth. *Thanksgiving: An AIDS Journal*. New York: Harper, 1990.

Critchley, Simon. *The Ethics of Deconstruction: Derrida and Levinas*. Oxford: Polity, 1992.

Critchley, Simon, and Peter Dews, eds. *Deconstructive Subjectivities*. Albany: State University of New York Press, 1995.

Culler, Jonathan. *On Deconstruction: Theory and Criticism after Structuralism*. Ithaca: Cornell University Press, 1982.

Dallery, Arleen, Charles Scott, and P. Holley Roberts, eds. *Ethics and Danger: Essays on Heidegger and Continental Thought*. Albany: State University of New York Press, 1992.

De Lauretis, Teresa, ed. *Feminist Studies/Critical Studies.* Bloomington: Indiana University Press, 1986.

———. "Eccentric Subjects: Feminist Theory and Historical Consciousness." *Feminist Studies,* no. 1 (1990).

Derrida, Jacques. *Speech and Phenomena.* Translated by David Allison. Evanston: Northwestern University Press, 1973.

———. *Of Grammatology.* Translated by Gayatri Chakravorty Spivak. Baltimore: Johns Hopkins University Press, 1976.

———. *Edmund Husserl's Origin of Geometry: An Introduction.* Translated by John P. Leavey. Stony Brook, N.Y.: Nicholas Hays, 1978.

———. *Writing and Difference.* Translated by Alan Bass. Chicago: University of Chicago Press, 1978.

———. *Spurs.* Translated by Barbara Harlow. Chicago: University of Chicago Press, 1979.

———. "The Law of Genre." Translated by Avital Ronell. *Glyph* 7 (1980).

———. *Dissemination.* Translated by Barbara Johnson. Chicago: University of Chicago Press, 1981.

———. "Economimesis." Translated by Richard Klein. *Diacritics* 11, no. 2 (1981).

———. *Positions.* Translated by Alan Bass. Chicago: University of Chicago Press, 1981.

———. *Margins of Philosophy.* Translated by Alan Bass. Chicago: University of Chicago Press, 1982.

———. "Geschlecht: Sexual Difference, Ontological Difference." Translated by Ruben Berezdivin. *Research in Phenomenology* 13 (1983).

———. *The Ear of the Other.* Edited by Christie V. McDonald. Translated by Peggy Kamuf and Avital Ronell. New York: Schocken Books, 1985. (A volume of the same name, including "Choreographies" and also edited by Christie V. McDonald, was published by the University of Nebraska Press in 1985.)

———. *Glas.* Translated by John P. Leavey Jr. and Richard Rand. Lincoln: University of Nebraska Press, 1986.

———. *The Post Card: From Socrates to Freud and Beyond.* Translated by Alan Bass. Chicago: University of Chicago Press, 1987.

———. *The Truth in Painting.* Translated by Geoff Bennington and Ian McLeod. Chicago: University of Chicago Press, 1987.

———. *Limited Inc.* Translated by Samuel Weber. Evanston: Northwestern University Press, 1988.

———. "A Number of Yes." Translated by Brian Holmes. *Qui Parle* 2, no. 2 (Fall 1988).

———. *Memoires for Paul de Man.* Translated by Cecile Lindsay, Jonathan Culler, Eduardo Cadava, and Peggy Kamuf. New York: Columbia University Press, 1989.

———. *Of Spirit: Heidegger and the Question.* Translated by Geoffrey Bennington and Rachel Bowlby. Chicago: University of Chicago Press, 1989.

———. "Rights of Inspection." Translated by David Wills. *Art and Text,* no. 32 (1989).

———. *Acts of Literature.* Edited by Derek Attridge. New York: Routledge, 1991.

———. *Cinders.* Edited and translated by Ned Lukacher. Lincoln: University of Nebraska Press, 1991.

———. *Given Time.* Vol. 1, *Counterfeit Money.* Translated by Peggy Kamuf. Chicago: University of Chicago Press, 1992.

———. *The Other Heading.* Translated by Pascale-Anne Brault and Michael B. Naas. Bloomington: Indiana University Press, 1992.

———. *Aporias: Dying—Waiting (for One Another) at the "Limits of Truth."* Translated by Thomas Dutoit. Stanford: Stanford University Press, 1994.

————. *Specters of Marx*. Translated by Peggy Kamuf. New York: Routledge, 1994.

————. *The Gift of Death*. Translated by David Wills. Chicago: University of Chicago Press, 1995.

————. *Points . . . : Interviews, 1974–1994*. Edited by Elisabeth Weber. Translated by Peggy Kamuf et al. Stanford: Stanford University Press, 1995.

Diacritics 25, no. 2 (Summer 1995).

Diamond, Irene, and Lee Quinby, eds. *Feminism and Foucault: Reflections on Resistance*. Boston: Northeastern University Press, 1988.

Dreyfus, Hubert L. *Being-in-the-World: A Commentary on Heidegger's "Being and Time," Division I*. Cambridge: MIT Press, 1991.

Elam, Diane. *Feminism and Deconstruction: Ms. en abyme*. New York: Routledge, 1994.

Ferguson, Kathy. *The Man Question: Visions of Subjectivity in Feminist Theory*. Berkeley and Los Angeles: University of California Press, 1992.

Flax, Jane. *Thinking Fragments: Psychoanalysis, Feminism, and Postmodernism in the Contemporary West*. Berkeley and Los Angeles: University of California Press, 1989.

Foucault, Michel. *The Order of Things*. New York: Vintage, 1973.

————. *Language, Counter-Memory, Practice*. Edited by Donald F. Bouchard. Translated by Donald F. Bouchard and Sherry Simon. Ithaca: Cornell University Press, 1977.

———— *The History of Sexuality*. Vol. 1, *An Introduction*. Translated by Robert Hurley. New York: Pantheon, 1978.

————. *Power/Knowledge: Selected Interviews and Other Writings, 1972–1977*. Edited by Colin Gordon. Translated by Colin Gordon, Leo Marshall, John Mephan, Kate Soper. New York: Pantheon, 1980.

Fraser, Nancy. *Unruly Practices: Power, Discourse, and Gender in Contemporary Social Theory*. Minneapolis: University of Minnesota Press, 1989.

————. *Justice Interruptus: Rethinking Key Concepts of a "Postsocialist" Age*. New York: Routledge, 1996.

Fraser, Nancy, and Sandra Lee Bartky, eds. *Revaluing French Feminism: Critical Essays on Difference, Agency, and Culture*. Bloomington: Indiana University Press, 1992.

Freeman, Barbara Claire. *The Feminine Sublime: Gender and Excess in Women's Fiction*. Berkeley and Los Angeles: University of California Press, 1995.

Gasché, Rodolphe. *The Tain of the Mirror: Derrida and the Philosophy of Reflection*. Cambridge: Harvard University Press, 1986.

Gauthier, Lorraine. "Truth as Eternal Metaphoric Displacement: Traces of the Mother in Derrida's Patricide." *Canadian Journal of Political and Social Theory* 13, nos. 1–2 (1989).

Grant, Judith. *Fundamental Feminism: Contesting the Core Concepts of Feminist Theory*. New York: Routledge, 1993.

Graybeal, Jean. *Language and "The Feminine" in Nietzsche and Heidegger*. Bloomington: Indiana University Press, 1990.

Grosz, Elizabeth. *Sexual Subversions: Three French Feminists*. Boston: Allen and Unwin, 1989.

————. *Volatile Bodies: Toward a Corporeal Feminism*. Bloomington: Indiana University Press, 1994.

————. *Space, Time and Perversion: Essays on the Politics of Bodies*. New York: Routledge, 1995.

Grosz, Elizabeth, and Elspeth Probyn, eds. *Sexy Bodies: The Strange Carnalities of Feminism*. New York: Routledge, 1995.

Haraway, Donna. *Simians, Cyborgs, and Women: The Reinvention of Nature.* New York: Routledge, 1991.

Hart, Kevin. *The Trespass of the Sign: Deconstruction, Theology, and Philosophy.* New York: Cambridge University Press, 1989.

Heidegger, Martin. *Being and Time.* Translated by John Macquarrie and Edward Robinson. New York: Harper, 1962.

———. *Poetry, Language, Thought.* Translated by Albert Hofstadter. New York: Harper, 1975.

———. *The Question Concerning Technology, and Other Essays.* Translated by William Lovitt. New York: Harper, 1977.

———. *Nietzsche, Eternal Resurrection of the Same.* Translated by David F. Krell. New York: Harper, 1984.

Hekman, Susan. *Gender and Knowledge: Elements of a Postmodern Feminism.* Boston: Northeastern University Press, 1990.

Hirsch, Marianne, and Evelyn Fox Keller. *Conflicts in Feminism.* New York: Routledge, 1990.

Holland, Nancy J. "The Treble Clef/t: Jacques Derrida and the Female Voice." In *Philosophy and Culture: Proceedings of the XVIIth World Congress of Philosophy.* Vol. 2. Montreal: Editions Montmorency, 1988.

———. *Is Women's Philosophy Possible?* Savage, Md.: Rowman and Littlefield, 1990.

hooks, bell. *Yearning: Race, Gender, and Cultural Politics.* Boston: South End, 1990.

Irigaray, Luce. *Speculum of the Other Woman.* Translated by Gillian C. Gill. Ithaca: Cornell University Press, 1985.

———. *This Sex Which is Not One.* Translated by Catherine Porter. Ithaca: Cornell University Press, 1985.

———. *An Ethics of Sexual Difference.* Translated by Carolyn Burke and Gillian Gill. Ithaca: Cornell University Press, 1993.

———. *Sexes and Genealogies.* Translated by Gillian Gill. New York: Columbia University Press, 1993.

Jardine, Alice. *Gynesis: Configurations of Woman and Modernity.* Ithaca: Cornell University Press, 1985.

Jardine, Alice, and Paul Smith. *Men in Feminism.* New York: Routledge, 1989.

Johnson, Barbara. *A World of Difference.* Baltimore: Johns Hopkins University Press, 1987.

Kamuf, Peggy, ed. *Reading Between the Blinds: A Derrida Reader.* New York: Columbia University Press, 1991.

Kaufman, Linda, ed. *Gender & Theory: Dialogues on Feminist Criticism.* Oxford: Basil Blackwell, 1989.

Kim, Maggie C. W., Susan M. St. Ville, and Susan M. Simonaitis, eds. *Tranfigurations: Theology and the French Feminists.* Minneapolis, Minn.: Fortress, 1993.

Kofman, Sarah. *The Enigma of Woman.* Translated by Catherine Porter. Ithaca: Cornell University Press, 1985.

———. *Nietzsche and Metaphor.* Translated by Duncan Large. Stanford: Stanford University Press, 1994.

Kristeva, Julia. *Desire in Language.* Translated by Thomas Gorz et al. New York: Columbia University Press, 1980.

Krupnik, Mark, ed. *Displacement: Derrida and After.* Bloomington: Indiana University Press, 1983.

Lacan, Jacques. "The Seminar on 'The Purloined Letter.' " *Écrits* (Paris: Le Seuil, 1966). Partially translated by Jeffrey Mehlman in *Yale French Studies* 48 (1972).

————. *Feminine Sexuality: Jacques Lacan and the Ecole Freudienne*. Edited by Juliet Mitchell and Jacqueline Rose. Translated by Jacqueline Rose. New York: Norton, 1982.

Laqueur, Thomas. *Making Sex: Body and Gender from the Greeks to Freud*. Cambridge: Harvard University Press, 1990.

Lawlor, Lawrence, ed. *Derrida's Interpretation of Husserl*. The Spindel Conference 1993. *Southern Journal of Philosophy* 32, supp.

Levinas, Emmanuel. *Totality and Infinity*. Translated by Alphonso Linguis. Pittsburgh: Duquesne University Press, 1969.

————. *Collected Philosophical Papers*. Edited by Alphonso Lingis. The Hague: Kluwer Academic, 1984.

Lévi-Strauss, Claude. *The Savage Mind*. Chicago: University of Chicago Press, 1966.

————. *The Elementary Structure of Kinship*. Translated by James Harle Bell, John Richard von Sturmer and Rodney Needham. Boston: Beacon, 1969.

Lyotard, Jean-François. "One of the Things at Stake in Women's Struggles." *Sub-Stance* 20 (1978).

————. *The Différend: Phrases in Dispute*. Translated by Georges Van Den Abbeele. Minneapolis: University of Minnesota Press, 1988.

MacKinnon, Catharine A. *Feminism Unmodified: Discourses on Life and Law*. Cambridge: Harvard University Press, 1987.

————. *Toward a Feminist Theory of the State*. Cambridge: Harvard University Press, 1989.

Madison, Gary B., ed. *Working Through Derrida*. Evanston: Northwestern University Press, 1993.

Magliola, Robert. *Derrida on the Mend*. West Lafayette: Purdue University Press, 1984.

Martin, Jane Roland. "Methodological Essentialisms, False Differences, and Other Dangerous Traps." *Signs* 19, no. 3 (Spring 1994).

McCarthy, Thomas. "The Politics of the Ineffable: Derrida's Deconstructionism." *Philosophical Forum* 21, nos. 1–2 (Fall–Winter 1989–90).

McNay, Lois. *Foucault and Feminism: Power, Gender, and the Self*. Oxford: Polity, 1993.

Mehuron, Kate, and Gary Percesepe. *Free Spirits*. Englewood Cliffs, N.J: Prentice-Hall, 1995.

Minh-ha, Trinh, ed. *She, The Inappropriate/d Other*. *Discourse* 8 (Fall–Winter 1986–87).

Modleski, Tania. *Feminist Without Women: Culture and Criticism in a "Postfeminist" Age*. New York: Routledge, 1991.

Moi, Toril. *Sexual/Textual Politics: Feminist Literary Theory*. New York: Routledge, 1988.

Murphy, Timothy F., and Suzanne Poirier, eds. *Writing AIDS: Gay Literature, Language, and Analysis*. New York: Columbia University Press, 1993.

Nancy, Jean-Luc. *The Inoperative Community*. Translated by Peter Connor et al. Minneapolis: University of Minnesota Press, 1991.

Nicholson, Linda J., ed. *Feminism/Postmodernism*. New York: Routledge, 1990.

O'Leary, Joseph. *Questioning Back: The Overcoming of Metaphysics in Christian Tradition*. New York: Winston, 1985.

Oliver, Kelly. *Reading Kristeva: Unraveling the Double Bind*. Bloomington: Indiana University Press, 1993.

Peabody, Barbara. *The Screaming Room*. New York: Avon, 1986.

Pearson, Carol Lynn. *Good-bye, I Love You*. New York: Random House, 1986.

Peavey, Fran. *A Shallow Pool of Time: A HIV + Woman Grapples with the AIDS Epidemic*. Philadelphia: New Society, 1990.

————. *By Life's Grace*. Philadelphia: New Society, 1994.

Poovey, Mary. "Feminism and Deconstruction." *Feminist Studies* 14, no. 1 (Spring 1988).

Rawlinson, Mary, Ellen Feder, and Emily Zakin, eds. *Derrida and Feminism*. New York: Routledge, 1996.

Rich, Adrienne. *On Lies, Secrets, and Silence: Selected Prose, 1966–1978*. New York: Norton, 1979.

Richards, Janet Radcliffe. *The Sceptical Feminist: A Philosophical Enquiry*. New York: Routledge, 1980.

Rorty, Richard. "Feminism, Ideology, and Deconstruction: A Pragmatist View." *Hypatia* 8, no. 2 (Spring 1993).

Ryan, Michael. *Marxism and Deconstruction: A Critical Articulation*. Baltimore: Johns Hopkins University Press, 1982.

Sabatier, Renee. *Blaming Other: Prejudice, Race and Worldwide AIDS*. Philadelphia: New Society, 1988.

———. *AIDS and the Third World*. Philadelphia: New Society, 1989.

Sallis, John, ed. *Deconstruction and Philosophy*. Chicago: University of Chicago Press, 1987.

Sawicki, Jana. *Discipling Foucault: Feminism, Power and the Body*. London: Routledge, 1991.

Scheman, Naomi. *Engenderings: Constructions of Knowledge, Authority, and Privilege*. New York: Routledge, 1993.

Scott, Joan W. "Gender as a Useful Category of Historical Analysis." *American Historical Review* 91, nos. 3–4 (November 1986).

———. "Deconstructing Equality-Versus-Difference: Or, the Uses of Poststructuralist Theory for Feminism." *Feminist Studies* 14, no. 2 (Spring 1988).

Sedgwick, Eve. *Epistemology of the Closet*. Berkeley and Los Angeles: University of California Press, 1990.

Sheets-Johnstone, Maxine. *The Roots of Power: Animate Form and Gendered Bodies*. Peru, Ill.: Open Court, 1994.

Silverman, Hugh J., ed. *Derrida and Deconstruction*. New York: Routledge, 1989.

Silverman, Hugh J., and Don Ihde, eds. *Hermeneutics and Deconstruction*. Albany: State University of New York Press, 1985.

Smith, Sidonie and Julia Watson, eds. *De/Colonizing the Subject: The Politics of Gender in Women's Autobiography*. Minneapolis: University of Minnesota Press, 1992.

Spelman, Elizabeth V. *Inessential Woman: Problems of Exclusion in Feminist Thought*. Boston: Beacon, 1988.

Spivak, Gayatri Chakravorty. *In Other Worlds: Essays in Cultural Politics*. New York: Methuen, 1987.

———. *Outside in the Teaching Machine*. New York: Routledge, 1993.

Thomas, Jennifer. "The Question of Derrida's Women." *Human Studies* 16, nos. 1–2 (April 1993).

Tong, Rosemarie. *Feminist Thought: A Comprehensive Introduction*. Boulder, Colo.: Westview, 1989.

Tuana, Nancy, ed. *American Philosophical Association Newsletter on Feminism and Philosophy*. Feminism and Postmodernism Issue, no. 91:2 (Fall 1992).

Tuana, Nancy, and Rosemarie Tong. *Feminism and Philosophy: Essential Readings in Theory, Reinterpretations and Application*. Boulder, Colo.: Westview, 1995.

Waters, Lindsey, and Wlad Godzich, eds. *Reading De Man Reading*. Minneapolis: University of Minnesota Press, 1989.

Watson, Stephen, and Lenore Langsdorf, eds. *Reinterpreting the Political: Continental Philosophy and Political Theory*, in *Selected Studies in Phenomenology and Existentialism*, vol. 20. Albany: State University of New York Press, 1997.

Weber, Samuel. *Institution and Interpretation*. Minneapolis: University of Minnesota Press, 1987.

Weedon, Chris. *Feminist Practice and Poststructuralist Theory*. Oxford: Basil Blackwell, 1987.

Whitford, Margaret. *Luce Irigaray: Philosophy in the Feminine*. London: Routledge, 1991.

Williams, Patricia J. *The Alchemy of Race and Rights*. Cambridge: Harvard University Press, 1991.

Wood, David, ed. *Derrida: A Critical Reader*. Oxford: Basil Blackwell, 1992.

Ziarek, Ewa. *The Rhetoric of Failure: Deconstruction of Skepticism, Reinvention of Modernism*. Albany: State University of New York Press, 1996.

Notes on Contributors

ELLEN T. ARMOUR is assistant professor of religious studies at Rhodes College in Memphis, Tennessee. She received her Ph.D. degree from Vanderbilt University in 1993. In addition to several articles, she is the author of a book manuscript currently under review entitled "Deconstruction, Feminist Theology and the Problem of Difference: Subverting the Race/Gender Divide."

PEG BIRMINGHAM is associate professor of philosophy at DePaul University. She is the co-editor, with Philippe van Haute, of *Dissensus Communis: Between Ethics and Politics,* and the author of several articles on the problem of thinking the ethical-political domain. Currently she is writing a monograph on Hannah Arendt, tentatively titled "The Predicament of Common Responsibility."

DRUCILLA CORNELL is a professor at the Benjamin N. Cardozo School of Law. The author of numerous articles on critical theory, feminism and postmodern theories of ethics, she spent the 1991–92 academic year at the Institute for Advance Study at Princeton University. She is the co-editor, with Seyla Benhabib, of *Feminism as Critique: On the Politics of Gender;* with Michel Rosenfeld and David Gray Carlson, of *Deconstruction and the Possibility of Justice;* and has published three books, *Beyond Accommodation: Ethical Feminism, Deconstruction and the Law, The Philosophy of the Limit,* and *Transformations: Recollective Imagination and Sexual Difference.*

JACQUES DERRIDA is directeur d'études, École des Hautes Études en Sciences Sociales, Paris. His most recently translated works include *Aporias: Dying—Waiting (for One Another) at the "Limits of Truth"*

240 Notes on Contributors

(Stanford University Press, 1994), *Specters of Marx* (Routledge, 1994), and *The Gift of Death* (University of Chicago Press, 1995). *Points . . . : Interviews, 1974–1994* was published by Stanford University Press in 1995.

NANCY FRASER is professor of political science in the Graduate Faculty of the New School for Social Research. Her new book, *Justice Interruptus: Rethinking Key Concepts of a "Postsocialist" Age*, will be published by Routledge in 1996. She is the author of *Unruly Practices: Power, Discourse and Gender in Contemporary Social Theory* (University of Minnesota Press and Polity Press, 1989), the co-author of *Feminist Contentions: A Philosophical Exchange* (Routledge, 1994), and the co-editor of *Revaluing French Feminism: Critical Essays on Difference, Agency, and Culture* (Indiana University Press, 1992).

ELIZABETH GROSZ teaches philosophy and critical theory at Monash University, Victoria, Australia. She is the author of *Sexual Subversions: Three French Feminists* (Allen and Unwin, 1989), *Volatile Bodies: Toward a Corporeal Feminism* (Indiana University Press, 1994), *Space, Time and Perversion* (Routledge, 1995) and is the co-editor, with Elspeth Probyn, of *Sexy Bodies* (Routledge, 1995).

NANCY J. HOLLAND is professor of philosophy at Hamline University. She is the author of *Is Women's Philosophy Possible?* (Rowman and Littlefield, 1990) and has published numerous articles on contemporary Continental philosophy and feminist theory.

PEGGY KAMUF teaches French and comparative literature at the University of Southern California. She is the author of *Fictions of Feminine Desire*, *Signature Pieces*, and *The Division of Literature*. In addition to translating numerous works of Derrida into English, she has also edited an anthology of his writings, *A Derrida Reader: Reading Between the Blinds*.

CHRISTIE V. MCDONALD is professor of Romance languages and literature at Harvard University. She is the author of *The Dialogues of Writing* (1985), *Dispositions* (1986), and *The Proustian Fabric* (1991); co-editor, with Claude Lévesque, of *The Ear of the Other: Texts and Discussions with Jacques Derrida* (1985) and co-editor, with Gary Wihl, of *Transformations in Personhood and Culture After Theory* (1994).

KATE MEHURON is associate professor of philosophy and women's studies at Eastern Michigan University. She is the co-editor of *Free Spirits: Feminist Philosophers on Culture* and the author of numerous articles on postmodernism, feminism, and cultural analysis.

DOROTHEA OLKOWSKI is associate professor of philosophy and former director of women's studies at the University of Colorado at Colorado Springs. She is co-editor, with Constantin Boundas, of *Gilles Deleuze and the Theatre of Philosophy* (Routledge, 1994) and has written numerous articles on aesthetics, feminism, and Continental philosophy. Her current project is a book that combines these interests with the philosophy of Gilles Deleuze, tentatively titled "Materiality and Language, Minor Consensus and Philosophical Variation.

GAYATRI CHAKRAVORTY SPIVAK is Avalon Foundation Professor in the Humanities at Columbia University. She has published *Of Grammatology* (1976), a critical translation of Jacques Derrida, *De la Grammatologie*, and *Imaginary Maps* (1994), a critical translation of Mahasweta Devi's fiction. Her own books are *Myself Must I Remake* (1974), *In Other Worlds* (1987), *The Post-Colonial Critic* (1988), and *Outside in the Teaching Machine* (1994). A *Spivak Reader*, edited by Donna Landry and Gerald McLean, will be out this year.

Index

Abgrund, force of law and, 158–59
abortion, feminist theory and, 120–21
ACT UP/New York (AIDS Coalition to Unleash Power), 169
Acts of Literature, 16
Adorno, Theodor, 3, 155n.11
affirmation, double affirmation: Derrida's concept of, 76–78, 98n.4; feminist theory and, 122–23, 126nn.24–25
African-Americans, AIDS activism and, 169–70
AIDS: counterfeit sentiment regarding, 179–88; elegaic context of testimony on, 167–70; feminist theory and, 18, 165–88; performative effect of testimony on, 170–79
Alchemy of Race and Rights, The, 163n.6
Alcoff, Linda, 16, 127
Alembert, Jean Le Rond d', 107
alterity: Derrida on, 206; Irigaray's concept of, 199–200
aperion, 130
aporetic structure, counterfeit sentiment and, 182–83
appropriation, politics of feminist theory and, 121–23
Arendt, Hannah, 151
Armour, Ellen T., 18–19, 193–211
"as if," Derrida on, 137
"At this Very Moment In this Work Here I Am," 89
Augenblick, 30, 143–45, 146n.13
Austin, J. L., 18, 172–74
autobiography, deconstructionism and, 118–19

Barthes, Roland, 70n.41
Baudelaire, Hector, 183–84

beauty, Derrida on, 218–29
Before the Law, 136–45
Being and Time (*Sein und Zeit*), 11, 36
Benhabib, Seyla, 152
Benjamin, Walter, 148, 155n.11
Bennington, Geoffrey, 101n.35
Benveniste, Emile, 182
Berg, Elizabeth, 124n.12
Birmingham, Peg, 16–17, 21n.10; on ethic of desire, 127–45; on Husserl, 9
Blanchot, Maurice, 15, 38, 63, 138; post-Holocaust writings of, 175–76
Bordo, Susan, 128
"bound ideality," Derrida's concept of, 132–36
Braidotti, Rosi, 21n.12, 78–82, 84, 99n.15, 212n.8
"Breast Giver, The," 187
Brodrib, Somer, 84, 100n.16
Bush, George (president), 189n.8
Butler, Judith, 124n.14

canon formation, male domination of, vii–viii
Carroll, David, 71n.39
castration: deconstructionism and, 52–53, 57–60, 70n.26; feminist theory and, 111, 124n.12; Lacan on, 13–14
categorical imperative, 137
causality, Heidegger on, 138–45, 146n.13
Cézanne, Paul, 215–18
"Choreographies" interview (Derrida), 10–11, 13–14, 23–40, 196
Christianity, Derrida and, 214n.21
civil disobedience, deconstructionism and, 149–54
class, feminist theory and, 197–200, 213n.20

colossal (*kolossos*), Derrida's concept of, 221–29
constellation metaphor, 155–56n.11
constitutional principles, force of law and, 161
Cornell, Drucilla, 3, 14, 17, 78; on civil disobedience and deconstruction, 149–54; on Derrida's view of sexuality, 92–93, 101n.30
Cox, Elizabeth, 167–68, 180–88
Crimp, Douglas, 178–79
Critchley, Simon, 100n.29
critique, force of law and, 157, 159–63
Critique of Judgment, 19, 217–29
"Critique of Violence," 148
cultural background, force of law and, 162

Dallmayr, Fred, 153
dance metaphor, Derrida's use of, 24–32, 39–40
Darstellung, 220–29
Dasein: Derrida on, 10–11, 15; gender neutrality and, 15–16, 35–37, 86–88; ontology of sexual difference and, 86–88
death, self-identity and, 112–15, 125n.18
deconstruction: activist discourse and, 18; autobiography and, 118–19; civil disobedience and, 149–54; Cornell's defense of, 101n.30; defined, 5–6; displacement and, 44–68; feminist theory and, 15, 103–23, 193–211; force of law and, 157–63; force of repetition and, 111–15; jealousy and, 111–23; politics of, 95–98; politics of equivocation and, 74–78, 98n.2; religion and, 12n.5, 194–211; singularity and, 116–18; suspicion of, among feminists, 78–85
Deconstruction and Theology, 194
Deleuze, Gilles, 99n.7, 217; postmodernism and, 83, 98n.1
de Man, Paul, 77, 167, 175–78
Derrida, Jacques: activist discourse and, 18; AIDS-related testimony and, 166–88; "Choreographies" interview, 10–11, 13–14, 23–40, 196; context to work of, 8–14; on counterfeit sentiment, 183–88; deconstruction and, 5–6, 84–85, 100n.19; deconstructive politics and, 95–98; ethics of desire, 127–45; feminist hostility towards, 78–85; feminist theory and, 1–2, 7–8, 14–20, 193–211; Irigaray and, 18–19, 196–200; law and fiction, 136–45; metaphysical/political aspects of law and, 157–63; ontology of sexual difference and, 85–95; on painting, 215–29; on performative utterance, 172–79; postmod-ernism and, 3, 98n.1, 151–52, 155n.11; on religion, 194–206
Descartes, René, 3; deconstructionism and, 5–6; Derrida's work and, 8; on envy and jealousy, 106–10
desire, ethic of, 127–45
Deutsch, Helene, 104
Devi, Mahasweta, 187
Diary of Adam and Eve, The, 32–33
Difficile liberté, 41n.5
Dionysius the Aereopagite, 200
discipleship, 70n.22
discourse, displacement and, in feminist theory, 43–68
displacement, Freudian theory on, 46–48
Dissemination, 200–206
dissymetry, Derrida's concept of, 39–40
double affirmation, Derrida's concept of, 76–78, 98n.4
double displacement theory, Derrida and, 48–51, 57–60, 63–64
double movement, deconstructionism and, 6, 21n.9, 32–40
La double séance, 32–33, 50, 54
Duras, Marguerite, 150
Du sacré au saint, 41n.5

"Economimemsis," 19, 228–29
Eckhart, Meister, 200
Emma Goldman Brigade, 40n.2
Engels, Friedrich, 70n.29
envy, jealousy and, 106–9, 123n.7
equivocation, politics of, Derrida on, 73–78, 174, 190n.20
ethics: Derrida on, 12; of desire, 127–45; symmetry in relationships and, 153–54
Ethique de la différence sexuelle (An Ethics of Sexual Difference), 207, 209, 214n.30
etymology, Derrida and, 32–33
Eumenides, 68

"*Le facteur de la vérité*," 13, 124n.15
fathers, Derrida on, 51–53
Felman, Shoshana, 175–76
"Female Sexuality," 104
"feminine silhouette," Derrida on law and, 138–45
femininity, Derrida on, 23–40, 92
feminist jurisprudence, 150–54
feminist theory, AIDS-related testimonies and, 166–88; counterfeit sentiment and, 179–88;

criticism of deconstruction in, 78–85; deconstructionism and, 15, 60–68, 104–23, 193–211; deconstructive politics and, 95–98; defined, 7–8; Derrida and, 1–2, 7–8, 14–20, 93–95; ethics of desire, 127–45; fiction and, 136–45; jealousy and, 103–23; Lacan and, 13–14; law and, 60–68, 150–54; Nietzsche and, 44–68; ontology of sexual difference and, 85–95; politics of equivocation and, 73–78, 98n.2, 99n.5; psychoanalysis and, 98n.3; religion and, 194–211; "subject" in, 107–11, 124nn.13–14; transformation of philosophical canon through, viii–ix

fetishism: deconstructionist discourse on, 52–54, 59–60, 64–68; Derrida on concept of, 30; jealousy and, 111, 124n.12

Feuerbach, Ludwig, 53, 209

fiction: Derrida on history and, 128–36; feminist theory and, 128, 136–45

finitude, Derrida on fiction and, 133–36

Fink, Eugen, 133

La folie du jour, 63–64

"Force of Law: The 'Mystical Foundation of Authority,' The," 17, 148–54, 157–63

Foucault, Michel: on biopower, 187–88; Derrida's work and, 8, 18; feminist interpretations of, 99n.7; postmodernism and, 98n.1; truth and power formations and, 166, 170, 172, 189n.13, 190n.17

Fox-Genovese, Elizabeth, 70n.33

Fraser, Nancy, 17–18, 84, 148, 157–63

"French Feminism in an International Frame," 67

Freud, Sigmund, 4; deconstruction and, 5–6; Derrida on, 8, 51–52, 70n.21; on displacement, 46–48; Irigaray on, 207–208; on jealousy, 109–10; Lacan and, 13, 195; legal theory and, 137; misogyny of, 82; on negation, 57–58; penis envy theory of, 16, 104–7; phallocentrism of, 51–53; Spivak on, 15

"gaine," 59, 70n.27

Gann Initiative, 171

Gasché, Rodolphe, 131

Gay Men's Health Crisis, 180–81

gender: AIDS and performative utterances and, 172, 190n.18; feminist theory, 197–200

geneaology, Foucault on, 190n.17

Genesis, role of woman in, 34–35

Genet, Jean, 15, 51–53, 225–26

genocide, AIDS pandemic as, 168–70, 189n.9

"Geschlecht: Sexual Difference, Ontological Difference," 86–89

Gift of Death, The, 12

Given Time: I. Counterfeit Money, 182, 183–84

Glas, 30, 51–54, 59, 64–65, 225

"God-the-Father" imagery: Derrida on, 200, 205–6, 213n.19; Irigaray on, 207–11

Goldman, Emma, 14, 23, 26

Grosz, Elizabeth, 2; deconstruction and, 5–6, 21n.9; on Derrida and feminist theory, 15–16; feminist theory and, 7–8, 21n.12; on Irigaray, 31, 214n.25; on postmodernism, 3; on sexual difference in Derrida, 73–98

Gynesis: Configurations of Woman and Modernity, 21n.10

hallucination, fiction and, 129–30

Hart, Kevin, 214n.21

Hegel, G. W. F.: on Adam and Eve, 43–44; deconstructionism and, 51–53, 70n.25; Derrida on, 8–10, 19, 33–34, 41; memory theory of, 176–79; on religion, 200; Spivak on, 15

Heidegger, Martin, 2; on causality, 138–45, 146n.13; Derrida on work of, 8–12, 15, 30–31, 35–37, 214n.22; fascism and, 77, 99n.6; Grosz on, 15; Irigaray on, 210–11, 214n.30; misogyny of, 82; on Nietzsche, 24; ontology of sexual difference and, 86–89; on poetic language, 182; on religion, 200

hermeneutics, feminist theory and, 44, 69n.3

heterosexuality: AIDS testimonies and, 180–88; Derrida on, 166–67, 188nn.1–2

history: Derrida on concept of, 128–29; feminist theory and, 62–68, 70n.33; fiction and, 128–36

Hobbes, Thomas, 3

Hoffman, Eve, 165

"home space," AIDS testimony and, 179–88

homosexuality: AIDS-related testimonies and feminist theory, 166–88; Derrida on, 51–52; jealousy and, 109–10

homosociality, feminist theory and, 166–88, 188n.1

Horney, Karen, 104

"How the 'True World' Finally Became a Fable: History of An Error," 56–60

Husserl, Edmund, 2; Derrida on, 8–10, 12, 16, 128–29, 138, 142; Kant compared with, 129–30; sign theory of, 111–15

hymen imagery: Derrida on, 32–40, 58–60, 63–64, 101n.34; double displacement and, 49–51, 70n.17
Hystera, 207–8, 214n.27

ideality, of self-identity, 111–15
identity: AIDS politics and, 178–79; Derrida on, 111–15, 124n.16; feminist theory and, 83
ideology, AIDS-related testimony and, 167–70
Imaginary, Lacanian concept of, 13
invagination imagery, Derrida on, 32–40, 41n.6, 101n.34
"invention of the possible," Derrida's concept of, 119–23, 125n.21
Irigaray, Luce: on Derrida, 128, 195–211; on female sexuality, 8, 18–19, 83, 104; feminist theory and, 196–200, 212n.8; on patriarchal order, 150; postmodernism and, 98n.1; on religion and feminism, 195–200, 206–11, 214n.32
"iterative reduction," 130–31

Jardine, Alice, 21n.10, 81
jealousy: envy and, 106–9, 123n.7; feminist theory and, 103–123; Freud on, 109–10
Johnson, Barbara, 78, 213n.18
Jones, Ernest, 104
"*jouissance*," 152, 156n.14, 195, 212n.7
Joyce, James, 4
judgment, force of law and, 159–63
justice: Derrida on law and, 138; violence and, 158–63
"Justice as Fairness: Political, not Metaphysical," 17–18

Kafka, Franz, 136
Kamuf, Peggy, 5, 16, 21n.12, 78, 103–23
Kant, Immanuel, 3–4; categorical imperative, 137; deconstructionism and, 5–6; Derrida on, 8, 19, 217–29; Hegel on, 53; Husserl compared with, 129–30
Kierkegaard, Søren, 12
Kirby, Vicki, 78
Klein, Melanie, 123n.7
Kofman, Sarah, 104–6, 109–10, 124n.12
Kristeva, Julia, 98n.1, 195–211

Lacan, Jacques, 2; Derrida's work and, 8–9, 13–14, 204; on Freud, 51, 195, 208; male-dominated discourse of, 17; patriarchal order and, 149–50; postmodernism and, 98n.1, 151–53, 155n.18; on sexual shame, 151
Lagache, Daniel, 107–9
language: counterfeit sentiment and, 182–88; deep grammar of legal reasoning, 161–62; Derrida on fiction and, 132–36, 142–45; Derrida on philosophy of, 9–10; in feminist theory, 197–200; performative utterance and, 172–79
law: Derrida on force and, 148; feminist theory and, 63–68, 150–54; fiction and, 136–45; metaphysical/political aspects of, 157–63
"Law of Genre, The," AIDS testimony and, 63–64, 70n.35, 172, 190n.18
legal reasoning, 161–62
Leviathan, 3
Levinas, Emmanuel, 2; Derrida on, 8–9, 11–12, 15, 34–35, 40n.5; feminist theory and, 17, 82; Grosz on, 15; messianic concept of justice, 152–54; ontology of sexual difference and, 86, 89–92, 100n.29; on suffering, 175
Lévi-Strauss, Claude, 20n.6; feminist theory and, 11
Limited, Inc., 172
literary criticism: AIDS-related testimonies and, 175–79; deconstructionism and, 62; Derrida on fiction, 128–36; fiction and feminist theory, 136–45
"Living On/Border Lines," 32, 63–68, 71n.36
Logical Investigations, 111–12
Luther, Martin, 194
Lyotard, Jean-François, law theory and, 150; postmodernism and, 98n.1; on sexual difference, 101n.31

MacKinnon, Catharine, 150–51
Madness of the Day, The, 141–42
Mallarmé, 31, 38, 49–51, 70n.21
Marx, Karl: Derrida and, 8–9, 52–53; Hegel and, 15, 70n.25
Marxism, patriarchy and, 69n.2
matrix, Derrida on concept of, 24–30
Mauss, Marcel, 182–83
"maverick feminism" concept, Derrida on, 26–27
McDonald, Christie V., 9, 14; interview with Derrida, 23–40, 93–94, 100n.26
meaning, Derrida on undecidability of, 115–16
Mehuron, Kate, 18, 165–88
Memoires for Paul de Man, 176–79

memory, Derrida on, 176–79
metaphysics: Derrida on, 12; feminist theory
    and, 197–200, 213n.20; force of law and,
    157–63; religion and, 200–206
"metaphysics of presence," 9–10
"Mimique," 49
modernism, defined, 3–4, 151, 155n.11
Moi, Toril, 212n.8
Montesquieu, 140
motherhood, deconstructionism and, 53–54,
    59–60, 67–68
Murphy, Timothy, 168

Nancy, Jean-Luc, 20, 124n.13
National Socialism, Derrida and, 177–78
"negation" (*Aufhebung*), 53, 57–60
"negative feminism," Derrida charged with,
    127–28
New Introductory Lectures on Psychoanalysis, 104
Nietzsche, Friedrich: deconstructionism and,
    55–60; Derrida on, 8, 14–15, 23–24, 26–29,
    45–68, 204; fascism and, 77; Heidegger and,
    11; Irigaray on, 210–11, 214n.30; misogyny
    of, 44–45, 50, 82; ontology of sexual differ-
    ence and, 86, 93–94; on power, 175; on
    religion, 200
nihilism: deconstruction and, 158–59; Derrida
    on religion and, 194
"nominalism" of Derrida, 17
"nonreturn" of subject (Derrida), 111, 124n.15

Oedipus complex: Freudian displacement theory
    and, 47; Lacan on, 51, 208
Of Grammatology, 198, 204–6
Of Spirit, 10, 214n.22
Olkowski, Dorothea, 19, 215–29
"On Being the Object of Property," 187
orgasm, double displacement theory and,
    61–62, 66–67; Nietzsche's misogyny and,
    44–45, 50
Origin of Geometry, 9, 16, 128–37, 142, 145
Othello, 16, 103
Other, Levinas on, 12, 89–92, 152–53

"parchment" (Derrida), 38–39
"parergon," 19, 220
participatory democracy, feminism and, 151–52
Passions de l'âme, 106–7
patriarchy, 44, 68n.2; civil disobedience and,
    149–54; counterfeit sentiment in AIDS testi-

mony and, 179–88; feminist rejection of, 76;
    in religious myths, 200–206
Peavey, Fran, 167–68, 170–71, 175, 178
penis envy: feminist theory and, 104–7, 208;
    Freud's theory of, 16
people with AIDS (PWAs), elegaic testimonies
    of, 167–70
performative utterance: Derrida on, 216–29;
    feminist theory and, 166–88
"personal is political," 119–23, 126nn.22–23
Phaedo, 203, 213n.18
Phaedrus, 201
phallocentrism: feminist deconstructionist dis-
    course on, 60–68, 209–11; fetishism and,
    53–54; Freudian displacement theory and,
    46–48, 58–60, 70n.26
phallogocentrism: AIDs testimony and,
    166–67, 182–88; Derrida on, 33–36, 51–52,
    190n.20; in Derrida's religious motif, 204–6;
    Heidegger and, 11; Lacan on, 13–14; Nietz-
    sche's misogyny and, 44–68; Spivak on Derri-
    da's concept of, 44
philosophical canon, male domination of,
    vii–viii
"philosophy of language," Derrida on Husserl
    and, 9–10
Philosophy of Right, 43
"phronesis," 160
pink triangle inconography, AIDS activism
    and, 169
Plato, 8; Derrida on, 19, 31, 200–206, 213n.18;
    Irigaray on, 207–11
"Plato's Pharmacy," 19
Politics, 182
politics: AIDS epidemic and, 170–79; decon-
    structive politics, 95–98; Derrida on equivo-
    cation and, 73–78; feminist theory and,
    119–23, 126n.22; force of law and, 157–63
Positions, 31
Post Card, The (La carte postale), 13, 30, 44,
    125n.16, 204
postmodernism: canons of, 4–5; defined, 3–5;
    feminist wariness of, 79–85; participatory de-
    mocracy and, 151–52, 155n.11; politics of
    equivocation and, 74–78, 98n.1
post-structuralism, feminist theory and, 127
"power/knowledge," AIDS testimony and,
    170–79, 189n.13
property rights, force of law and, 161
psychoanalysis, feminist theory and, 98n.3, 195

"Psychogenesis of a Case of Homosexuality in a Woman," 105–6

quasi-transcendentalism, force of law and, 158–63
La question du style, 46

race, feminist theory and, 197–200, 213n.20
Rawls, John, 17, 149
Reagan, Ronald (president), 171, 189n.8
Real, Lacanian concept of, 13
"reductions," Derrida's concept of, 9
religion, deconstruction, feminism and, 193–211
reproduction: deconstructionism and, 60, 70n.29; Derrida on law and, 143–45
Republic, 203
Rich, Adrienne, 1–2
Richards, Janet Radcliffe, 99n.5
Rilke, Rainer Maria, 11
Rorty, Richard, 1–2
Rose, Jacqueline, 156n.14
Rousseau, Jean-Jacques, Derrida on, 31, 70n.21, 204
Ryan, Michael, 84

Saussure, Ferdinand de, 6, 173, 182, 190n.19
Savage Mind, The, 20n.6
Searle, John, 172
self, Derrida on role of, 111–23
Self-defense, force of law and, 162
self-love, jealousy and, 107–10
Sexes et Parentés (Sexes and Genealogies), 206–7, 209–11
sexual difference: deconstructionism and, 5–6, 60–68, 70n.30; deconstructive politics and, 95–98; Derrida on, 32–40, 73–98; Heidegger on, 86–89; Irigaray's concept of alterity and, 199–200, 206; jealousy and envy regarding, 103–10; Kamuf on, 16; law and, 136–45; Levinas on, 89–92; ontology of, 15–16, 85–95
sexual harassment, 151, 162
sexuality: Derrida's ambiguity regarding, 34–36, 89–95; Levinas' concept of sexual difference and, 90–91; postmodernism and, 4–5
Shakespeare, William, 8, 16, 103–4
Shallow Pool of Time: An HIV + Woman Grapples with the AIDS Epidemic, A, 167–68, 170
sign, Husserl's theory of, 111–15
"Signature Event Context," 172

significance, concept of, 152–53, 156n.15
singularity, Derrida's concept of, 116–18, 124n.20; Derrida on law and, 144–45
Socrates, 201–6
Speculum of the Other Woman, 128, 207–8
speech-act theory, 216–29
Speech and Phenomena, 9, 16
"spiritual corporeality," Derrida's concept of, 132–33
Spivak, Gayatri, 15, 18, 78, 226; AIDS-related testimony and, 166, 168, 180–81, 185–88, 188n.6; on discourse and deconstruction, 43–64
Spurs/Eperons, 15, 23, 27–30, 46, 225; feminist theory and, 54–60, 80–81, 93–95; religious motif in, 204
storytelling, Derrida on, 176–79
subjectivity: deconstructionism and, 5–6; feminist theory and, 7–8, 111–23; Irigaray on, 150, 208–9; jealousy and, 107–10, 124n.13; role of, in postmodernism, 3–5, 80–81, 99n.12; sexual difference and, 16
sublime, Kant's sense of, 218–29
supplémentation, 198–200, 207–11, 212n.13
Symbolic, Lacanian concept of, 13

"Taboo of Virginity," 106
Tain of the Mirror, 131
taste, Derrida on, 218–29
testimonial utterance, elegaic context of, 167–70; feminist theory and, 166–88
Textes pour Emmanuel Lewis, 41n.5
Thanksgiving: An AIDS Journal, 167–68, 180–88
Third World countries, AIDS discourses and, 168–70, 187
This Sex Which Is Not One, 196
Totality and Infinity, 12, 89
transgender issues, AIDS testimony and, 179–88
truth, AIDS and politicization of, 171–79
Truth in Painting, The, 19, 41n.7, 215–29
Twain, Mark, 32
Twilight of the Idols, The, 56

Vernant, Jean-Pierre, 221–22
violence, force of law and, 157–63
violence against women, 150–51
"Violence and Metaphyics," 12–13
La Voix et le phénomène, 111
Vorstellung, 220–21

Weber, Samuel, 124n.16
West, Robin, 150
"What are Poets For?," 11
Whitford, Margaret, 81–84, 128, 212n.8,
   214n.25
Williams, Patricia J., 163n.6, 187–88
woman, Derrida on concepts of, 33–40
women, defined in male-dominated philosophical canon, vii–viii

"Women in the Beehive," 196, 212n.9
writing: deconstruction and, 31–32; Derrida's
   hymen imagery and, 50–51
Writing AIDS: Gay Literature, Language, and
   Analysis, 168
Writing and Difference, 12–13
Writing and the Disaster, 176

Zarathustra imagery, Nietzsche on, 56–57